Pragmatic Neuroethics

Improving Treatment and Understanding of the Mind-Brain

Eric Racine

The MIT Press
Cambridge, Massachusetts
London, England

For information about special quantity discounts, please email special_sales@ mitpress.mit.edu

This book was set in Sabon by Westchester Book Group. Printed and bound in the United States of America.

Library of Congress Cataloging-in-Publication Data

Racine, Eric, 1976–
Pragmatic neuroethics : improving treatment and understanding of the mind-brain / Eric Racine.
    p. ; cm. — (Basic bioethics)
Includes bibliographical references and index.
ISBN 978-0-262-01419-9 (hardcover : alk. paper) 1. Neurology—Moral and ethical aspects. 2. Neurosciences. I. Title. II. Series: Basic bioethics.
[DNLM: 1. Neurosciences—ethics. 2. Behavior—ethics. 3. Bioethical Issues. 4. Morals. 5. Neurology—ethics. WL 100 R121p 2010]
RC343.R16   2010
174.2'968—dc22
                                                              2009037816

10 9 8 7 6 5 4 3 2 1

Contents

Preface   ix

Acknowledgments   xv

1   Salient Challenges in Modern Neuroethics   1

2   Reviewing Past and Current Neuroethics: Definitions, Attributes, and Perspectives   27

3   Pragmatic Naturalism in Bioethics   53

4   Neuroethics: Exploring the Implications of Pragmatic Naturalism   71

5   Public Understanding of Neuroscience Innovation and Emerging Interpretations of Neuroscience Research   97

6   Enhancement of Performance with Neuropharmaceuticals: Pragmatism and the Culture Wars   121

7   Disorders of Consciousness in an Evolving Neuroscience Context   139

8   Communication of Prognosis in Disorders of Consciousness and Severe Brain Injury: A Closer Look at Paradoxical Discourses in the Clinical and Public Domains   161

9   Social Neuroscience: A Pragmatic Epistemological and Ethical Framework for the Neuroscience of Ethics   179

10 Conclusion: Neuroethics and Future Challenges for Neuroscience, Ethics, and Society   215

References   223

Index   255

Handwritten annotations in right margin: Background on Neuroethics; Policy Approaches. Making decisions on NeuroEthical questions

Series Foreword

I am pleased to present the twenty-seventh book in the series Basic Bioethics. The series presents innovative works in bioethics to a broad audience and introduces seminal scholarly manuscripts, state-of-the-art reference works, and textbooks. Such broad areas as the philosophy of medicine, advancing genetics and biotechnology, end-of-life care, health and social policy, and the empirical study of biomedical life are engaged.

Arthur Caplan
Basic Bioethics Series Editorial Board
Joseph J. Fins
Rosamond Rhodes
Nadia N. Sawicki
Jan Helge Solbakk

Preface

Pragmatic Neuroethics is a book based on the reasonable hope that if clinicians and researchers from various disciplines work together in collaboration with different stakeholders, the chances of making a difference for patients suffering from neurological and psychiatric disorders can be increased. It relies on the belief that ethics is a crucial part of this endeavor, and that ethics, the search for the good and for what Aristotle called moral excellence, is inherently part of social and medical acts aiming to alleviate suffering, pain, and daily difficulties for patients. This view is at the heart of this book and of what I describe as "pragmatic neuroethics," a view of bioethics influenced by various thinkers that emphasizes the pluralistic nature of ethics and society and the value of interdisciplinary collaboration and research to further knowledge and institute beneficial practice changes in healthcare, science, and society.

The need for an interdisciplinary and collective response to ethical challenges in neuroscience and clinical care—neuroethics—has surfaced in the past years in response to important social, medical, and scientific changes. In many developed countries today, as illustrated by data of the World Health Organization, the combined "health burden" of neurological and mental health disorders matches and even surpasses that of any cluster of health conditions (World Health Organization 2001, 2006). Developing countries are spared neither from this prevalence of neuropsychiatric conditions nor from issues of stigma associated with mental illness and the need for better treatments for neurological disorders. The term "health burden," often measured in days of lost productivity, may seem overly administrative. Nonetheless, it is a convenient way to illustrate the costs of caregivers without appropriate support and resources; stigma and discrimination; lives that are shattered by illness and isolated suffering; lack of research efforts; and, in some unfortunate cases, suicide. Today, almost everyone can look around and identify, if not themselves, a friend or relative that has faced not only a mental health or neurological problem but the challenges of being respected as a person and finding the internal resources to carry forward. These are the familiar stories of depressed friends or colleagues who never came back to work after falling ill and elderly parents coping with dementia. In proportion to other serious illnesses, diseases of the brain and mind now represent one of the greatest—and still increasing—public health burdens faced by both higher- and lower-income nations.

This book presents neuroethics as an unprecedented opportunity to integrate healthcare neurospecialties such as neurology, psychiatry, neurosurgery, the humanities, neuroscience research, social science, and allied healthcare professions to tackle the emerging challenges in neuroscience and to improve patient care. There are signs that we are making some headway. Scientists, governments, advocacy groups, and public health authorities are intensely pursuing research to address the causes and consequences of neurological and psychiatric disease and to search for "cures." The clinical translation of neuroscience is not straightforward, and as neuroscience research progresses and strives to improve clinical practices and public understanding, many scientific unknowns make it difficult to produce practical clinical neuroscience applications. In addition, once some clinical changes are introduced, the pluralistic nature of contemporary societies means that not everyone will always unanimously agree on what is an "advance" or "progress." For example, if we could know with more accuracy our future risk of developing depression or Alzheimer's disease—based on a combination of structural brain measures, brain activity patterns, and neurogenetic testing—would everyone feel that it is in their best interest to know? What about the potential of neuropharmacology to generate medicines that can not only treat illnesses but also improve cognitive function in the healthy? And when are scientific advances dealing with complex and sensitive issues or health conditions such as disorders of consciousness ready to be shared with the broader public? Neuroethics signals that promising advances are surfacing but, as they percolate to healthcare and public stakeholders, questions surface about how new insights and new interventions will find their proper place in society to serve individuals and the public good.

Neuroethics, alongside other initiatives, has surfaced to tackle head on some of the challenges created by advances in neuroscience. However, to date, there have been few theoretical perspectives on this new field and scarce in-depth discussion about its nature and scope. In response, this book provides such a perspective as well as examples of research that attempts to bridge different disciplines to provide frameworks for elucidating and attending to important neuroethics issues. These include, for example, the increasing use of neuropharmacology to enhance performance and the incursion of functional neuroimaging in the world of the humanities and social sciences beyond conventional clinical neuroscience research. I hope that readers will find this book enlightening and stimulating, enough so to encourage reflection, action, or research that will contribute to meeting the broad ethical, scientific, medical, and social challenges that we collectively face.

Pragmatic Neuroethics pursues a number of goals: (1) to thoroughly review diverging perspectives within neuroethics and provide a constructive critical analysis of the latest literature; (2) to provide a consistent view of the field with compelling arguments that yield a theoretical approach to tackling several problems within neuroethics; (3) to address several key neuroethics issues using empirical research data and a pragmatic approach; and (4) to identify future challenges for neuroscience and society and discuss possible directions for the field of neuroethics. The limitations of this book include the focus on some salient challenges to the detriment of others as well as perspectives that reflect my training in bioethics, social science, and philosophy. For example, legal issues related to neuroscience are not addressed, and I will be the first to admit that many more issues, especially clinically relevant ones, such as stigma, neurodegenerative disease, and aging, pose huge challenges to society. Further, given the range of topics, some will require more attention in the future.

Pragmatic Neuroethics is divided in two parts. The first section, chapters 1 through 4, reviews recent neuroethics scholarship, provides background on neuroethics, and introduces pragmatism and pragmatic neuroethics. The second section, chapters 5 through 9, presents a series of essays on salient topics in neuroethics such as decision making in disorders of consciousness; public understanding of neuroscience; and policy approaches to "cognitive enhancement."

Chapter 1 ("Salient Challenges in Modern Neuroethics") provides a thematic overview of neuroethics and explains some of the key areas currently under discussion. By gaining acquaintance with these topics, the reader should get a clear sense of why modern neuroethics has surfaced to systematically examine emerging challenges. Chapter 2 ("Reviewing Past and Current Neuroethics: Definitions, Attributes, and Perspectives") analyzes some early definitions of neuroethics and identifies some distinct views of the field. A review of neuroethics attributes and the ethical, legal, and social issues associated with it in peer review literature, on the Internet, and in print media gives an overall sense of how the field has been characterized in formal academic definitions and beyond. Chapter 3 ("Pragmatic Naturalism in Bioethics") presents and discusses different waves of naturalism in bioethics, including how neuroethics has reinitiated discussions on the relationship between the biological sciences and the humanities. This chapter argues that bioethics in itself is a form of pragmatic naturalism as illustrated by the field's commitment to interdisciplinary collaborations and its practical focus. Finally, chapter 4 ("Neuroethics: Exploring the Implications of Pragmatic Naturalism") explores the implications of pragmatic naturalism by addressing several controversies surrounding neuroethics. It concludes by highlighting some of the characteristics of pragmatic neuroethics, such as the integration of pluralism, bottom-up research approaches, and a focus on practical issues that distinguish this approach from other, more theoretical or more monodisciplinary views of the field.

The second part of this book presents a series of essays that are nourished by both the background material and the theoretical framework of pragmatic neuroethics laid out in chapters 1 through 4. Chapter 5 ("Public Understanding of Neuroscience Innovation and Emerging Interpretations of Neuroscience Research") highlights the importance of public understanding from a pragmatic perspective in order to take into consideration not only expert opinions about ethics in neuroscience but also public concerns and emerging lay interpretations of neuroscience research. This chapter discusses various forms of media coverage of neuroscience innovation. Chapter 6 ("Enhancement of Performance with Neuropharmaceuticals: Pragmatism and the Culture Wars") stems from a context of increasing prevalence and salience of nonmedical uses of neuropharmaceuticals for performance enhancement. This chapter examines critically

some of the assumptions behind the conservative and liberal moral-
political approaches to this issue and makes the case from a pragmatic
standpoint for the recognition of pluralism and for approaches that minimize harm, promote autonomy, and urge considerations for the public
good. Chapter 7 ("Disorders of Consciousness in an Evolving Neuroscience Context") provides background information and some discussion of
different clinical conditions such as the vegetative state and the minimally
conscious state, called collectively disorders of consciousness, in an evolving neuroscience context that challenges some assumptions about these
disorders. Chapter 8 ("Communication of Prognosis in Disorders of Consciousness and Severe Brain Injury") builds on the material presented in
chapter 7 to discuss in more detail why there are lingering sources of confusion in disorders of consciousness. Specifically, I argue that there is a strong
tension at work between, on the one hand, intuitive notions about consciousness and behavior and, on the other hand, scientific understanding
and medical language describing consciousness and behavior. Chapter 9
("Social Neuroscience: A Pragmatic Epistemological and Ethical Framework for the Neuroscience of Ethics") builds on the naturalism inherent
to pragmatic naturalism and discusses the possibility that neuroscience
provides powerful insights into the mechanisms underlying moral reasoning, cooperative behavior, and emotional processes such as empathy. This
chapter briefly introduces social neuroscience and the neuroscience of ethics and highlights some potential benefits and misunderstandings created
by this area of research. It then presents a pragmatic framework based on
the philosophy of emergentism. This framework yields conditions and
guideposts for the meaningful contribution of neuroscience to ethics. This
emergentist and pragmatic framework also debunks common arguments
against the introduction of neuroscience research into ethics as well as
overstated promises. The conclusion of *Pragmatic Neuroethics* ("Neuroethics and Future Challenges for Neuroscience, Ethics, and Society") revis-
its some major issues discussed in this book and sketches recommendations
and strategies for moving ahead.

I hope that readers of this book will enjoy these neuroethics contributions. It is also my hope, even though I realize much still needs to be
done, that each chapter will stimulate reflection, action, and ideas for
research that embrace pragmatic goals while remaining open to genuine
dialogue in the search for collaborative and practical solutions.

Acknowledgments

Although it bears the signature of one man, this book, which captures some of my basic opinions, would have been absolutely impossible without the support of many colleagues and students. This is an opportunity for me to acknowledge the help and support of colleagues, family, and friends who have directly or indirectly inspired and supported my work in the last years.

I would like to sincerely thank Nicole Palmour for reviewing this manuscript on several occasions and providing constructive and helpful comments. I want to thank former and current trainees and assistants of the Neuroethics Research Unit: Amaryllis Ferrand, Cynthia Forlini, Constance Deslauriers, Emily Bell, Ghislaine Mathieu, Bruce Maxwell, William Affleck, Zoë Costa-von Aesch, Marie-Josée Dion, Marta Karczewska, Matthew Seidler, David Bouvier, David Risse, Catherine Rodrigue, Lila Karpowicz, and Danaë Larivière-Bastien. Their work and presence have inspired me along the way and are truly appreciated. My work reflects part of the ongoing daily conversations and exchanges I have had with them, and I am immensely indebted to them.

I consider myself privileged to have received the mentorship of outstanding individuals along the years. I have been fortunate to cross paths with senior scholars who possess extraordinary energy, creativity, and commitment. I would like to thank in particular Judy Illes, Hubert Doucet, and Bartha Knoppers for their generous time, ongoing support, and encouragements. Nothing can replace the mentorship and advice a young scholar receives from senior colleagues or the intellectual exchanges that occur within collegial and respectful environments. I would like to thank particularly Walter Glannon for his helpful guidance throughout this project, James Bernat for helpful comments on this manuscript, and an additional anonymous reviewer.

The idea for writing this book originates partly from the days of my postdoctoral fellowship at the Stanford Center for Biomedical Ethics (SCBE). I would like to thank accordingly the leadership of the SCBE, in particular David Magnus, Henry Greely, and Mildred Cho, for support and the staff members (Anne Footer, Paula Bailey, Joyce Prasad, and Shobha Kumar) who helped me in many different ways to make this a successful journey. I want to thank the students who worked with me on various projects at the SCBE, including Sarah Waldman, Adri Van der Loos, Ofek Bar-Ilan, Stacey Kallem, Neil Mukhopadhyay, Allyson Mackey, Vivian Chau, Rakesh Amaram, Marisa Gallo, and Tessa Watt. I am indebted for their assistance in numerous research projects, and the exchanges I have had with them are marked in my past and present and will remain with me for the future.

Pragmatic Neuroethics materialized during a visiting fellowship at the Brocher Foundation in August 2007, where I had the privilege to put on paper the project for this book. The beautiful and inspiring settings provided by the foundation's location on the shores of Lake Geneva and the friendly exchanges with colleagues helped me prepare the proposal and nourished this project as it unfolded. I would like to thank the leadership of the Brocher Foundation, in particular Cécile Caldwell Vulliéty, and the friendly staff, especially Raji Sultan for his kind assistance. I would also like to acknowledge the support of colleagues I met during my enjoyable stay there (Anthony Mark Cutter, Thomas Douglas, Bert Gordijn, Rouven Porz, Michael Selgelid); they made this a remarkable and inspiring experience for me and my family members (Nathalie, André-Anne, Gabrielle, and Amélie). The foundation's generous support for the publication of this book deserves special recognition.

During the writing of this work and the work that preceded it, I received fellowships, awards, and grants from several agencies, including the Social Sciences and Humanities Research Council, the Fonds de la recherche en santé du Québec, the National Institutes of Health (grant awarded to Judy Illes), the Greenwall Foundation (grant awarded to Judy Illes), the Canadian Institutes of Health Research (Ethics Office; Institute of Neurosciences, Mental Health and Addiction; Institute of Human Development, Child and Youth Health), the CIHR-funded States of Mind Network (Françoise Baylis), and the CIHR-funded Pediatric Neuroimaging Ethics Network (Jocelyn Downie). The support from these agencies and from various peer communities has made much of the work underlying this book possible.

I am grateful for the support from the unique Institut de recherches cliniques de Montréal (IRCM), especially Louis-Gilles Durand, who has been an invaluable source of inspiration and advice in the past three years. Jeannine Amyot's impressive administrative skills and commitment to supporting the Neuroethics Research Unit need to be underscored and acknowledged. I thank all my IRCM colleagues who have provided feedback on material presented in this book and who believe in the legacy of Jacques Genest, the founder of the institute, who was committed early in the 1970s to creating the first Canadian Bioethics Center. The example and vision he has set to bridge research, healthcare, and ethics in the service of humankind will be with us for decades and hopefully centuries. Thanks to Claudia Jones and Nicole Campeau at the library, and to the IRCM leadership, in particular its director, Tarik Möröy, for his confidence in and ongoing support of this project and others.

Material in this book has been presented at several occasions during seminars, talks, and scientific congresses. I would like to acknowledge the feedback given by audiences and colleagues at the University of Tokyo, the University of Delaware, Uppsala Universitet, Université Laval, Université de Montréal, the University of Minnesota, McGill University, Stanford University, the University of Toronto, Universidade do Estado do Rio de Janeiro, the Alden March Bioethics Institute, the Montreal Neurological Institute, Université du Québec à Montréal, the National Research Council of Canada, the Jewish Rehabilitation Hospital, the University of Pennsylvania, the University of Alberta, the University of Western Ontario, York University, Universidade Federal de Rio de Janeiro, and Concordia University. I am also indebted to audiences at various scholarly meetings, including the Canadian Bioethics Society, the American Society for Bioethics and Humanities, the Society for Neuroscience, the International Conference in Clinical Ethics, the Society for Social Studies of Science, the Canadian Association for Neuroscience, the International Association for Bioethics, Association Francophone pour le Savoir, the Neuroethics Society, the International Academy of Law and Mental Health, the American Philosophical Association, and the International Society of History, Philosophy, and Social Studies of Biology. I would like to thank students from the neuroethics seminars at Université de Montréal and at McGill University for stimulating exchanges in 2008 and 2009.

Portions of chapters 1, 4, and 5 have previously appeared in E. Racine and C. Forlini, "Cognitive Enhancement, Lifestyle Choice or Misuse of Prescription Drugs? Ethics Blind Spots in Current Debates," *Neuroethics* (2008).

Portions of chapter 1 have previously appeared in E. Bell, G. Mathieu, and E. Racine, "Preparing the Ethical Future of Deep Brain Stimulation," *Surgical Neurology* (2009).

Portions of chapters 1 and 8 have previously appeared in E. Racine and E. Bell, "Clinical and Public Translation of Neuroimaging Research in Disorders of Consciousness Challenges Current Diagnostic and Public Understanding Paradigms," *American Journal of Bioethics* 8 (2008): 13–15.

Portions of chapters 2 and 4 have previously appeared in E. Racine, Comment on "Does It Make Sense to Speak of Neuroethics?" *EMBO Reports* 9 (2008): 2–3.

Portions of chapter 3 have previously appeared in E. Racine, "Which Naturalism for Bioethics? A Defense of Moderate (Pragmatic) Naturalism," *Bioethics* 22 (2008): 92–100.

Portions of chapters 4 and 9 have previously appeared in E. Racine, "Interdisciplinary Approaches for a Pragmatic Neuroethics," *American Journal of Bioethics* 8 (2008): 52–53.

Portions of chapters 6 and portions of the conclusion have previously appeared in E. Racine, O. Bar-Ilan, and J. Illes, "fMRI in the Public Eye," *Nature Reviews Neuroscience* 6 (2005): 159–64.

Portions of chapters 6 have previously appeared in E. Racine, O. Bar-Ilan, and J. Illes, "Brain Imaging: A Decade of Coverage in the Print Media," *Science Communication* 28 (2006): 122–142.

Portions of chapter 8 have previously appeared in E. Racine, R. Amaram, M. Seidler, M. Karczewska, and J. Illes, "Media Coverage of the Persistent Vegetative State and End-of-Life Decision-Making," *Neurology* 71 (2008): 1027–1032.

Portions of chapter 9 have previously appeared in E. Racine and J. Illes, "'Emergentism' at the Crossroads of Philosophy, Neurotechnology, and the Enhancement Debate," in J. Bickle, ed., *Handbook of Philosophy and Neuroscience*, New York: Oxford University Press (2009): 431–453.

I want to acknowledge the outstanding support of MIT Press, especially that of Clay Morgan, Laura Callen, Katherine Almeida, Susan Clark, and Meagan Stacey, and the editor of the Basic Bioethics Series, Arthur Caplan. Their encouragement and understanding are tremendously appreciated. Thanks to Nathalie for years of ongoing support and belief in the importance of this project and my scholarly work. I look forward to the future and seeing the lives of our children unfold. Thanks to my parents and my family members who encouraged me and who will for my life long be a daily source of inspiration.

This book is dedicated to those who have suffered and still suffer in silence.

1

Salient Challenges in Modern Neuroethics

Overview

The field of neuroethics is associated with an increasing amount of scholarly work, workshops, conferences, symposia, governmental and regulatory output, and other activities. This chapter provides a thematic overview of neuroethics and explains some of the key topics. By gaining acquaintance with these topics, the reader should get a clearer sense of why modern neuroethics has surfaced to systematically examine and tackle those challenges. Definitions of neuroethics and diverging perspectives on the field are reviewed in chapter 2, which provides an analytic overview of neuroethics.

The nervous system is the most complicated biological organ we know of and not surprisingly the one we least understand. The importance of the nervous system as a biological system is paradoxically matched by the limited understanding we have of it and of its interaction with other (inner) biological systems (e.g., immune system, endocrine system) as well as other external systems (e.g., social systems). The ethical landscape of healthcare and biomedical research on neurological and psychiatric disorders is shaped by this paradox. If we had good treatments for devastating neurodegenerative diseases such as Alzheimer's disease (AD); public comprehension of the complexity of mental health problems; and a general scientific understanding of brain function and dysfunction, perhaps many of the current ethical and social challenges we face would greatly diminish in size and scope. However, the actual context is one where we typically have limited treatments for many common and severe mental health and neurological disorders; where there is much stigma related to mental illness and cognitive and motor disability; and where available tools to understand the nervous system are imperfect.

The flip side of this bleak depiction is that the evolution of neuroscience, the area of biomedical research dedicated to understanding the nervous system, has now reached an exciting level of maturity. Work examining the biological underpinnings of neurological and psychiatric disorders is flourishing with unprecedented support and interest. The brain is often depicted metaphorically as one of the last frontiers of science, a *terra incognita*, and will likely remain a substantial challenge for scientists and healthcare professionals. Consequently, thousands of neuroscience researchers worldwide are engaged in research aimed at understanding the normal and pathological functions of the brain. The work of neuroscientists is comprehensive and ranges from genetic analysis (neurogenetics), to physiological examination of neuronal activity (neurophysiology), up to the higher-level investigation of the neural underpinnings of behavior and cognition (cognitive neuroscience). Some of the basic knowledge generated by neuroscience is now translating into opportunities to apply discoveries to and test novel insights in clinical care in AD and Parkinson's disease (PD), to name just a few conditions.

In other instances, translation of research results is moving beyond the scope of the traditional boundaries of the biomedical sciences to touch upon the biological basis of behavior (e.g., learning, deception) and personality (e.g., introversion, empathy). This research has laid the foundations for using neuroscience to inform practices of child education and judicial proceedings. In the former domain, brain-based education is being explored to improve how children are taught in the classroom and beyond (Gura 2005). What if neuroscience could determine which teaching methods are "best suited" to the biology of human brains? Could we identify the neuronal profile of future over- and under-achievers? Although these possibilities are captivating, some researchers have raised questions about the readiness of neuroscience results to inform child education (Bruer 1998), while others have highlighted the risk of favoring biological understandings and approaches to learning disabilities over social approaches and public health interventions (DiPietro 2000).

In matters of courtroom procedures, research and related discussion have surfaced about the potential of functional neuroimaging to provide evidence to exculpate defendants and mitigate responsibility for criminal acts (President's Council on Bioethics 2004). Will neuroscience be conducive to "my brain made me do it" arguments that could diminish legal responsibility (Gazzaniga 2005)? (*Functional* neuroimaging techniques attempt to measure brain activity, in contrast to *structural* neuroimaging techniques, which examine brain structure.) This raises important issues about the meaning of legal and ethical responsibility as well as the real, that is, scientifically and legally warranted, value of neuroscience to legitimately inform judicial proceedings. Under which conditions (if any) should an "abnormal" functional brain scan be factored into the equation to diminish legal responsibility? Another controversial use of neuroscience-based techniques in law relates to lie detection using functional neuroimaging. One start-up company, No Lie MRI (www.noliemri.com), based in San Diego, California, is already offering lie-detection tests using functional magnetic resonance imaging (fMRI); and in India, other imaging techniques (not fMRI) have started to be used to "reveal signs that a suspect remembers details of the crime in question" (Giridharadas 2008), even though the evidence supporting these uses is hotly debated. For example, Wolpe and colleagues have raised important questions about the lack of sufficient validity and reliability to support the use of functional neuroimaging techniques for lie detection (Wolpe, Foster, and Langleben 2005). These questions include test design issues (e.g., measuring concealed information may not be the same as measuring active lying) and countermeasures (e.g., how do you know someone is not thinking about something else while being interrogated in the scanner?). Similarly, Greely and Illes have noted the urgent need for regulation of neuroimaging lie detection before such uses become more widespread and taken up by courts (Greely and Illes 2007). Some concerns regarding the appropriateness and readiness of neuroscience-based lie-detection could also apply to the use of such techniques in brain-based education and to broader social uses of neuroscience.

With these examples in mind, one can already get a sense of the scope and far-reaching ethical and social implications of neuroscience advances in healthcare and beyond. The field of neuroethics has evolved in response to the current context to address issues related to advances in neuroscience and their potential applications. Even though much smaller in number and size than neuroscience itself, the field of neuroethics is also complex, pluralistic, multifaceted, and, contrary to some misperceptions,

considerably varied in perspective and approach. This first chapter introduces areas of neuroethics scholarship and practice as well as some common topics discussed in the field. This content should convey to the
reader a sense of the range of ethical and social challenges discussed in
neuroethics. Nonetheless, this chapter should be considered in no way
an exhaustive depiction of topics covered in the field but only an illustration of some important ethical, legal, and social issues related to
advances in neuroscience. For a more extensive review of the issues sum-
marized below, notably in neuroimaging, neuropharmacology, and
neurostimulation, please consult Walter Glannon's excellent *Bioethics
and the Brain* (Glannon 2007) and Judy Illes's edited volume, which offers
a rich diversity of perspectives on these topics and others (Illes 2006).
The following chapter (chapter 2) explores how the field of neuroethics
has developed to address some of the issues discussed in this first chapter
and reviews different perspectives on the field.

Areas of Neuroethics Scholarship and Practice

Neuroethics can be defined as a new field of contemporary bioethics
that focuses on the ethics of neuroscience research and related clinical
specialties such as neurology, neurosurgery, and psychiatry (Marcus 2002;
Wolpe 2004; Glannon 2007; Racine and Illes 2008). This new field is often
viewed as an interdisciplinary endeavor based on the contributions of
neuroscience, medical specialties (neurology, psychiatry, and neurosurgery), law, philosophy, and allied healthcare fields. The goals of neuroethics
are many; the backgrounds of stakeholders are diverse; and, accordingly,
several reasons have been put forward to justify this new field. These reasons range from concerns of neglecting the needs of specific psychiatric
and neurological patient populations to addressing social and philosophical challenges created by advances in neuroscience and neurotechnology
(Racine 2008a). I will come back to this pluralism in the next chapters.

Several areas of neuroethics scholarship and practice have surfaced.
Before introducing illustrative examples of these topics, it is useful to first
highlight distinct (but overlapping) areas of neuroethics, that is, research
neuroethics; clinical neuroethics; public and cultural neuroethics; and
reflective and theoretical neuroethics (figure 1.1).

Research Neuroethics
Ethical challenges in the responsible conduct of neuroscience research

Clinical Neuroethics
Ethical challenges in the delivery of accessible and respectful healthcare to neurological and psychiatric patients

Public and Cultural Neuroethics
Ethical challenges in the public understanding of neurological and psychiatric conditions; public engagement and the cultural representation of mental illness

— *Media*

Theoretical and Reflective Neuroethics
Theoretical and epistemological foundation of neuroethics and the impact of neuroscience research on bioethical concepts and principles

—*future of theory*

Figure 1.1
Overview of neuroethics scholarship and practice. This figure should be interpreted as an illustration of major areas of interest in neuroethics and not as a definitive categorization restricting interactions between these areas.

Research Neuroethics

Some challenges encountered in neuroethics relate to the responsible conduct of neuroscience research and the sensitive nature of research on the biological basis of cognition, emotion, and motor function. Issues range from considering how patients can provide informed consent after severe brain injury to the banking of data concerning the biological basis of personality. One revealing key issue speaking to both the sensitivity of brain data and the complexity of this information is the management of incidental findings in neuroimaging research. These incidental findings are infrequent but occur in 2 to 8 percent of "healthy" volunteers (Katzman, Dagher, and Patronas 1999; Kim et al. 2002; Weber and Knopf 2006). Important ethical and legal dilemmas surface in establishing what should be done with these incidental findings (Illes et al. 2002; Illes 2008). Are researchers obligated to report those findings to volunteers? Should the significance of findings be reviewed systematically by medical experts prior to deciding to communicate with the volunteer? Functional neuroimaging research is often conducted by researchers and students with an

yes!

ok!

interest in basic cognitive processes in nonclinical contexts, that is, research that has no purported clinical benefit for the volunteer and that is potentially conducted in nonclinical facilities. If the researchers are nonclinicians, what are their obligations to the volunteers' health, and are they responsible for reporting their observation of an anomaly to clinicians (e.g., the volunteer's primary care physician)? What if the volunteer does not want to know? Should that decision be respected? What if the volunteer does want to know but the finding suggests a life-threatening anomaly (e.g., a large brain aneurysm)? Does the researcher have a "soft paternalism" obligation to disclose the incidental finding? Should the volunteer's choice be bypassed or be respected? I have singled out incidental findings in neuroimaging as one issue in research neuroethics, but there are of course many other important challenges in conducting neuroscience research, including, for example, the management of confidentiality and privacy in brain banks (Hulette 2003) and neuroimaging databases (Toga 2002) and the establishment of sound guidelines for neuropharmacological (Macciocchi and Alves 1997) and interventional neuroclinical trials (Mathews et al. 2008).

Clinical Neuroethics

Another area of neuroethics bears on the need to address ethical issues in neurological and psychiatric care, that is, "clinical," or "healthcare," neuroethics. Issues related to healthcare can differ considerably from those surfacing in research because healthcare professionals are bound by deontological codes and have different responsibilities toward their patients than researchers have toward volunteers. Patients have the right to be informed and to exercise their own choices in matters of healthcare. Nonetheless, this imperfectly translates into practice due to potential challenges related to "information processing" and information understanding in patient populations (Beauchamp and Childress 2001). However, given that neurological and psychiatric illnesses can affect (but not necessary eliminate) decision-making capacity (e.g., later stage AD and PD, severe depression), there are important issues in the assessment of this capacity as well as in the use of specific approaches to obtain an informed decision for patients or their proxy decision makers. In addition, given uncertainties regarding the understanding of brain function, medical decisions can be plagued by diagnostic and especially prognostic uncertainties (Bernat 2004). In such cases, proxy decision making can be vexingly difficult and challenging for those who have to decide on behalf of a loved one. For example, the saga of Terri Schiavo, who was in a persistent vegetative state (PVS) following anoxic brain injury, can serve as a bleak reminder of how things can go wrong. Challenges in decision making and the communication of poor prognosis of severe neurological illness to family members, between healthcare providers, within families, and even in the general public domain can shape proxy decision making and the end-of-life process in cases of life-support withdrawal (Racine et al. 2008). The scope of clinical neuroethics issues is great given the number and diversity of patients and healthcare providers involved.

Public and Cultural Neuroethics

"Public neuroethics" includes topics related to health policy for mental health and neurology, such as resource allocation decisions as well as topics related to the "public understanding" of neuroscience research and public engagement. We know from various national and international sources such as the World Health Organization (WHO) that the public health burden of psychiatric and neurological disorders represents a key challenge for healthcare delivery in the twenty-first century (World Health Organization 2001, 2006). In many respects, neurological and mental health is essential to nations and communities for their further economic and social well-being (Beddington et al. 2008). Yet developed countries face an epidemic of depression and work-related mental health problems. When treatments and therapies do not support recovery and reintegration of daily activities, chronic illness may impose a huge toll on patients, their families, and society at large. Developing countries are also hard hit with the high prevalence of HIV-related depression and other neurological disorders such as epilepsy as well as the management of stigma associated with brain-related illnesses and disabilities. This issue has been underscored in the WHO's annual report on mental health (World Health Organization 2001) and in its more recent report on neurological disorders (World Health Organization 2006). For instance, the WHO writes that sometimes "coping with stigma surrounding the disorder is more difficult than living with any limitations imposed by the disease itself" and the organization underscores how stigma can detrimentally affect the "social prognosis" of patients because of reduced opportunities and support (World Health Organization 2006). Consequently, public understanding endeavors that foster multidirectional approaches to improve communication and mutual understanding will be crucial to alleviating stigma and discrimination. In this regard, the Australian depression-focused program beyondblue can be informative for future initiatives. This broad project has yielded palpable gains in reducing stigma and in increasing opportunities for individuals suffering or who have suffered from depression (Hickie 2004). Given the future impact of neuroscience on neurological and mental health, it is unavoidable that neuroscience progress will cross paths with broader social and economic issues with international ramifications. Accordingly, the efficient use and just allocation of health resources and the establishment of priorities in research and healthcare for mental and neurological health will likely further penetrate the broader political and international health policy landscape.

Theoretical and Reflective Neuroethics
Finally, "theoretical and reflective neuroethics" designates work examining the foundation and meaning of the field of neuroethics and, more broadly, ethics itself. For example, could new neuroscience research on the biological basis of moral reasoning and the role of emotions in decision making change how we view ethics or the approaches and methodologies we use to resolve ethical problems? For example, in a landmark study conducted at Princeton University, Joshua Greene and his collaborators examined neuronal activation in a series of ethical scenarios. They used the example of the trolley problem well known by philosopher-ethicists to illustrate how traditional moral theory poorly captures the complexity of actual moral reasoning. Briefly, the trolley problem features a runaway trolley that will, if let free to pursue its course, kill five individuals. However, if a switch is activated to change the tracks on which the trolley is running, it will kill one individual instead of the five on the first set of tracks. Generally, most respondents would think it is ethically acceptable to activate the switch if this is the only means by which the five individuals can be saved. However, in the footbridge dilemma, a variant of the trolley scenario, one has a choice between allowing the trolley to kill the five individuals on the track or pushing an innocent bystander

from a bridge onto the track to stop the trolley and save the five individuals. In this case, most would hesitate and say that this is not ethically acceptable. From a theoretical perspective, it is difficult to understand why responses would differ based on traditional ethical theories (e.g., utilitarian or deontological). Greene found that these dilemmas varied systematically in the extent to which they engaged emotional processing and that these variations in emotional engagement influenced moral judgment in ways that are ill captured by conventional moral theories (Greene et al. 2001).

Other neuroscience findings have also provoked discussions on the nature of moral reasoning. Neurologists Paul Eslinger and Antonio Damasio encountered in their practice a patient who, after suffering a lesion to the orbito-frontal cortex, could not conduct himself in socially and ethically acceptable ways (Eslinger and Damasio 1985). Damasio has hypothesized that "somatic markers," markers that evaluate the emotional bodily feeling in decision making, are absent in this patient, which leads to a form of callousness and inappropriate behaviors. Damasio has argued that emotions are key in rational decision making, contrary to rationalist claims (Damasio 1994). If Damasio is right, does this fundamentally change currently held views about moral decision making? In addition to work on the affective aspects of moral decision making, other areas of neuroscience research have provoked debates on the existence (or nonexistence) of free will (Levy 2007) and the nature of concepts such as personhood (Farah and Heberlein 2007).

These are some questions encountered in the area of theoretical and reflective neuroethics. Some scholars have named this area the "neuroscience of ethics" (Roskies 2002), but I argue later in this work that no straightforward path leads from neuroscience to ethics. True "intertheoric reduction" is likely to be very challenging if not impossible in most areas of cognitive neuroscience research because the concepts that this research starts with are so fuzzy that they need further clarification and critical analysis before any "reduction" can occur. This is one of the reasons I prefer to broaden this area of neuroethics to a more general discussion of neuroscience's impact on the foundations of ethics and on the epistemological issues associated with this discussion. I present arguments to further this perspective in chapter 9.

Salient Challenges in Modern Neuroethics

Challenge 1. Neuropharmacology to Enhance Mood and Cognition

A wide array of neuroscience-based technologies could lead to potential improvements of treatments for individuals suffering from neurological and psychiatric disorders. Among the different technologies, pharmaceuticals are an obvious and well-known therapeutic strategy, although non-biological approaches exist and can add to the efficacy of pharmacological approaches. The complexity of the brain's biochemistry and the interaction of various neurotransmission systems defy any simple approach to neuropharmacological treatments, especially for mental health problems. In addition, there are some important ethical issues in the research, development, and marketing of neuropharmaceuticals, including publication bias (Turner et al. 2008), direct-to-consumer advertising to vulnerable populations (Racine, Van der Loos, and Illes 2007), and the ethical and social issues related to the prescription of common stimulants and anti-depressants (Singh 2008). These are only a few of the ethically salient features characterizing the landscape of modern neuropharmacology.

One provocative set of issues surfaces when prescription drugs are used beyond medical indications to improve cognitive performance and manage what we usually consider lifestyle issues, such as jet lag and academic performance. Managing jet lag or improving academic results beyond average performances are not typically viewed as being within the purview of medicine and healthcare, unlike, for example, the treatment of narcolepsy and learning disabilities. The use of pharmaceuticals for reasons other than those medically intended, such as to deal with such lifestyle choices, or lifestyle goals, is commonly referred to as "cognitive enhancement" or "neurocognitive enhancement" in bioethics discussions (Farah et al. 2004). Yet the description of these practices shifts toward "prescription drug misuse" or "prescription drug abuse" in the public health literature (Racine and Forlini 2008). Already one can sense the radical divergence in attitudes reflected by the different terms "cognitive enhancement" and "prescription abuse."

Diverging attitudes toward cognitive enhancement practices has brought fierce reactions and debates. One point of view is that individuals should be free to decide if they want to pursue cognitive "enhancements"; that is, there are no substantial differences between improvements gained through pharmacological means and those gained through nonpharmacological means, such as tutoring, exercising, and the like. For example, bioethicist Arthur Caplan has argued, based on such a "liberal" perspective, that "the answer is not prohibiting improvement. It is ensuring that enhancements always be done by choice, not dictated by others" (Caplan 2003). In the same vein, Greely and colleagues have more recently argued that "a proper societal response will involve making enhancements available while managing their risks" (Greely et al. 2008). Proponents of a contrasting, more "conservative" view highlight the potential broad impact of cognitive enhancers. For example, would pharmacological enhancements have a detrimental impact on cultural traditions that have been created and handed down through generations to tackle some of the challenges that cognitive enhancers are used to surmount (e.g., anxiety, lack of sleep, developing focus and attention). Eric Cohen, a fellow at the Ethics and Public Policy Center in Washington, DC, has commented, "At stake is the very meaning and nature of human excellence and human happiness—the meaning of what we do at our best, and the connections between our real experiences and our inner understanding of the world" (Cohen 2006). This stance reflects a radically different take on cognitive enhancement beyond considerations for the respect of individual choices and preferences. The conservative view also highlights the potential impact of cognitive enhancement on the nature of human achievement, on the humanities, and on the traditions that have supported the development of human cultures across centuries.

The current debates on cognitive enhancement are complex and have important potential practical implications because diverging views on the ethical acceptability of cognitive enhancement could yield distinct policy and public health approaches ranging from *laissez-faire* to prohibition. Nonetheless, it is important to know that in the United States, 48 million individuals (approximately 20 percent of the U.S. population) over the age of twelve have misused prescription drugs in their lifetime (National Institute on Drug Abuse 2005). Practices of prescription misuse for purposes that include enhancement are not uncommon and actually seem to be gathering momentum. From 2002 to 2004, 11.3 million Americans reported nontherapeutic use of prescription drugs (McCarthy 2007). The misuse of prescription stimulants (e.g., methylphenidate, or Ritalin) in particular has been found to range from 5 to 35 percent in American college students (Wilens et al. 2008). Rates of misuse for the specific goal of cognitive enhancement (e.g., enhancing concentration, enhancing studying) range from 3.7 to 11 percent in American college students (reviewed in table 1.1). The causes underlying this evolution are not well understood, but potential contributing factors to the spread of prescription misuse include the low cost of prescription drugs relative to illegal drugs and the availability of drugs through nonmedical channels such as online pharmacies (National Institute on Drug Abuse 2005). A wide range of pharmaceuticals are being misused, such as opioids, central nervous system depressants, and stimulants (National Institute on Drug Abuse 2005). One of the most commonly discussed cases is the misuse of stimulants because of their alleged potential to "enhance" function in healthy individuals, a practice that is supported by a few studies on the cognition-enhancing effects of methylphenidate, notably on memory and planning (Elliott et al. 1997; Mehta et al. 2000; Barch and Carter 2005). However, conflicting perspectives exist. At this point, it is not impossible to exclude a form of placebo effect, as Bray and colleagues have commented in their study: "Benefits perceived by abusers may relate to increased confidence and sense of well-being, as well as to sympathetic nervous system stimulation" (Bray et al. 2004; Coveney, Nerlich, and Martin 2009).

There are several issues associated with the emergence of prescription misuse for cognitive enhancement. One is pinning down the complex nature of the phenomenon. Some descriptions (e.g., cognitive "enhancement") may suggest prematurely that there are beneficial effects to using nonmedically prescribed drugs beyond medical indications. Consequences of this include misperception of risks and potential neglect of unknown and long-term consequences of prescription misuse. Other descriptions (e.g., "prescription abuse") may imply strongly negative connotations that do not reflect how the public has integrated and accepted the nonmedical use of prescription drugs. Consider, for example, media portrayal of nonmedical use of methylphenidate as "better living through chemistry" (Zernike 2005), a "brain steroid" (Garreau 2006), or a "smart drug" (Phillips 2006). Consider also the not uncommon, but provocative, comparison of Ritalin to "study tools, just like tutors and caffeine pills" (Khan 2003). These statements do not correspond to some assumptions of public health approaches that emphasize nonmedical use as drug misuse and abuse. Hence, current public health approaches may incorporate a moral-

Table 1.1
Brief review of studies reporting prevalence rates of lifetime prescription stimulant (PS) misuse and PS misuse specifically for cognitive enhancement (CE) in college student populations

Study	Sample population	PS misuse (%)	PS misuse for CE (%)*
Teter et al., *Pharmacotherapy*, 2006	4,580 college students in a large midwestern university	8.3	5.4 (enhance concentration) 5.0 (enhance studying) 4.0 (enhance alertness)
Prudhomme White, Becker-Blease, and Bishop, *J Am Coll Health*, 2006	1,025 students at the University of New Hampshire	16.2	11.0 (enhance concentration) 8.7 (enhance studying) 3.2 (enhance grades)
Teter et al., *J Am Coll Health*, 2005	9,161 undergraduate students at the University of Michigan	8.1	4.3 (enhance concentration) 3.2 (enhance alertness)
Hall et al., *J Am Coll Health*, 2005	381 college students from the University of Wisconsin–Eau Claire	13.7	3.7 (enhance studying)
Graff Low and Gendaszek, *Psychol Health Med*, 2002	150 undergraduate students at a small, competitive college in the United States	35.3	8.2 (enhance intellectual performance) 7.8 (enhance studying)

Source: First published in *Neuroethics* (Racine and Forlini 2008)
*Data for this column are calculated based on data presented in the studies

izing or negative view of prescription misuse that is not shared by the general public. It is also of interest to note that illicit drugs would not likely be glamorized in this way; and other forms of enhancement (e.g., bodily enhancements) have received more critical reception in academia and in medical professions (Olshansky and Perls 2008).

While the debate rages over the misuse of neuropharmaceuticals and other drugs for lifestyle-fulfillment purposes, several lingering questions will need to be addressed. National Institutes of Health data suggest that over 40 percent of physicians feel challenged by discussions on prescription drug abuse with their patients, a rate similar to that for alcohol dependence discussions and far greater than for depression, where fewer than 20 percent state that they have difficulties discussing the topic (National Institute on Drug Abuse 2005). Will trends of prescription drug misuse keep growing? Will public acceptance of such practices defy the common conceptual dualistic dyads of good/bad, medical/nonmedical, licit/illicit, use/abuse? Broad social and economic forces are no doubt shaping an environment of social pressures for cognitive performance in competitive environments. For example, the Foresight Project of the UK Government Office for Science described the pressures created by international competition and relentless demands for greater ability to handle knowledge by workers in the context of social changes (e.g., changing family structures; Government Office for Science 2008). However, it is unlikely that the nature of these pressures or the motivations underlying them would be questioned by a libertarian laissez-faire approach and its attitude toward cognitive enhancement. This approach would also potentially conflict with governmental drug-approval mechanisms and professional societies, especially if current regulations are substantially modified to reflect proconsumer attitudes and diminish what some view as undue paternalism on the part of the U.S. Food and Drug Administration (FDA) and the medical profession.

Challenge 2. Informed Consent and Resource Allocation for Deep Brain Stimulation

Deep brain stimulation (DBS) is a form of neurosurgery that is now widely used to treat PD and essential tremor (ET) and is emerging as a potential treatment for some neuropsychiatric disorders (Benabid 2007). DBS involves the implantation of at least one electrode, typically in thalamic, subthalamic, or globus pallidus regions (for PD or ET), which is con-nected by very small wires (leads) and electrically stimulated by an implanted pulse generator in the upper portion of the chest (the sub-clavicular region; other sites are generally targeted in neuropsychiatric conditions). DBS was approved by the FDA in 1997 for the treatment of tremor in ET and PD, and in 2002 was more widely approved for the management of refractory PD. DBS is now an established therapy for PD and ET patients whose disease is severe and drug refractory (Greenberg 2002). A more recent humanitarian-device exemption for the use of DBS in obsessive-compulsive disorder (OCD) has been granted (U.S. Food and Drug Administration 2009). Apparently, over 35,000 patients world-wide have received DBS for those indications (Kuehn 2007). The current scientific and medical knowledge surrounding the DBS mechanism of action is still incomplete, but a widespread hypothesis is that DBS repli-cates the effects of neurosurgical lesioning (Benabid 2007). In comparison to ablative neurosurgery, however, DBS is generally considered reversible and nondestructive (Larson 2008), although it may have some irrevers-ible short-term (e.g., hemorrhage) and long-term effects (e.g., reshaping synaptic connectivity) that cannot be easily reversed.

Some neurosurgical research groups are exploring the use of DBS in severe refractory cases of major depressive disorder (MDD), Tourette's syndrome (TS), OCD, chronic pain, and multiple sclerosis (McIntyre and Mazzolini 1997; Kopell, Greenberg, and Rezai 2004; Lozano and Hamani 2004). An emerging literature documents the promises of DBS in treating these disorders (Benabid 2007). Interestingly, case reports of DBS to treat a generalized anxiety disorder (Kuehn 2007) and obesity (Hamani et al. 2008) have lead to unexpected relief of comorbid alcohol dependence in the first case and memory enhancement in the second case (without any effects on the anxiety disorder or the obesity problem). Clinical trials (see table 1.2) are under way to investigate DBS in MDD, TS, and OCD.

With the extension of DBS to neuropsychiatry, costs and resource allo-cation could become major issues. The costs of DBS devices and proce-dures for PD run several tens of thousands of dollars (approximately fifty thousand dollars for the implant, not including the expensive batteries that need to be replaced after a few years of use; Fraix et al. 2006). The costs may create challenges for patients, providers, and publicly funded healthcare services. Obtaining consent for last-resort innovative interventions is another area of ethical significance given the enthusiastic media response to DBS in PD (Racine, Waldman, Palmour, et al. 2007). A study of U.S. and UK media coverage of neurostimulation with a focus on DBS procedures found increasing coverage and marked enthusiasm for the clinical translation of DBS, with many articles emphasizing "miracle stories" where patients were literally cured (Racine, Waldman, Palmour, et al. 2007). This study also showed that the public discussion on the ethical, legal, and social issues of neurostimulation techniques differs from the extensive media coverage of such issues in genetics research. For the former, only 14 percent of the analyzed papers included ethical content, while this figure is closer to 40 percent for print media coverage of genetics and genomics research (Racine et al. 2006). Headlines emphasized strong treatment claims based on DBS as well as the "scientific breakthrough" nature of DBS procedures for a wide array of conditions. Although the impact of the media on patient behaviors and expectations is hard to assess, the history of neuroscience suggests some possible detrimental consequences. For example, Diefenbach and colleagues (1999) have presented evidence that the infamous lobotomy benefited from optimistic media coverage in the 1930s and 1940s. Hence, enthusiastic media depiction of neuroscience innovation could affect patient and public behaviors even though the extent to which this is true is very hard to determine precisely.

Ethical issues of DBS have been acknowledged and are starting to be discussed by leaders in the fields of DBS neurosurgery (Benabid 2007) and neurosurgical ethics (Fins 2000; Fins 2003; Fins, Rezai, and Greenberg 2006; Kubu and Ford 2007). Further attention is needed on the modalities of neurostimulation approval and trial initiation; allocating resources for DBS and managing waiting lists when a limited number of implants are available; ensuring sound surgical and ethical selection criteria for surgery candidates to avoid unnecessary risks and harms and to maximize output of surgery; avoiding conflicts of interest in a lucrative segment of the medical device industry; determining how future uses of DBS in psychiatry are likely to interact with issues of informed patient choice, competency, compliance, and, finally, public understanding given the precedent in psychosurgery and the enthusiastic media coverage of DBS (Racine, Waldman, Palmour, et al. 2007).

Table 1.2

Registered deep brain stimulation trials for neuropsychiatric disorders

Clinical trial	Condition	Start date	Status
Reclaim Deep Brain Stimulation Clinical Study for Treatment-Resistant Depression	MDD	Feb. 2009	Recruiting
Berlin Deep Brain Stimulation Study	MDD	Sept. 2007	Recruiting
Deep Brain Stimulation for Treatment Resistant Depression	MDD	Sept. 2006	Recruiting
Deep Brain Stimulation for Treatment-Refractory Major Depression	MDD	July 2005	Active Not Recruiting
Deep Brain Stimulation for Depression	MDD	Jan. 2004	Enrolled by invitation
Deep Brain Stimulation for Refractory Major Depression	MDD	June 2002	Completed
Effectiveness of Deep Brain Stimulation for Treating People with Treatment Resistant Obsessive-Compulsive Disorder	OCD	Mar. 2008	Recruiting
Subthalamic Nucleus (STN) Stimulation and Obsessive-Compulsive Disorder (OCD)	OCD	Oct. 2005	Completed
Unilateral Deep Brain Stimulation (DBS) of the Nucleus (Nucl.) Accumbens (Acc.) in Patients with Treatment Resistant Obsessive Compulsive Disorder (OCD)	OCD	Feb. 2004	Completed
Deep Brain Stimulation for Treatment-Resistant Obsessive Compulsive Disorder	OCD	Jan. 2001	Active Not recruiting
Pallidal Stimulation and Gilles de la Tourette Syndrome	TS	Nov. 2007	Recruiting
Thalamic Deep Brain Stimulation for Tourette Syndrome	TS	June 2005	Completed
Chronic Electrical Stimulation of Hypothalamus/Fornix in Alzheimer's Disease	AD	June 2009	Not yet recruiting
Deep Brain Stimulation (DBS) for Alzheimer's Disease	AD	Mar. 2007	Recruiting

Source: Clinical Trials Database, http://clinicaltrials.gov
Notes: Updated May 4, 2009. MDD, major depressive disorder; OCD, obsessive-compulsive disorder; TS, Tourette syndrome; AD, Alzheimer's disease

Challenge 3. Ethical and Clinical Implications of Neuroscience Research on Consciousness

The diagnosis of what are now recognized as distinct disorders of consciousness (DOC), such as coma, the vegetative state (VS), and the minimally conscious state (MCS), has a fascinating and complex history marked by the constant challenge of establishing sound diagnostic categories and appropriate clinical examinations (Koehler and Wijdicks 2008). Recent advances in neuroimaging research into the VS and the MCS have brought renewed attention to the scientific understanding of those states, assumptions regarding them, and attitudes toward treatment for those patients. In particular, sound diagnosis and prognostication (determining the patient's likely outcomes) are fundamental in the care of severely brain-injured patients. This is also true of patients in DOC such as coma, PVS, and MCS. Coma is usually a transient state of unconsciousness that rarely lasts more than thirty days. The comatose patient can awaken, move to brain death (death determined by neurological criteria, which is by all means understood as the death of the patient), or move into a VS (Stevens and Bhardwaj 2006). The VS is similar to coma but patients experience sleep-wake cycles and can open their eyes (Jennett and Plum 1972).

The common medical and scientific understanding is that vegetative patients do not have any conscious experience, do not feel pain, and do not hear or understand language (American Academy of Neurology 1989; Multi-Society Task Force on PVS 1994). They display only reflex behaviors. The VS is said to be "persistent" after one month and "permanent" after three months if it is caused by a nontraumatic injury (e.g., stroke) or twelve months for a traumatic injury (e.g., cranial trauma; Multi-Society Task Force on PVS 1994). This difference in the time needed to establish permanency of a VS reflects that nontraumatic injury is usually caused by damage to the gray matter (cell bodies), which recovers less well than white matter (the axons), usually damaged in traumatic injuries (Bernat 2006a). The MCS is a more recently accepted diagnostic category of vegetative patients that display some limited signs of repeated conscious behavior (e.g., responding to a command, such as lifting one's arm, when the patient hears his or her name; Giacino et al. 2002). DOC should not be conflated with brain death, which is death of the brain based on the whole brain death concept accepted in many countries. (In the

UK, the cessation of brain stem function is considered sufficient to diagnose brain death.) There are still many unknowns regarding the treatment of vegetative patients, and medical and scientific knowledge is still severely limited—a situation that is changing with investigations on neuronal functions in PVS and MCS. Topics under scrutiny include, for example, the true absence of consciousness of patients in PVS and their inability to feel pain.

A number of research groups have begun to examine brain activation in patients with DOC using neuroimaging techniques such as fMRI. One hope is that these techniques could identify signs of awareness, consciousness, or meaningful response in vegetative patients when the clinical examination has not. Current practice to identify signs of awareness requires careful examination by a clinician to determine if behaviors are "simply reflex responses that do not require awareness or are cognitive or intentional responses that could be made only by an aware person" (Fins et al. 2008). Hence, much hinges on the care taken by the examining physician, the state of the patient at the time of examination, and the experience of the physician in conducting such examinations. Unfortunately, misdiagnosis of vegetative patients appears to be surprisingly frequent, with some studies showing figures neighboring 40 percent (Childs, Mercer, and Childs 1993; Andrews et al. 1996; Wilson et al. 2002; Andrews et al. 2005). This context explains part of the interest in improving treatment and understanding of DOC. In addition, severe brain injury and subsequent DOC can lead to lifelong impairments, and thus, the potential to spend in some cases many years with severe cognitive or motor disability becomes a fundamental aspect to consider.

Recent research in this area has provided results that are both astonishing in their insights and intriguing in the ethical and medical questions they leave open. One of the most discussed reports was published in 2006 in *Science* by Adrian Owen and his research group, the Cognition and Brain Sciences Unit, based at the Medical Research Council in the UK. Owen and colleagues examined brain function in a twenty-three-year-old female vegetative patient who had been in a car accident. They then presented to the patient some mental imagery tasks such as imagining playing tennis and navigating in her house. They found that her brain activation patterns were comparable with a normal healthy individual performing the same tasks (Owen et al. 2006). Owen and colleagues concluded, "These results confirm that, despite fulfilling the clinical criteria for a diagnosis of VS, this patient retained the ability to understand spoken commands and to respond to them through her brain activity, rather than through speech or movement." They even interpreted their results as evidence that the patient made a "decision to cooperate with the authors." In their view, this "confirmed beyond any doubt that she was consciously aware of herself and her surroundings," a very controversial conclusion given standard views on PVS (Multi-Society Task Force on PVS 1994; Royal College of Physicians 2003). The researchers envisioned that such patients could perhaps eventually use their "residual cognitive capabilities to communicate their thoughts to those around them by modulating their own neural activity" (Owen et al. 2006). Needless to say, Owen and his colleagues' paper sparked a lot of discussion and debate in the scientific and public domains.

Owen's study is one of the most controversial studies and interpretations to date, but many other studies of patients in vegetative and minimally conscious states have sparked interest and enthusiasm in the scientific community and beyond. These have reached different stakeholders, including relatives of patients in PVS or MCS, and have led to medical and ethical questions. Can such research improve the diagnostic accuracy of DOC? Could we now be in a position to more accurately access the level of consciousness of patients and their thought processes? Are we in a position to obtain better insights into their chances of an eventual recovery? Could we even communicate with patients to learn about their end-of-life preferences if they have sufficient "residual cognitive capabilities," and if so, would patients be able to convey more complex messages to their loved ones? These questions and several others related to the potential use of neuroimaging in DOC raise important issues, especially given the vulnerability of the patients, the limited understanding of DOC, and the sometimes desperate state of parents and friends of patients. Before initiating clinical applications beyond current research uses, however, we need to examine several important scientific challenges with ethical purport, such as better standardizing of task designs used to illicit brain activation, validating current procedures on a greater number of patients, and establishing guidelines for the interpretation of brain activation in the PVS and the MCS (Bernat and Rottenberg 2007). As Nicolas Schiff, neurologist and scientist from Cornell University, commented, perhaps this research is "not ready for prime time" (Hopkin 2006). Indeed, one of the key challenges concerns the acquisition and interpretation of the data yielded by functional neuroimaging, particularly neuroimaging's ability to reveal signs of consciousness in response to simple tasks (Racine and Bell 2008). Are the responses observed really signs of awareness or consciousness or are they simply mechanical neuronal activation? How would competency and the informed nature of any expressed choice be assessed if abilities to communicate with patients were so severely limited? Other issues that need to be tackled include clarifying how scientific limitations should be taken into account before public dissemination of findings in a domain where desperation may clash with the tremendous hope conveyed in the media; establishing criteria for the ethical and clinical use of functional neuroimaging in DOC patients; determining if research guidelines intended to protect vulnerable patients lacking decision-making capacity do not prevent their participation in research that could improve their condition (Fins, Rezai, and Greenberg 2006); and determining how the clinical use of concepts like awareness and consciousness interact with various preexisting cultural, religious, and philosophical traditions.

Challenge 4. Addressing "Mind Reading" and "Mind Control"
The use of neuroimaging research creates many potential benefits and challenges, and this brief section cannot do justice to all of them (for reviews see Downie and Marshall 2007; Racine and Illes 2007; Tovino 2007). Some of the most extensively discussed topics concern the management of incidental findings (Illes 2008) or the proper scientific and sociocultural interpretation of neuroimaging research given that some concepts and behaviors investigated with neuroimaging are culturally laden (Illes and Racine 2005a). By this I mean that some behaviors and attitudes can be substantially shaped by the environment, context, and background of research participants in ways that complicate their scientific examination—social scientists refer to the "social construction of research objects" to convey this complexity.

For my purposes, I will focus on the evolution of neuroscience research based on the use of functional neuroimaging procedures such as fMRI, positron emission tomography (PET), and magnetoencephalography (MEG), which have brought some ethical and social challenges to the forefront of neuroscience research (Racine and Illes 2007). This occurred under various circumstances, including the potential benefits and risks of using these techniques beyond health research, such as to investigate the neural underpinnings of personality and behavior, that is, "neurosocial studies," mostly conducted with fMRI. Research by my colleague Judy Illes of the University of British Columbia has shown that neurosocial studies on higher-order cognition, emotions, and decision making were responsible for a small but increasing proportion of fMRI neuroimaging research in the first years of its development (Illes, Kirschen, and Gabrieli 2003). Examples of this area of research are landmark studies that have examined, for example, brain activation in moral decision making (Greene et al. 2001); deception (Langleben et al. 2002); race-based categorizations (Lieberman et al. 2005); economic decision making (McClure et al. 2004; Plassmann, O'Doherty, and Rangel 2007); and aggressive reaction (Kramer et al. 2007). For now, much of this research has remained theoretical in the sense that it has been conducted for scholarly purposes and the pursuit of basic knowledge. Some of this research, however, may eventually lead to real-world applications in lie detecting, improving efficiency of marketing strategies with neuroscience, and predicting susceptibility for engaging in aggressive behavior. How and by whom will such research be used? Should for-profit companies be allowed to commercialize these techniques and, if so, for which purposes? If not, what would be the rationale to exclude neuroscience from the marketplace of ideas and products in liberal economic and political environments? Would the combination of neuroimaging and neuropharmacological interventions create mind-controlling tools and interventions that should be scrutinized? Will the limits of current knowledge based on neuroimaging be acknowledged to prevent hasty "neuropolicy" (Racine, Bar-Ilan, and Illes 2005) based on the belief in the "mind-reading" potential of functional neuroimaging?

This last question points to the need to clarify what neuroimaging approaches can actually do versus what we sometimes think they can do. This is not necessarily a simple task. There are still many unknowns regarding what commonly used techniques like fMRI actually measure (e.g., oxygen consumption) and the measured variable's relation to neuronal activity (e.g., peaks of oxygen consumption occur after or before actual neuronal activity; Logothetis 2007). Such fundamental issues persist in the scientific interpretation of fMRI data while its research uses are expanding. This is not necessarily unusual considering the many unknowns about some current standard treatments and procedures for complex neuropsychiatric disorders like attention deficit/hyperactivity disorder and depression. So we should not exaggerate or overemphasize the limitations of neuroimaging tools, but at the same time, these tools yield results that are ripe for overinterpretations by the media and by those eager to use neuroimaging research results. As Jennifer Kulynych warned early on in contemporary neuroethics discussions, "As policymakers, the courts, and the public become aware of imaging techniques and intrigued by this window on the living brain, researchers must avoid inadvertently fueling misconceptions about the power and promise of neuroimaging. This task is complicated by media accounts that portray brain imaging technology as the functional equivalent of a polygraph, a Rorschach test, or a Ouiji board" (Kulynych 2002).   *Balance is key*

In addition to scientific and epistemological issues in the interpretation of neuroimaging research, there are particular challenges in the design of studies that investigate brain activation related to personality traits and social behaviors. Some of these challenges are familiar to psychological research and the social sciences, particularly for neuroimaging research that explores neuronal correlates for concepts that are sometimes difficult to define or are culturally laden. For example, intelligence is a multidimensional concept that can be viewed as much broader than what standard intelligence measures reveal, thus creating challenges for neuroscience studies examining the neural underpinnings of intelligence (Gray and Thompson 2004). This challenge is also apparent in the study of deception and the use of neuroimaging for lie detection. Neuroimaging applications in this domain confront major epistemological issues related to the neuroimaging paradigms used to measure the behavior of deception itself and the task dependency of most fMRI studies (the fact that activations are observed in response to tasks performed in an artificial setting; Illes 2004a; Wolpe, Foster, and Langleben 2005; Bell and Racine 2009). The potential ethical use and misuse of neuroimaging depends partly on addressing the validity of the constructs underlying research and its broader interpretation and application. Bioethicists Paul Wolpe, Kenneth Foster, and Daniel Langleben wrote, regarding the use of neuroimaging for lie detection, "Separation of a deception-related signal from the host of potentially confounding signals is a complicated matter, and depends on the careful construction of the deception task rather than the measurement technology. Sophisticated application of the technology and interpretation of results will therefore be crucial to the successful translation of these technologies outside the laboratory" (Wolpe, Foster, and Langleben 2005).

Both the scientific and the sociocultural aspects of neuroimaging research interpretation have potentially important consequences. First, this research creates challenges for meaningful integration within current social sciences and humanities approaches to objects of research (e.g., economic behavior, moral decision making). These research objects are more commonly examined in the humanities and investigated using techniques such as focus groups, interviews, or questionnaires. The emergence of different "neuro" subfields such as neuroeconomics, neuromarketing, neurotheology, and neurophilosophy is representative of a movement in that direction. The impact of neuroscience on the humanities and social practice could be profound, and neuroscience evidence, in the public's eye, could supersede all other scientific research results or discourses (Racine 2007). I have previously shown with colleagues Ofek Bar-Ilan and Judy Illes that different expectations can interact and shape the landscape for the interpretation and application of neuroimaging research. For example, we found in fMRI media coverage a belief that we humans are our brains, that the brain defines the essence of who we are, what can be called "neuroessentialism." I also encountered the belief that neuroimaging techniques can reveal direct pictures of brain function, what I have called "neurorealism" (Racine, Bar-Ilan, and Illes 2005). These aspects of public understanding of neuroscience innovation are discussed in more detail in chapter 5. Similar beliefs have been found in the marketing of neuroimaging services directly to consumers (through the Internet)—a strategy used by healthcare companies called direct-to-consumer advertising (Racine, Van der Loos, and Illes 2007).

The consequences of neurorealism and neuroessentialism could also affect how neuroimaging research is used in clinical care. As Brendel argues in *Healing Psychiatry*, sweeping philosophical reductionism could bring unnecessary or unwelcome support to biological approaches in psychiatry (Brendel 2006). Indeed, if the use of nonbiological approaches in healthcare such as psychotherapy is jeopardized on such ideological grounds, some treatment options could be dismissed hastily without there being any good biological alternative available. In a study of speech acts, Rodriguez has identified a flourishing public discourse conveying various forms of reductionism and biologization of the mind (Rodriguez 2006).

Other important questions regarding the field of neuroimaging include the use of neuroimaging and potential new, more powerful imaging techniques to inform social practices as well as the concrete handling by institutional review boards of the salient issues created by the potential uses of functional neuroimaging (e.g., "mind reading" and brain privacy).

Conclusion

This first chapter introduced salient examples of challenges created by advances in neuroscience. On the one hand, the lifestyle use of neuro-pharmaceuticals, the expanding use of neurostimulation, insights into DOC, and the potential of functional neuroimaging highlight both the promises and the wide-ranging issues that need to be tackled in neuroethics. On the other hand, the nervous system is still poorly understood, and patients and families are sometimes desperate for treatments that could make a difference. Between the hopes for the future created by advances in basic and clinical neuroscience and the current clinical and social contexts in which these technologies are applied lie many important gray zones. Some are specific to individual neurotechnologies (e.g., risks related to neurosurgical procedures of neurostimulation), while others find a home in several neuroscience contexts (e.g., uncertainties about scientific understanding of the brain). I have laid out in this first chapter some of the reasons why modern neuroethics has emerged in reaction to important ethical, social, and legal challenges. In doing so, I have left out many important questions as well as some of the previous work in "historical neuroethics" (e.g., brain death, neuroscience Nazi experiments, psychosurgery). The next chapter reviews some historical and contemporary views of neuroethics and highlights some of the perspectives in recent scholarship.

2

Reviewing Past and Current Neuroethics: Definitions, Attributes, and Perspectives

Overview

Although neuroethics is nascent as a thriving interdisciplinary endeavor, many views of the field coexist. Some views emphasize theoretical neuroethics issues raised by neuroscience while others insist on the need to address clinical neuroethics challenges of specific patient populations. In this chapter, I present and analyze some early definitions of neuroethics and identify some distinct views of the field. I also present a review of attributes of neuroethics and the ethical, legal, and social issues associated with it in peer review literature, on the Internet, and in the print media to give an overall sense of how the field has been characterized beyond formal academic definitions. This chapter and the previous prepare the subsequent discussion of pragmatic neuroethics.

What Is Neuroethics?

The previous chapter introduced some common neuroethical topics to broadly portray the field and illustrate some of the issues further discussed and analyzed in this book. Chapter 1 (purposely) did not provide an overview of various definitions of neuroethics or explain the various meanings of this field. That will be the focus of this chapter, which prepares for the two subsequent chapters' introduction of a specific view of neuroethics that I call "pragmatic neuroethics."

I am often asked by colleagues, students, policy makers, stakeholders, and curious nonacademics what neuroethics is. This apparently simple question has in fact no simple and straightforward answers. In fact, it naturally leads to challenging questions: What are the goals of neuroethics? Is neuroethics really new? Should there be a neuroethics? To acknowledge pluralism in the development of neuroethics and the absence of straightforward answers to those questions is crucial to avoid simplifications and premature judgments based on sweeping or superficial views. The most obvious reason for such prudence is that there are currently many views of the field, including what it should be doing as well as key problems that should be tackled.

Pluralism in neuroethics is often not fully or well conveyed. For example, Fins has argued that there are two views: one "focused on scientific inquiry and clinical utility," which Fins identifies as his view, and another that is "more speculative and expansive," which he identifies as the view of many contemporary authors (Fins 2008a). Fins' description captures well the media coverage and Internet portrayals of neuroethics, but much less the extent of scholarly discussions in peer review literature. Others like Parens and Johnston have criticized neuroethics for being focused almost entirely on the ethics of neurotechnology (Parens and Johnston 2007), but the closer analysis in this chapter reveals that this is only partially true. Given persisting discussions and potential misunderstandings, it is therefore crucial to review in some detail various historical and contemporary views of neuroethics to convey the complexity and pluralism within the field and thereby dispel monolithic descriptions. And as I further argue in chapter 4, and that I have mentioned elsewhere, a truly pragmatic perspective does not need to commit to monolithic or inflexible views, especially given that neuroethics is still in its infancy and some of the contributions that will flesh out this field still lay ahead of us (Racine 2008c).

Historical Definitions of Neuroethics

Despite the recent activities in the field, it is important to keep in mind precursor views of neuroethics. This is particularly important since the contributions of pioneers like Anneliese Pontius and Ronald Cranford are rarely acknowledged (for a rare exception, see Bernat 2008). This chapter does not review the history of ethics in neuroscience or related clinical specialties (which would be an enormous task) but simply identifies views about neuroethics, which in this case is understood as a vehicle that captures a specific endeavor and approach to the ethics of neuroscience and related clinical specialties.

The Harvard physician Anneliese A. Pontius, to my knowledge, coined the term "neuroethics." Pontius used it in the early seventies to highlight how different forms of early interventions to accelerate walking in the newborn could provoke detrimental long-term consequences (Pontius 1973). Pontius argued that such attempts were not cognizant of the neurophysiology of the newborn. In addition, she highlighted that such experimentation with young children could lead to ethically problematic consequences for their future development. Pontius concluded her 1973 paper on these interventions by calling attention to neuroethics: "By raising such questions, attention is focused on a new and neglected area of ethical concerns—neuroethics. In the present context, this concept stresses the importance of being aware of neurological facts and implications while experimenting with the newborn's motility" (Pontius 1973). To my knowledge, Pontius's discussions on ethics and the physiology of the newborn have remained marginal. However, and interestingly, Pontius's view hinted at other aspects of future developments of neuroethics, notably (1) the ethical issues raised by the attempts to accelerate the acquisition of behaviors (what could now be called a form of performance enhancement); (2) the importance of neurological facts for ethics because hasty interventions can be counter to neuroscience knowledge; and (3) neuroethics as a concept stressing neglected issues in mainstream medical ethics.

In the late 1980s, Ronald Cranford, an American neurologist who was extensively involved in discussions of ethics in neurology, used the term "neuroethicist" or "neuroethics consultant" to designate "a neurologist who has taken a specific interest in bioethical issues and becomes an active member of [his] IEC [Institutional Ethics Committee] or becomes an individual consultant" (Cranford 1989). Cranford had apparently used the term even in the early eighties (Bernat 2008). In his 1989 paper, Cranford discussed the ethical and legal issues in which the neurologist is often involved (e.g., infant anencephaly, brain death, acute brain injury, and dementia; this paper was in a special issue of the journal *Neurologic Clinics* dedicated to ethics). After discussing such topics, Cranford concluded, "The neuroethicist, because he or she understands the neurologic facts and has extensive clinical experience in dealing with these neuroethical dilemmas at the bedside, serves in a significant educational and consultative capacity by clarifying the neurologic facts and integrating them with the ethical and legal issues" (Cranford 1989). Cranford's view of the "neuroethicist" emphasized (1) the role of the neurologist in ethics discussions, especially to clarify neurological facts, and (2) the importance of ethical issues surfacing in neurological care. Cranford hinted in his writings that from an ethics perspective, there was something unique about both the brain and the neurologist's knowledge of it. As will be seen in the next pages, Cranford's view of the neuroethicist does not completely correspond to the discussions of neuroethics in the 2000s, but like Pontius's, it is not entirely incongruent with contemporary neuroethics. For example, Cranford's emphasis on the importance of facts maps to Pontius's view and is not foreign to Roskies' contemporary view as described below. Cranford's comments on the unique nature of the brain (and of the neurologist's knowledge of it) are also akin to modern neuroethics' frequent emphasis on the specificity of the brain.

Contemporary Definitions of Neuroethics

The modern use of the term neuroethics was reinvigorated and propelled by the writings of *New York Times* journalist William Safire, who was also chairman of the Dana Foundation, an organization dedicated to promoting neuroscience. The 2002 Neuroethics: Mapping the Field Conference, held in California, was probably the key factor leading to today's developments and to some of the current views on neuroethics (see figure 2.1). This meeting assembled dozens of experts in neuroscience, law, ethics, and other fields, including some leading scholars, to discuss wide-ranging topics (e.g., the impact of neuroscience on the self; neuroscience and social policy; neuroscience and public discourse; Marcus 2002). At that meeting Safire defined neuroethics "as a distinct portion of bioethics, which is the consideration of good and bad consequences in medical practice and biological research. But the specific ethics of brain science hits home as research on no other organ does" (Safire 2002b). This was not the first meeting dedicated to such issues; one other such meeting occurred in Europe, and the proceedings were published in 1996 in a volume edited by philosopher-psychologist Gérard Huber (1996).

Shortly after the 2002 Dana Foundation meeting, philosopher Adina Roskies was one of the first to define the field of contemporary neuroethics in a paper published in *Neuron* (Roskies 2002). Roskies argued that neuroethics is different from other areas of biomedical ethics because of "the intimate connection between our brains and our behaviors, as well as the peculiar relationship between our brains and our selves" (Roskies 2002). Roskies distinguished two parts of neuroethics: the "ethics of neuroscience" and the "neuroscience of ethics." Although she acknowledged that "each of these can be pursued independently to a large extent," she also stated "most intriguing is to contemplate how progress in each will affect the other" (Roskies 2002). Roskies parsed the "ethics of neuroscience" into two divisions: "the ethics of practice" and the "ethical implications of neuroscience." The first division of the ethics of practice deals with issues related to clinical trial design and privacy rights for neurological testing; the second division deals with the consequences of neuroscientific insights for society (e.g., criteria for life and death, determination of liability in the presence of brain injury). The second part of neuroethics (the neuroscience of ethics) deals with fundamental concepts (e.g., free will, self-control, personal identity) and how neuroscience could change them based, for example, on neuroimaging research (as discussed briefly in the last section of chapter 1 of this book; Roskies 2002): "As we learn more about the neuroscientific basis of ethical reasoning and self-awareness, we may revise our ethical concepts" (Roskies 2002).

Roskies' "knowledge-driven" (see figure 2.1) perspective is comprehensive and based on the belief that neuroethics is a legitimate endeavor that can extend beyond the reaches of traditional philosophical ethics to foster interdisciplinary collaborations and public debate. This view is not without precedent. Van Rensselaer Potter, who explicitly coined the term "bioethics" in 1970, integrated into his work this form of two-way dialogue between the humanities and the biological sciences (Potter 1970). As will be seen in chapter 3, this is why Potter saw bioethics not only as a response to the challenges posed by advances in science and technology but also as a bridge between the "two cultures," the humanities and the biological sciences. Potter's conception emphasized that bioethics was also a biologically informed naturalistic ethics. The 2002 conference and Roskies' writing have consolidated this naturalistic influence in modern neuroethics reflection and reconnected with some of Potter's original insights.

Another early definition of neuroethics was provided by sociologist and bioethicist Paul Wolpe in the third edition of the *Encyclopedia of Bioethics*. In his entry, Wolpe characterized neuroethics as a "content field," that is, one "defined by the technologies it examines rather than any particular philosophical approach." Wolpe stated that "the term *neuroethics* is used by European neurologists to refer to ethical issues in brain disorders, such as stroke or epilepsy, and it has been used at times for ethical concerns in psychiatry, child development, and brain injury rehabilitation" (Wolpe 2004). Wolpe stressed, "Neuroethics encompasses both research and clinical applications of neurotechnology, as well as social and policy issues attendant to their use" (Wolpe 2004). For Wolpe, the field's distinctive nature derives from novel questions stemming from the application of neurotechnology, because the brain is "the seat of personal identity and executive function in the human organism" (Wolpe 2004). Wolpe discussed a number of topics such as the proper medical use of psychopharmaceuticals as well as their nonmedical uses for lifestyle purposes. He also alluded, among other issues, to the impact of neuroimaging for predicting disease and the use of brain-computer interfaces. Wolpe's definition differs from the one articulated by Roskies since the neuroscience of ethics is, for Wolpe, not part of neuroethics. This divergence of views is clear in one of Wolpe's papers, co-written with neuroscientist Martha Farah, where it is stated, in reference to both Roskies 2002 paper and Wolpe's 2004 encyclopedia entry, that "the term neuroethics, which originally referred to bioethical issues in clinical neurology, has now been adopted to refer to ethical issues in the technological advances of neuroscience more generally. (Unfortunately, the term is also used to refer to the neural bases of ethical thinking, a different topic.)" (Farah and Wolpe 2004). Similar to the arguments in genomics and genetics research that called for a distinct ethics endeavor, Wolpe and Farah sustained that the field should address concerns related essentially to neurotechnological interventions because the brain is the biological basis of personality and higher-order cognition. This definition resembles Roskies'; however, Wolpe's definition emphasizes how the new technologies are changing the landscape for healthcare and social practices. This is partly why I dub this view "technology-driven" (see figure 2.1).

Knowledge-Driven Perspective (Roskies 2002)

"As I see it, there are two main divisions of neuroethics: the ethics of neuroscience and the neuroscience of ethics... The ethics of neuroscience can be roughly subdivided into two groups of issues: (1) the ethical issues and considerations that should be raised in the course of designing and executing neuroscientific studies [the ethics of practice] and (2) evaluation of the ethical and social impact that the results of those studies might have, or ought to have, on existing social, ethical, and legal structures [the ethical implications of neuroscience]... The second major division I highlighted is the neuroscience of ethics. Traditional ethical theory was centered on philosophical notions such as free-will, self-control, personal identify, and intention. These notions can be investigated from the perspective of brain function" (Roskies 2002).

Technology-Driven Perspective (Wolpe 2004)

"Neuroethics involves the analysis of ethical challenges posed by chemical, organic, and electrochemical interventions in the brain... Neuroethics encompasses both research and clinical applications of neurotechnology as well as social and policy issues attendant to their use... Neuroethics is a content field, defined by the technologies it examines rather than any particular philosophical approach. The field's distinctiveness derives from novel questions posed by applying advanced technology to the brain, the seat of personal identity and executive function in the human organism" (Wolpe 2004).

Healthcare-Driven Perspective (Racine and Illes 2008)

"Neuroethics is a new field at the intersection of bioethics and neuroscience that focuses on the ethics of neuroscience research and the ethical issues that emerge in the translation of neuroscience research to the clinical and public domain. Although there are lively discussions on the nature of this new field, the single most important factor supporting it is the opportunity for an increased focus and integration of the ethics of medical specialties (neurology, psychiatry and neurosurgery) and of the ethics of related research to improve patient care" (Racine and Illes 2008).

Figure 2.1
Three contemporary perspectives on neuroethics. The labels should be considered areas of emphasis in the different views, not implication that other aspects are neglected by these authors.

Finally, my colleague Judy Illes and I have proposed a definition of neuroethics that profiles the field as at the intersection of neuroscience and bioethics defined by a general practical goal, that of improving patient care for specific patient populations (Racine and Illes 2008). According to this view, neuroethics is a new field defined by both scholarly and practical goals to tackle challenges emerging in areas such as neuroimaging and neuropharmacology. Since much of chapter 4 is dedicated to better defining pragmatic neuroethics, I will avoid getting into further details about this view. However, one of its features is a deliberate attempt to consolidate some of the earlier historical meanings (e.g., Pontius and Cranford), focusing on the clinical aspects, with some of the contemporary views (e.g., Roskies, Wolpe) that emphasize the philosophical challenges posed by neuroscience as well as the ethical challenges of neurotechnology use. Another distinct feature of this view is its insistence on describing neuroethics as both a scholarly and a practical endeavor, akin to medicine, which attempts to understand and intervene.

Brief Overview of Definitions, Views, and Attributes of Neuroethics

Many distinct views and definitions of neuroethics have been proposed—much as the general field of bioethics is still defined in various ways. To better assess the range of attributes of neuroethics and the ethical, legal, and social issues (ELSI) discussed under the umbrella of neuroethics beyond the few historical and formal contemporary definitions that have been put forward, this section reports a review of published peer review literature from the early seventies to June 2007, thus including the five years of activity after the landmark 2002 Neuroethics: Mapping the Field Conference (Marcus 2002). The review I am presenting also includes an analysis of Web sites and media reports discussing neuroethics (search criteria for this review can be found in table 2.1).

Keep in mind that this review deliberately employed a focused strategy. Since my goal was to examine the field of neuroethics itself and related activities, I retained for analysis only sources that explicitly used the term "neuroethics." However, much ethics discussion of neuroscience happened and is happening without being explicitly tied to the concept of "neuroethics." Hence, the review captures only part of the discussion on neuroscience and ethics and should be considered a review of neuro-

Table 2.1
Search strategies and samples for review of neuroethics in peer review literature, on the Internet, and in print media*

	Peer review literature	Internet	Print media
Dates of searches	May 4 to May 15, 2007	June 22, 2007	June 20, 2007
Databases	Pubmed		
	Ovid current content	Google**	Factiva
	ISI Web of science	Alta Vista**	
	Philosopher's index	Yahoo**	
	LegalTrac		
	ETHXWeb		
Documents***	83	16	36

*Search terms were "neuroethic" and "neuro-ethic" with truncation operation allowing for variants of the term
**200 first occurring Web sites were considered
***Number of relevant documents retrieved and retained for final analysis

ethics itself rather than an exhaustive discussion on the ethics of neuroscience. Because much of the content corresponds to the years of activity after 2002, this review can also be taken as one of neuroethics activities in the early years of development.

Literature searches yielded a total of 83 peer review articles published in scientific sources, 16 institutional Web sites (e.g., research groups, professional societies), and 36 print media articles. My first goal was to identify attributes of neuroethics itself, that is, how neuroethics was viewed and depicted as an area of scholarship and practice. Table 2.2 shows that neuroethics is generally viewed across sources as (1) a new field of scholarship; (2) dedicated to examining ethical issues in neuroscience; and (3) focusing on philosophical or metaphysical issues. This is what I will refer to in later discussion as the "common view of neuroethics," that it is a new field of scholarship examining ethical issues in neuroscience, particularly those with high philosophical salience. It is interesting to note how the media depiction of neuroethics boils down to only a few attributes while the peer review discussion and even the Web site presentation are richer and more complex.

Figure 2.2 presents qualitative examples of the attributes defining neuroethics in peer review literature, on Web sites, and in print media that

Table 2.2
Common attributes of neuroethics in peer review literature, on the Internet, and in print media*

Attribute	Peer review literature (%)	Internet (%)	Print media (%)
Ethics of neuroscience	23**	81**	11**
New field	23**	75**	22**
Pluridisciplinary***	17**	25	0
Branch of bioethics	14	13	0
New discipline	13	13	0
Neuroscience of ethics	12	13	0
Philosophical concerns	11	31**	11**
New movement	1	0	0
Practical	2	6	0

*See figure 2.2 for qualitative data on the attributes of neuroethics
**One of three most frequent attributes mentioned in specific source
***Pluridisciplinary or interdisciplinary

are quantified in table 2.2. Although the terms "new field," "new discipline," and "branch of bioethics" are all represented in neuroethics, much of the discussion focuses on specific definitions of these terms and what they would mean for neuroethics. For example, if neuroethics is a new discipline, does this mean it already specific has theories, methodologies, and training programs? Or does it only mean that neuroethics is basically a new field of research? Some attributes are much more marginal, such as describing neuroethics as a new movement or as a practical field, that is, one that is driven by the desire to change practices.

The idea that neuroethics constitutes a "new field" is surely one of the most heated sources of debate. The majority of arguments sustaining the novelty of this field are based on the opinion that the brain is a special or unique organ that constitutes the biological basis of cognition and affect, consciousness and self-awareness. For example, in the peer review literature, Fukushi and colleagues have argued that "the brain and its functions are unique and should not to be treated in the same way as other biological organs and vital functions" (Fukushi, Sakura, and Koizumi 2007). Farah and Wolpe have presented a similar argument:

The brain is the organ of the mind and consciousness, the locus of our sense of selfhood. Interventions in the brain therefore have different ethical implications than interventions in other organs. In addition, our growing knowledge of mind-brain relations is likely to affect our definitions of competence, mental health and illness, and death. Our moral and legal conceptions of responsibility are likewise susceptible to change as our understanding of the physical mechanisms of behavior evolves. (Farah and Wolpe 2004)

Web sites and print media reports have disseminated this argument. For example, one European Web site stated that "not all of neuroethics is continuous with traditional medical ethics. The reason for this is that the brain is a very special organ" (3TU Centre for Ethics and Technology 2007), and a Canadian Web site claimed that "it is widely held that the brain is the organ that most defines us as human beings, both as a species and as unique individuals. . . . It follows that brain interventions are significantly different from other medical interventions, given their potential to alter our sense of self relative to certain higher order mental functions, consciousness and personal identity" (Novel Tech Ethics 2007).

Some scholars have countered that "there is still the serious question of whether the brain deserves special consideration or not. If not, there is no reason to develop neuroethics" (Fukushi, Sakura, and Koizumi 2007). Others have highlighted some of the continuity between bioethics and neuroethics. For example, with my colleague, Judy Illes, I have emphasized the many constructive avenues to bridge precedent in bioethics with innovation in neuroethics: "Why should neuroethics follow a completely different path than bioethics has for the last 35 years? It should not" (Illes and Racine 2005b).

Another important question bears on the ethical topics discussed in the neuroethics literature. What are they and which are most frequently discussed? Are fairly common bioethics topics, such as confidentiality and privacy, or respect for person and autonomy, most frequently discussed? Do novel issues raised by neuroscience (e.g., thought privacy) dominate discussions? Table 2.3 shows the five most common clusters of ELSI discussed in the peer review literature: (1) consent, autonomy, and decision-making capacity; (2) privacy and confidentiality; (3) enhancement and medicalization; (4) meaning and direction of ethical debates in neuroscience; and (5) readiness of neurotechnology. The issue of enhancement and medicalization was a common topic across the peer review literature, Web sites, and print media. Again, a fairly rich peer review

Neuroethics is pluridisciplinary or interdisciplinary

PR: "To attain such understanding, and be able to use it well, knowledge from many academic domains is required that meet in the interdisciplinary field of neuroethics" (Evers 2005).

W: "Neuroethics encompasses a wide array of ethical issues emerging from different branches of clinical neuroscience (neurology, psychiatry, psychopharmacology) and basic neuroscience (cognitive neuroscience, affective neuroscience)" (Center for Cognitive Neuroscience at the University of Pennsylvania 2007).

Neuroethics is a branch of bioethics

PR: "Bioethics, of which neuroethics is a part, is indeed a question of interpreting scientific data and placing these in ethical, legal and social contexts, but it is also a question of carrying out broad and thorough conceptual analyses of key notions" (Evers 2005).

W: "Neuroethics is most commonly understood to be the bioethics subcategory concerned with neuroscience and neurotechnology" (Wikipedia 2007).

Neuroethics deals with ethical issues in neuroscience

PR: "Neuroethics intersects with biomedical ethics in that, broadly defined, neuroethics is concerned with ethical, legal and social implications of neuroscience research findings, and with the nature of the research itself" (Illes and Bird 2006).

W: "Neuroethics covers ethical problems raised by advances in functional neuroimaging, brain implants, brain-machine interfaces and psychopharmacology as well as by our growing understanding of the neural bases of behaviour, personality, consciousness and states of spiritual transcendence" (Neuroethics New Emerging Team 2007).

PM: "At a gathering of brain scientists and philosophers hosted by Stanford and the University of California, San Francisco, and sponsored by the Dana Foundation, in which I'm involved, participants zeroed in on one portion of the world of worry about unbridled science called 'neuroethics.' It deals with the benefits and dangers of treating and manipulating our minds" (Safire 2002b).

Neuroethics is a new field or a new area of scholarship

PR: "Current efforts to delineate the field of 'neuroethics' reflect an emerging view that ethical problems in the neurosciences merit a distinct domain within the broader arena of bioethics" (Kulynych 2002).

W: "These developments give rise to numerous ethical and legal problems. As a result, the relatively new field of neuroethics is currently undergoing an explosive

Figure 2.2
Representative examples of neuroethics attributes as described in peer review literature (*PR*), on Web sites (*W*), and in print media (*PM*)

growth. Some issues discussed in neuroethics are special cases of problems which are familiar from traditional medical ethics. However, not all of neuroethics is continuous with traditional medical ethics" (3TU Centre for Ethics and Technology 2007).

Neuroethics is a new movement

PR: "Yet, from a 21st century partnership among disciplines including medical imaging and bioethics, such a movement has emerged. It has been coined 'neuroethics,' and it has connected the very earliest debates about physiological processes and psychological states dating back to the ancient philosophers to the anatomo-clinical approaches to cerebral localization and functional specialization beginning in the 16th and 17th centuries with present-day thinking" (Illes 2004b).

Neuroethics is a new discipline

PR: "As a new discipline, the terrain for 21st-century neuroethics was first formally defined in a meeting sponsored by the Dana Foundation called 'Neuroethics: Mapping the Field' held in San Francisco in May 2002" (Illes 2004b).
W: "This portal aims at providing a complete and up-to-date overview of all publications in the discipline of 'Neuroethics' from 1985 until today" (Johannes Gutenberg-University of Mainz 2007).

Neuroethics deals with the neuroscience of ethics

PR: "Neuroethics includes both the 'ethics of neuroscience' (i.e., ethical issues raised by emerging neurotechnology such as neuropharmaceutical enhancement) and the 'neuroscience of ethics' (i.e., understanding moral reasoning with the help of neuroscience methods; Roskies 2002)" (Racine, Bar-Ilan, and Illes 2006).
W: "This section is divided into two subcategories, because neuroethics, which can be understood as 'ethics of neuroscience (normative) and neuroscience of ethics (descriptive),' can focus on either normative or descriptive research" (Johannes Gutenberg-University of Mainz 2007).

Neuroethics deals with philosophical and metaphysical issues

PR: "Other neuroethical issues are more specific to neuroscience, specifically cognitive neuroscience, which concerns the human mind most directly. Like the field of genetics, which has evoked decades of ethical analysis and debate, our field concerns the biological foundations of who we are, of our 'essence'" (Farah 2007).
W: "Neuroethics confronts us with profound questions about human existence: What does it mean to be human?" (Center for Cognitive Neuroscience at the University of Pennsylvania 2007).

Figure 2.2
(continued)

PM: "We now step into the world of neuroethics. This is the field of philosophy that discusses the rights and wrongs of the treatment of, or enhancement of, the human brain" (Safire 2003).

Neuroethics deals with practical issues

PR: "Neurologists will play an increasingly important role as members of institutional ethics committees or as individual ethics consultants. The neuroethicist, because he or she understands the neurologic facts and has extensive clinical experience in dealing with these neuroethical dilemmas at the bedside, serves in a significant educational and consultative capacity by clarifying the neurologic facts and integrating them with the ethical and legal issues" (Cranford 1989).
W: "Neuroethics represents an unprecedented opportunity to integrate healthcare specialties (neurology, psychiatry and neurosurgery), the humanities and social science to improve patient care" (Neuroethics Research Unit 2007).

Figure 2.2
(continued)

discussion ($N = 21$ different issues) translated into a selective list of topics emphasized in the print media ($N = 8$ different issues) and on the Internet ($N = 10$).

The numbers found in table 2.3 convey an overview of themes emphasized (e.g., consent and autonomy, privacy and confidentiality) as well as those which are the object of marginal discussion (e.g., dignity and integrity, resource allocation, animal rights, eugenics). Closer examination of specific qualitative examples (figure 2.3) suggests that these different issues can be grossly clustered into groups of concerns and issues.

Neuroscience and Neurotechnologically Grounded Issues

First, some issues bear on the limitations of current neurotechnologies and the risks posed by the early use of clinically unproven concepts or approaches (e.g., readiness; safety, side effects, and discomfort; validity of research; reliability of research). This often reflects the fairly primitive understanding we generally have of brain function coupled with the unparalleled complexity of the nervous system.

Context-Based Issues

Second, some issues extend previous bioethics discussion in the context of neuroscience (e.g., enhancement and medicalization; evolution and

Table 2.3
Ethical, legal, and social issues (ELSI) discussed in peer review literature, on Web sites, and in print media

ELSI	Peer review literature (%)	Web sites (%)	Print media (%)
Consent, autonomy, and decision-making capacity	45**	19**	3
Privacy and confidentiality	39**	19**	0
Enhancement and medicalization	35	38**	11
Meaning of ethical debate in neuroscience	30	0	0
Readiness of neurotechnology	27	0	6**
Public involvement and understanding	23	0	19**
Responsibility	23	13	0
Commercialization and conflicts of interest	20	0	0
Identity, personhood, and spirituality	18	19**	3
Safety, side effects, and discomfort	18	13	3
Validity of research and neurotechnologies	16	6	0
Governance and regulation	16	13	0
Interpretation of research	13	0	0
Deontological and professional obligations	12	0	0
Discrimination and stigmatization	11	0	0
Reliability of research and neurotechnologies	11	0	0
Justice, access, and equity	8	0	3
Dignity and integrity	2	19**	3
Resource allocation	2	6	0
Animal rights	1	0	0
Eugenics	1	0	0

*See figure 2.3 for qualitative data on ELSI
**Two most frequently discussed ELSI per source

future direction of ethical debate in neuroscience; public involvement and understanding; commercialization and conflicts of interest; deontological and professional obligations; justice, access, and equity; resource allocation; animal rights; eugenics). This is not to say that this discussion is uninteresting or a mere replication of previous scholarship. Rather, these discussions often illustrate how new contexts of contemporary neuroscience have not been examined systematically and across disciplines. For example, public understanding of neuroscience creates some interesting ethical challenges given the problem of overinterpretation of neuroimaging research (Racine, Bar-Ilan, and Illes 2005). One also finds that the relationship between historical neuroscience and the Nazi eugenic practices (Shevell 1999) is not often acknowledged. Resource allocation is a longstanding challenge in chronic neurological and psychiatric care but is also not widely discussed. In sum, many of the issues in this second category reflect substantial challenges, based partly on new contexts created by neuroscience and partly on previous bioethics discussion.

Uniqueness of Brain Issues
Finally, a third cluster of issues is informed by some "traditional" bioethics scholarship but takes a specific twist in the context of current neuroethics discussion (e.g., consent, autonomy, and decision-making capacity; responsibility and free will; identity, personhood, and spirituality; meaning and interpretation of research; discrimination and stigmatization). Often this is the case because the brain is viewed as partly defining who we are, and hence, neuroscience has the ability to bring access to our personal thoughts and intimate lives and experiences. For example, in the discussion of respect for persons and autonomy, one finds that informed consent for incidental findings in neuroimaging research as well as consent for covert mind reading are discussed. Discussion of privacy often highlights the risk posed by viewing intimate knowledge of our brains as a source of information on who we are as individual human beings with unique personal histories and experiences. The focus here is often on the unprecedented potential access to human thought. The discussion surrounding dignity and integrity of human beings, for example, is informed partly by the potential of neuroscience to reveal who we are and partly by the "mind-control" capability of individuals or groups that could access such information.

Consent, autonomy, and decision-making capacity

Concerns about informed consent, right not to know, and disclosure of incidental findings to research participants

PR: "The fact that brain disordered individuals are often particularly vulnerable poses another set of special concerns. Issues of informed consent, for example, are often complicated by cognitive impairment or susceptibility to coercion or incentives" (Leshner 2005).

W: "New issues are surfacing such as the responsible management of unexpected incidental findings and the protection of confidentiality in neuroimaging databases" (Neuroethics Research Unit 2007).

PM: "What are the consequences of a machine being able to 'read' brains? Should it be allowed without a person's knowledge or consent? Is it an invasion of privacy, an illegal—even if noninvasive—search and seizure?" (Nut 2005).

Privacy and confidentiality

Risks and concerns related to potential harms due to sharing confidential data, privacy of research data, and privacy of thought

PR: "Risks related to the crossing of information and the limits of deidentification and anonymization are considerable, even if the most effective methods are used. What is novel and particularly interesting about privacy and confidentiality with neuroimaging (and for which there is no adequate precedent in the ethics and genetics literature) is the predicted—and unprecedented—access to human thought" (Illes et al. 2007).

W: "Similarly, law enforcement agencies are interested in brain-based lie-detection, arguing that 'the brain does not lie.' It is hard to think of a more drastic breach of privacy" (3TU Centre for Ethics and Technology 2007).

PM: "Using magnetic resonance imaging machines that detect the ebb and flow of brain activity, researchers have become so good at peering into the workings of the human mind that their work is raising a new and deeply personal ethical concern: brain privacy" (Goldberg 2003).

Enhancement and medicalization

Risks and concerns related to cognitive enhancement, overuse of medications, and concerns about socioeconomic effects of enhancement on personhood, personal identity, and authenticity

PR: "Should society be worried about the medicalisation of normal physiological processes, such as forgetfulness? Is it ethically acceptable to embrace technology to make ourselves as good as we possibly can be?" (2006).

W: "Concerns about drugs like Prozac and Ritalin being overprescribed have long raised questions about what kind of emotions and behaviors a 'normal' life

Figure 2.3

Representative examples of ethical, legal, and social issues (ELSI) discussed in peer review literature (*PR*), on Web sites (*W*), and in print media (*PM*)

is supposed to entail. Newer drugs with the potential to significantly enhance cognitive abilities, such as modafinil (Provigil) raise a host of new questions, issues" (Centre for Ethics 2007).

PM: "For example, few will dispute the benefits of the regulated use of drugs to treat diseases of the brain. But what about drugs to enhance memory or alertness, to be taken before a test—isn't this akin to an athlete unethically taking steroids before a race? If we quiet the broadest range of inattentive, hyperactive children with compounds such as Ritalin, do we weaken the development of adult concentration, character and self-control?" (Safire 2002a).

Evolution and future direction of ethical debate in neuroscience

Concerns related to the meaning and direction of neuroethics and bioethics and the influence of public groups, politics, religion, and culture on bioethics

PR: "As individuals and as a profession, we should consider the role(s) we want to play in the ethics of neurocognitive enhancement and take action before technology and market forces eliminate our options. However, scientists should be encouraged to take moral responsibility for their research and to monitor and foresee, as far as possible, the consequences of their work. It can be very difficult for scientists to anticipate the implications of their work, particularly at the discovery stage. Nevertheless, consideration for the ethical implications of research could be further encouraged by funding bodies, in the same way that scientists have been urged to engage in the public dissemination of their results" (Bush 2006).

Readiness

Risks and concerns about premature applications of research, especially in legal and socioeconomic contexts, and concerns about public pressure on hasty translation of research

PR: "As a result, it is conceivable that market interest in neurocognitive enhance-ment drugs could result in the drugs being commonly used before the potential long-term effects are sufficiently understood" (Bush 2006).

Public involvement and understanding

Concerns related to "public autonomy" and responsibility, such as lack of public consultation; absence of public debate; manipulation of public opinion; and undemocratic procedures

PR: "As the field of neuroethics emerges, it will be critical to bring members of the public into its discussions early on so that future research proceeds in a manner that is sensitive to public hopes and concerns. Any effort at public engagement should be grounded in a genuine dialogue, where each party listens to and respects the hopes, fears, and unique perspectives of the other. Scientists

Figure 2.3
(continued)

must reach out to the public for help with framing the research agenda, for posing scientific questions we might ask to help clarify issues of public concern. Finally, there should be mechanisms established to enable the public to help shape the regulatory framework that will guide the conduct of research and how the products of neuroscience research are used" (Leshner 2005).

PM: "The conference 'mapping the field' of neuroethics this week showed how eager many scientists are to grapple with the moral consequences of their research. It's up to schools and media and Congress to put it high on the public's menu" (Safire 2002a).

Responsibility and free will

Concerns about the meaning of free will and responsibility of individuals, especially for being legally and morally responsible for their actions

PR: "A core issue with clinical, ethical, and legal characteristics concerns personal responsibility in brain-disordered individuals. If we understand schizophrenia to be a brain disorder, how do we deal with the violent and sometimes criminal behavior that can be exhibited by these patients? Should they be held personally responsible for the workings of their disordered brains? The same question is often asked when talking about addiction as a brain disease. If addicts commit crimes to procure drugs necessary to assuage their compulsions, how should they be held responsible or dealt with?" (Leshner 2005).

W: "We perceive this as relevant to the defendant's responsibility for his or her behavior, and it seems reasonable to punish a person less harshly if they are less responsible. This may put us on a slippery slope, however, once we recognize that all behavior is 100% determined by brain function, which is in turn determined by the interplay of genes and experience" (Center for Cognitive Neuroscience at the University of Pennsylvania 2007).

PM: "Future developments involving lie detection, psychoactive drugs, brain mapping and other topics could change the law even more, forcing lawyers and scientists to rethink fundamental concepts such as privacy and personal responsibility" (Tamber 2005).

Commercialization and conflicts of interest

Concerns about the relationship between neuroscience research and various conflicting interests (e.g., for-profit sector), and concerns related to intellectual property and patents

PR: "A competitive health care marketplace can tempt professionals to employ extreme marketing strategies to entice consumers. Under pressure to generate or increase revenue, individual practitioners or organizations may chose to make exaggerated or unsubstantiated claims about the effectiveness of a novel service or neurocognitive enhancement procedure" (Downie and Hadskis 2005).

Figure 2.3
(continued)

Identity, personhood, and spirituality

Concerns related to the incompatibility of spiritual or implicit views and neuro-science discoveries regarding mind and brain

PR: "Mapping or intervening in the brain can reveal and affect the nature and content of our mind and thus who we essentially are. The incompatibility between the intuitive or religious view of persons and the neuroscience view is likely to have broad social consequences" (Glannon 2006a).

W: "These issues concern significant issues at the core of how we understand what it means to be human. Our brain is more directly related to our notions of self than any other part of our body" (Centre for Ethics 2007).

PM: "Our generation has outlived science fiction. Just as we have anti-depressants today to elevate mood, tomorrow we can expect a kind of Botox for the brain to smooth out wrinkled temperaments, to turn shy people into extroverts, or to bestow a sense of humor on a born grouch. But what price will human nature pay for these nonhuman artifices? What does the flattening of people's physical and mental differences, accompanied by a forced fitting of mental misfits, do to the diversity of personality that makes interpersonal dynamics so fascinating?" (Safire 2002a).

Safety, side effects, and discomfort

Concerns regarding side effects of clinical procedures, unintended physical and psychological consequences for patients or volunteers, long-term effects, psycho-logical unease or discomfort, and protection of subjects enrolled in protocols

PR: "How safe are the new methods of neuroscience, such as transcranial magnetic stimulation or high-field MRI, and who should decide?" (Farah 2002).

W: "Side effects and unintended consequences are a concern with all medications and procedures, but in comparison to other comparably elective treatments such as cosmetic surgery, neuroscience-based enhancement involves intervening in a far more complex system" (Center for Cognitive Neuroscience at the University of Pennsylvania 2007).

PM: "Even enhancement advocate Hughes agrees that safety remains important. The Food and Drug Administration needs to certify drug safety 'and it needs to be independent of the biomedical industry in a way that it hasn't been,' he says" (Lamb 2004).

Validity of research and neurotechnologies

Concerns related to appropriate and rigorous research design, and concerns about poorly designed studies, lack of standards, small numbers of research subjects

PR: "Before any test is offered clinically for which counseling will be needed, the validity of the test, including psychometric reliability and sensitivity, must be in place" (Illes et al. 2007).

Figure 2.3
(continued)

W: "Project 2 will develop methods to deal with two significant problems encountered in pediatric MRI research: the anxiety and discomfort MRI scans cause children and the low quality imaging data resulting from the tendency for children to move during MRI procedures" (Neuroethics New Emerging Team 2007).

Governance and regulation

Concerns about government control over research and governmental efficiency in managing research; concerns about nonexistent or insufficient legislation and related fears of the public about ethics governance by ethics committees

PR: "The individual, not corporate or government interests, should have sole jurisdiction over the control and/or modulation of his or her brain states and mental processes. How will these emerging technologies, with an enhanced capacity to monitor and control cognitive function, be restricted or applied? How will the law cope with discoveries and revelations from brain science that call for a revision of some of its most basic core assumptions of human autonomy and freedom?" (Sententia 2004).

W: "A strong legal and ethical foundation needs to be constructed upon which sound policy decision, clinical guidelines and best practices, and research protocols can be built in the neuroimaging field" (Neuroethics New Emerging Team 2007).

Meaning and interpretation of research

Concerns about the meaning and direction of neuroscience research; concerns about misinterpretation of research and use of partial data; and concerns that neurosciences threaten morals and ethics and social, cultural, and family values

PR: "Further, these trends bring to the foreground what would appear to be a strict epistemological challenge at the core of neuroethics—proper interpretation of neuroimaging data" (Illes and Racine 2005a).

Deontological and professional obligations

Concerns about doctors' responsibility for patients; concerns about rigorous clinical practice, false beliefs of clinicians, lack of knowledge of clinicians, negligence of clinicians, and integrity of researchers and healthcare professionals

PR: "Clinicians must not overstep the boundaries of their professional competence by offering recommendations related to pharmacologic or other enhancement options for which they are not adequately trained or do not have statutory authority" (Bush 2006).

Discrimination and stigmatization

Concerns about prejudice or damage caused by exclusion or negative labeling; concerns about vulnerability of individuals with brain disease or mental illness

PR: "The possible benefit of predictive imaging would have to be carefully

Figure 2.3
(continued)

weighed not only against possible harm but also against the burden of knowledge and the possible discriminations caused by being an at-risk patient. In the future, however, it might be possible to more reliably 'read' personality features, psychiatric history, truthfulness and hidden deviations from a brain scan. This could be exploited for such purposes as screening job applicants, assessing insurance risks, detecting a vulnerability to mental illness, determining who qualifies for disability benefits, and so on" (Fuchs 2006).

Reliability of research and neurotechnologies
Concerns related to reproducibility of results and sustainability of technology
PR: "Standardized, reproducible protocols in which sensitivity and specificity of different measures are well established will be crucial in making decisions for individual patients" (Illes et al. 2007).

Justice, access, and equity
Concerns related to the just treatment of persons and equal access to technology and healthcare
PR: "Testing might exacerbate existing disparities, largely through access. If predictive imaging becomes commercialized, those who cannot afford tests may not be able to get them" (Illes et al. 2007).
PM: "In a world where rich economies have denied cheap AIDS drugs to Africa, where they could save millions of human lives, it's unrealistic to think people will lose any sleep over an unfair distribution of 'smart' drugs. So relatively speaking, the rich will get smarter and the poor will get stupider, a cognitive divide. Of course, this is not different from rich people sending their children to the best schools. Or is it?" (Evenson 2003).

Dignity and integrity
Concerns related to treating humans as mere means and not ends; concerns based on the sanctity of life; concerns related to mischievous uses, inhumane or cruel uses, uses that jeopardize human dignity
PR: "By prodding into our brains and studying our reactions, people may discover how best to make us buy something we don't need and that will, perhaps, run us heavily into debt. Worse, though, shrewd politicians might exploit these psychological 'highways' to get elected against our best interests or beliefs. As Dr. Kennedy said, 'I don't want my employer or insurance company to know about my genome; even less so about my brainome.' And although many claim to respect individual privacy, how will society ensure that our brainomes don't find their way into some politicians' or marketers' offices, ready for the next mass-market campaign? Humans represent a unique species as they are endowed with thought, self-awareness, and free volition. How can we avoid allowing that others, by accessing our brainomes, may change our sense of

Figure 2.3
(continued)

ourselves, how we fit into the world, how we treat others, and how we decide between right and wrong?" (Mariani 2003).

W: "Research on electronic brain enhancement conjures up frightening scenarios involving mind control and new breeds of cyborg" (Center for Cognitive Neuroscience at the University of Pennsylvania 2007).

PM: "But what of the hooking up of software with what computerniks call 'wetware' (the human nervous system) to combine human imagination with a machine's computational speed? Is this the next logical step of evolution, or an invitation to a controlling organization, as a NASA neuroethicist put it, 'to hack into the wetware between our ears'?" (Safire 2002a).

Resource allocation

Concern regarding the ethical distribution of resources (i.e., finances, procedures, services) and insufficient resource provision by institutions (i.e., government, university, hospital).

PR: "However, if everybody has the right to fulfill their potential, this surely must also include 'already-clever' people who choose to enhance. The medical profession has a duty to service those in need. But it is not inconceivable that limited healthcare resources could mean that, in the future in the UK, certain people would be able to receive cognitive enhancement on the National Health Service while others would be urged to 'go private'" (Turner and Sahakian 2006).

W: "Another such question might be: Is it fair for the wealthy to have access to neurotechnology, while the poor do not?" (Wikipedia 2007).

Animal rights

Concerns for animal rights and animal welfare; respectful and ethical treatment of animals in research

PR: "We engaged in a discussion of a possible new frontier for animal neuroethics, hearing proposals for more humane means of acquiring neural signals using optical imaging techniques rather than conventional electrode implants, achieving motivational effects using social competition paradigms instead of food deprivation paradigms, and even of a 401K-type retirement plan for monkeys once their involvement in experiments is complete (as the alternative is not conducive to their longevity) (Fujii 2006)" (Illes 2007b).

Eugenics

Risks and concerns related to selection of individuals based on cognitive abilities, and concerns about the desire to enhance humans based on the selection of features of the brain

PR: "Historical precedent illustrates how researchers in neuroscience have supported infamous acts such as those leading to the extermination of the most vulnerable in the German Third Reich" (Racine and Illes 2006).

Figure 2.3
(continued)

The presentation of previous neuroethics discussion under these three clusters should be viewed as a general overview of how current ethical discussions have tended to aggregate.

Conclusion

In this chapter's review of different definitions of neuroethics, I have underscored how the philosophical, technological, and clinical challenges of neuroscience yield distinct views of the field. This pluralism is not atypical of bioethics, where competing views on the goals and methods of the field have sparked heated debates for several years. One of the key challenges for neuroethics, however, is to remain an open field where different perspectives about ethical issues and about the field itself can find room to grow (Racine 2008a).

In my review of previous work in neuroethics as well as coverage of the field on the Internet and in print media reports, focusing on the first five years following the landmark 2002 Neuroethics: Mapping the Field Conference, I found that although the field of neuroethics carried a number of defining attributes in the peer review literature, the translation to the public domain emphasized that neuroethics is an interdisciplinary field that addresses highly philosophical issues (in contrast to practical topics) related mostly to neuroscience research (in contrast to clinical care). This is an important finding that partly supports critical comments like those of Fins, suggesting that neuroethics has strong philosophical components (Fins 2008a). However, this is much truer for the media coverage and Internet depictions of the field than for the scholarly discussions. Other attributes, such as neuroethics being a practical field or one that captures not only an ethics of neuroscience but also a neuroscience of ethics, are more marginal even though, as I will argue, they are constitutive of the field. I also found that a wide range of ethical, legal, and social issues were discussed in the peer review literature (figure 2.2), but that again, the discussion of these on Web sites and in the print media boiled down to a much more limited set of issues. Grossly speaking, there were three clusters of issues: those that focused on scientific and epistemological limitations of current neurotechnologies; those that examined "traditional" bioethics issues in the contexts created by neuroscience; and those that were discussed in light of the uniqueness of the brain and the

potential mind-reading capabilities of neuroscience tools, with, consequently, heightened concerns of thought privacy and the integrity of the
person. At this point, I have not argued for any specific perspective but
rather presented several important neuroethical topics (chapter 1) and
reviewed aspects of the field of neuroethics itself (this chapter). The next
two chapters lay the foundation for the presentation of pragmatic neuroethics. Specifically, chapter 3 presents a specific view of bioethics called
"pragmatic naturalism," which highlights how bioethics distinguishes
itself, among other forms of ethics and social regulation (e.g., philosophical ethics, theological ethics), by its commitments to practical outcomes
and its interdisciplinarity. This view is then used to discuss, in chapter 4,
how pragmatic naturalism yields a distinct view of neuroethics and how
it addresses a number of controversies surrounding the field.

3

Pragmatic Naturalism in Bioethics

Overview

The two previous chapters introduce and review the field of neuroethics to give an overview of topics of concern and different perspectives on neuroethics. This chapter highlights how different forms of pragmatism are at work in bioethics and argues for a more explicit pragmatic take that extends bioethics' commitments to interdisciplinarity, collaboration, and beneficial practice changes. First, I present different waves of naturalism in bioethics, including how neuroethics has reinitiated discussions on the relationship between the biological sciences and the humanities. I then argue that bioethics itself is a form of pragmatic naturalism as illustrated by bioethics' commitment to interdisciplinary collaborations and its practical focus. This sets the stage for developing a view of neuroethics informed by moderate and pragmatic naturalism.

"Naturalism," sometimes called "pragmatism" in bioethics, is a source of debate within the bioethics community and beyond. Naturalism is a general term used to designate various philosophical approaches and epistemological commitments, including some that emphasize the importance of establishing bridges between the humanities and the biological sciences; proclaim that some social and moral phenomena can be explained by the biological sciences; sustain that ethical norms have a biological basis in natural laws; or argue for the role of qualitative research based on symbolic interactionism. Jonathan Moreno has argued that bioethics is an unacknowledged form of naturalism inasmuch as bioethics is a practical field heavily influenced by forms of American pragmatism that support interactive methodologies and practical goals, such as the social engagement of bioethics and openness to marginalized voices (Moreno 1999). Others prefer the term pragmatism to designate some of these characteristics of bioethics and do not emphasize epistemological relationships to naturalism (Fins, Bacchetta, and Miller 1997). In France, Anne Fagot-Largeault has argued a similar point to Moreno's, based on her view that bioethics constitutes an adaptive case-based social regulation movement (Fagot-Largeault 1987, 1993). This feature of bioethics brings it more in line, for example, with Aristotle's naturalistic philosophy than with Sartre's antinaturalistic existentialism. Others have contended that bioethics has taken a neopragmatic turn (Wolf 1994), while some scholars have been engaged in clarifying the methodological implications of naturalism in bioethics (Donnelley 2002). Finally, others have highlighted the challenges of pragmatism, such as its practical usefulness (Bellantoni 2003) and relationship to existing moral theory (Jansen 1998).

Interestingly, the initial definition of bioethics by Van Rensselaer Potter in the early seventies captured a form of naturalism promoting the integration of biology and the humanities. At the core of Potter's concept of bioethics, nature and the study of biological phenomena had a key role in informing ethics and the humanities, much as the biological sciences needed values and guidance from the humanities. This naturalistic approach, and the two-way relationship between the life sciences and the humanities it implied, now represents a highly marginal view within contemporary bioethics even though it is revived within the emerging field of neuroethics (Roskies 2002; Evers 2007b). Indeed, most of bioethics is a form of "interdisciplinary biomedical ethics" that has no explicit commitment to Potter's naturalism and his views on the relationship between the biological sciences and the humanities, which he intended to reflect in the compound neologism "bio-ethics."

In spite of current debates about naturalism and pragmatism in bioethics, little clarification has been put forward to identify different epistemological stances and concomitant theoretical commitments regarding naturalism. In an effort to further this debate and provide some foundation for the following discussions in this book, I present three epistemological stances: antinaturalism, strong naturalism, and moderate pragmatic naturalism. I recall that the dominant paradigm within philosophical ethics has been antinaturalism, that is, the rejection of the idea that facts and experience can contribute meaningfully to ethical inquiry. This explains partly why Toulmin argued that "medicine saved the life of ethics," since ethics was pursued for some decades mainly as a highly theoretical philosophical endeavor (Toulmin 1982). Rejection of antinaturalism and acceptance of naturalism, however, is often associated with strong forms of naturalism that commit the naturalistic fallacy and threaten to reduce the normative dimensions of bioethics to biological imperatives. These are rightly dismissed as pitfalls since ethics is in part a struggle against what is viewed as the course of nature. This rejection of strong naturalism, however, often carries bioethicists away from acknowledging some of their implicit moderate naturalistic commitments.

In this chapter, I argue that a moderate pragmatic form of naturalism represents an epistemological position that embraces the tension between antinaturalism and strong naturalism; bioethics is neither disconnected from empirical knowledge nor is it subjugated to it. I provide examples showing that this position is in fact the underlying implicit epistemological paradigm of much of mainstream bioethics. I first provide a quick background by identifying successive but loosely connected waves of debate on naturalism in bioethics. Second, I identify and discuss three relevant epistemological paradigms and highlight the value and relevance of pragmatic naturalism.

Naturalistic Epistemology in Bioethics

First Wave Naturalism: Bioethics as Strong Naturalism
The first wave of naturalism in bioethics begins with the concept of bioethics itself, first proposed by Van Rensselaer Potter in a 1970 paper entitled "The Science of Survival" (Potter 1970). Potter wrote on bioethics keeping in mind Charles Percy Snow's then popular analysis of the uneasy relationship between the "two-cultures": the life sciences and the humanities. Potter suggested that a new science of survival requiring a two-way relationship between the life sciences (bio) and the humanities (ethics) be fully developed into the discipline of bioethics (Potter 1971, 1972; like Charles Snow, Potter largely left out the third culture of the social sciences). For Potter, bioethics would take into account knowledge of the natural world and yield a new form of wisdom to ensure the survival of

the human species. The metaphor he constantly used to describe the new relationship between the two cultures was that of a bridge, one that would establish and sustain channels of communication between the two cultures:

The purpose of this book is to contribute to the future of the human species by promoting the formation of a new discipline, the discipline of Bioethics. If there are "two cultures" that seem unable to speak to each other—science and the humanities—and if this is part of the reason that the future seems in doubt, then possibly, we might build a "bridge to the future" by building the discipline of Bioethics as a bridge between two cultures. (Potter 1971)

For Potter, bioethics was therefore an ethics of the biological sciences as we often view bioethics today but also a new form of ethics informed by biology, especially cybernetics and systems biology, which greatly influenced Potter's thought. This naturalistic root of bioethics, where the biological sciences were to play a key role, is at odds with much of contemporary bioethics, perhaps best described as "an interdisciplinary biomedical ethics" without any explicit commitment to naturalism in the sense of Potter's "bio-ethics"—an ethics informed by biology.

Second Wave Naturalism: Revisiting Antinaturalism

As bioethics moved forward, it rapidly lost collective memory of Potter's work and evolved with its own set of progressively defined goals and approaches. By the early nineties, a second wave of naturalism surfaced to question some of the then traditional antinaturalistic commitments of ethics. Some leading authors in bioethics started to discuss the relationship between pragmatism and bioethics, mainly putting into question the apparent predominance of antinaturalistic epistemology found in some of the early versions of principle-based approaches. Bioethicists started to feel estranged from conventional moral theories. For example, in 1994, Susan Wolf reviewed bioethics advances at that time, suggesting the emergence of a form of neopragmatism in the field (Wolf 1994). Wolf argued that, among other things, bioethics' own liberal commitments and disregard for context in the early form of "principlism" led to the creation of alternative theoretical frameworks such as narrative ethics, casuistry, and feminist ethics:

This growing attention to context, to empirical realities, and to difference has been diagnosed as "inductivism" or sometimes Rawlsian "coherentism" in bioethics. However, placed side-by-side with the comparable shift in health law, it seems part of larger trends. This is not just parochial ferment in the limited ranks of bioethicists. Instead, it seems linked to the rise of a new paradigm. John Dewey, William James, and Charles Sanders Peirce have come to visit the clinic and find much to criticize. (Wolf 1994)

In 1996, Daniel Callahan sparked a debate on naturalism in the pages of the *Hastings Center Report*. In his paper entitled "Can Nature Serve as a Moral Guide?" Callahan questioned the validity of the naturalistic fallacy and the strong distinction between "is" and "ought" (Callahan 1996). Other authors brought forward additional arguments, highlighting some of the problems with the classic distinction. For example, Norton indicated, based on the heritage of American pragmatism, that facts are always informed by values and that all values refer to concrete experiences (Norton 1996). Donnelley warned that ethics needs to be attentive to the movement of reality and should shy away from static and dualistic concepts, for example, mind and body, nature and nurture (Donnelley 1996).

In France in the 1980s, independently of American bioethics scholarship, Anne Fagot-Largeault sustained that bioethics represents a naturalism inasmuch as bioethics is an auto-regulation process based on social adaptation. In this sense, bioethics was, for her, closer to Aristotle's thought than Sartre's insofar as elaborations of norms and codes represent a type of "phronesis" in the search for appropriate solutions to particular cases (Fagot-Largeault 1987). She considered bioethics to be part of the normalization of the powers humankind acquires through self-knowledge gained in the biological and health sciences (Fagot-Largeault 1987). Interestingly, and without there being any formal connection, this view of bioethics as an adaptive, quasi-evolutionary process to achieve a new form of wisdom corresponds, in part, to Potter's conclusion that contemporary culture's solutions to new ethical problems were inadequate to tackle emerging challenges.

These writings did not refer to Potter's initial naturalistic view of bioethics and its intended meaning. However, they represent key moments of a second and independent wave of naturalism where bioethicists started discussing some of their implicit commitments to some forms of pragmatism and naturalism and the often unquestioned acceptance of antinaturalism. At the same time, other scholars started exploring pragmatic approaches to bioethical theory (Mahowald 1994).

Third Wave Naturalism: Bioethics' Naturalistic Pragmatic Commitments
A third wave of naturalism, building on the previous one, brought a
pragmatic form of naturalism to the foreground. For example, Jonathan
Moreno explicitly argued that bioethics is a naturalism (Moreno 1999).
Moreno claimed that bioethics feeds on the American pragmatic philosophical tradition of John Dewey and George Herbert Mead, among
others. Moreno (1999) differentiated, much like Fagot-Largeault (Fagot-
Largeault 1993), between a strong and a more moderate form of naturalism. Following Moreno's terminology and analysis are epistemological
naturalism (following Quine) and philosophical naturalism (inspired by
pragmatism). Both forms of naturalism reject foundationalism, the belief
in fundamental ethical principles that rely on a priori inquiry (Moreno
1999). The first form of naturalism takes the natural sciences as an epistemological model and relies on a theory of knowledge where there is a
strong distinction between subject and object. The second acknowledges
interactions between subject and object and considers knowledge to be a
dynamic and interactive process between the observer and the phenomenon observed (Moreno 1999). This epistemological stance implied, for
Moreno, that the natural sciences are not the only model of inquiry even
if the scientific method based on the experiential nature of knowledge
should be preferred (Moreno 1999):

In rejecting epistemological naturalism, American philosophic naturalism also
rejects the notion that the ultimate authority on the nature of the world is natural
science, and the only questions that can legitimately be framed about the world
must be expressed in the terms of natural science. The philosophic naturalist
stresses the method of science rather than the content of science. Too great an
emphasis on the content of science can lead to scientism, which is the substitution
of dogma derived from current scientifically validated ideas for the open-minded
inquiry and critical thinking of the method of science. (Moreno 1999)

Judith Andre has also written eloquently on the nature of bioethics as
a practice and how this makes it a form of ethics, in nature and in commitments, quite different from traditional academic forms of ethics
(Andre 2002). This third wave of naturalism has generated many debates
as well as much scholarship on the nature of bioethics and the role
of theory and methods in bioethics. For example, some scholars have
proposed pragmatism as an explicit methodology for clinical ethics
(Fins, Bacchetta, and Miller 1997), and others have started to systemati-

cally explore the thought of Dewey and James and their possible contribution to bioethics on specific epistemological topics (Schmidt-Felzman 2003).

Fourth Wave Naturalism: The Bridges between Mind and Brain

Neuroethics was yet another moment when naturalistic commitments surfaced in bioethics. For example, Roskies views neuroethics, as discussed in the previous chapter, as a field that integrates both the neuroscience of ethics and the ethics of neuroscience (Roskies 2002). This perspective strikingly resembles Potter's definition of bioethics. Likewise, several authors have started to explore and discuss the contribution of neuroscience to ethics. For example, in an interesting paper, Farah and Heberlein (2007) discussed the potential implications of cognitive neuroscience on our understanding of personhood. More than three decades after Potter, the view of bioethics as a two-way dialogue between the life sciences and the humanities is gaining interest, especially as neuroscience research approaches topics such as moral reasoning, responsibility, and higher-order cognition and calls for further interdisciplinary exchanges (Schmidt-Felzman 2003). Under the impetus of scientific advances, and after a tradition of scholastic antinaturalism in philosophy of mind, the discussion on the mind–body relationship is reconnecting (Smith 2001) with its broader implications for the future of the humanities, our understanding of moral behavior, and the ability of biological knowledge to contribute to ethics.

This brief and, I will be first to acknowledge, selective sketch of naturalistic epistemology in bioethics would of course need to be further detailed. For my purposes, it clearly shows how different debates and scholarship on naturalism in bioethics have been only loosely connected and therefore call for further theoretical clarification. Neuroethics needs to build on these debates and define more clearly how it contributes to naturalism in bioethics.

Bioethics and Naturalism

Building on and borrowing from the different successive waves of naturalism in bioethics, I now introduce and discuss three broad epistemological stances on the field. Each epistemological posture is described according to its commitments and views relative to the following seven epistemological and metaethical issues. It should be noted that the stances described here are ideal types: no author has sustained all of these theoretical commitments together but most of these have been argued for separately in the literature by various authors.

1. The "is"-"ought" distinction
2. The reduction of ethical predicates to natural properties
3. The nature of ethical knowledge
4. The nature of ethical principles
5. The sources of ethical principles (a priori or a posteriori)
6. The disciplinary status of bioethics
7. The nature of normative ethics and metaethics

Antinaturalism

Antinaturalism (AN) can be characterized by the following seven epistemological commitments:

(AN$_1$)   There is a strong distinction between "is" and "ought."

(AN$_2$)   Ethical predicates are irreducible to natural properties.

(AN$_3$)   Ethical knowledge is not reducible to empirical knowledge.

(AN$_4$)   Ethical norms are not natural laws.

(AN$_5$)   Ethical norms stem a priori from human reason and theoretical reflection.

(AN$_6$)   Ethics is an autonomous discipline.

(AN$_7$)   Normative ethics and metaethics are conceptual and not empirical.

Antinaturalism has long-inspired Anglo-American philosophical ethics. This stance is supported by the philosopher David Hume's historical distinction between "is" and "ought," facts and values. On the one hand, there are facts and their descriptions, and on the other, "oughts" and prescriptions. An evaluation or an axiological judgment based on normative principles is required to ensure the argumentative transition (AN$_1$). The naturalistic fallacy of deducing an "ought" from an "is" was identified by Hume and is still widely considered to be an illegitimate and illogical form of ethical reasoning:

In every system of morality . . . I have always remark'd, that the author proceeds for some time in the ordinary way or reasoning, and establishes the being of a God, or makes observations concerning human affairs; when all of a sudden I am surpriz'd to find, that instead of the usual copulations of propositions, is, and is not, I meet with no proposition that is not connected with an ought and ought not. . . . how this new relation can be a deduction from others, which are entirely different from it. (Hume 1975 [1739])

Hume's distinction was radicalized by one of the first analytic philosophers, G. E. Moore. Moore upheld in his *Principia Ethica* that the *good* is the ethical concept *par excellence*, a non-natural property to which all ethical propositions refer. Any naturalization of the good begs the question of whether the naturalized term is good or not. For example, to argue like the hedonist that "the good is pleasure" raises the question of determining if pleasure is itself good. Any reduction of the good to a natural property, for example, "is pleasant," "is useful," "is in accordance with the laws of evolution," implies this naturalistic fallacy, a confusion of distinct categories according to Moore (1971). Accordingly, antinaturalism implies that ethics predicates are irreducible to natural properties and that the analysis of facts is not necessary to support and apply moral norms (AN$_2$). It also follows that normative knowledge is not reducible to empirical knowledge, and most often this argument supports the rejection of any empirical contribution to bioethics (AN$_3$). Knowing what we ought to do is a form of knowledge that cannot be described in the language of the empirical disciplines because these examine only natural properties, and ethics deals with non-natural properties.

These clarifications further explain why, for antinaturalists, ethical norms should not be confused with natural laws (AN$_4$). Indeed, ethical norms can even be opposed to biological laws like the survival of the fittest. A historical example of this antinaturalistic stance is found, for example, in Thomas Huxley's *Evolution and Ethics*. Huxley argued that, contrary to Herbert Spencer and other early twentieth-century theorists of social Darwinism, progress of society depends not on our capacity to imitate biological processes, but on our ability to fight against some of these processes.

If ethics concerns the "ought" and cannot follow from the "is," then the source of ethics must be a form of pure reason external to the world of being. The source of norms is therefore in theoretical reflection and a priori thinking (AN$_5$) both of which have important consequences relative to the disciplinary status of ethics. Indeed, ethics is an autonomous discipline (AN$_6$), and its preferred method is conceptual analysis. Given this commitment to the disciplinary autonomy of ethics and the irreducible character of ethical knowledge, both normative ethics and metaethics are conceptual, that is, nonempirical, because only the philosophical method of conceptual analysis is ideally suited to address metaethical questions (AN$_7$) and clarify the nature of non-natural ethics predicates.

Critical Assessment of Antinaturalism in Bioethics
Antinaturalism and the strong distinction between "is" and "ought" were highly relevant in the early twentieth century, when Spencer and others were proposing a form of conservative social Darwinism, implying that human beings had to mimic biological laws in their social and ethical conduct. Today, the distinction remains highly relevant because it warns that the issues raised by biomedical advances overwhelm the scope and normative resources of biomedicine. Even if the distinction is useful, however, it was part of an antinaturalistic philosophical movement that sustained the estrangement of philosophy from real-world objects as well as from other disciplines (Toulmin 1982). Even if ethics predicates are different from other predicates, and even if ethical norms cannot be reduced to laws or explanation, this does not necessarily imply incommensurability. In fact, it still does not explain the fundamental distinction between "is" and "ought" itself, which may be a "philosophical fiction," as suggested by Norton, given that all facts can be considered laden with some values (Norton 1996). Daniel Callahan has argued that this fundamental antinaturalistic argument renders any "ought" unachievable since the world is made only of "is." Hence, the distinction is useful but cannot foreclose discussion on naturalistic epistemological commitments. "Since 'is' is all the universe has to offer, to say that it cannot be the source of an 'ought' is tantamount to saying *a priori* that an ought can have no source at all—to say that is no less than to say there can be no oughts" (Callahan 1996).

In bioethics, many have found antinaturalism and its commitments a hard position to defend or practice. Taken literally, this position is incompatible with one of bioethics' admitted tasks—to clarify and offer concrete solutions to ethical problems occurring in various clinical and biomedical contexts. Callahan wrote early on in the history of bioethics that abstract analytic philosophical discourse, detached from facts and experience, was unable to reestablish a useful link with the concrete world of experience, which compromised its ability to tackle real-world issues (Callahan 1976). Moreover, Callahan argued, such problems are most usefully tackled by interdisciplinary collaboration to increase the scope with which we can understand the various dimensions of an ethical problem. These observations highlight the shortcomings of radical antinaturalism, the fundamental distinction between "is" and "ought," and monodisciplinary ethics. This was also historically observed by John Dewey: "Since morals is concerned with conduct, it grows out of specific empirical facts. Almost all influential moral theories, with the exception of the utilitarian, have refused to admit this idea" (Dewey 1922).

Other bioethicists, without explicitly questioning antinaturalism, have implicitly rejected some of its commitments. For example, the process of specifying ethical principles, as in Beauchamp and Childress' account, is opposed to the epistemological commitment that ethical predicates have no relationship to natural properties (see, for example, the critique of "top-down" justification by Beauchamp and Childress 2001). These authors, who are often (and abusively) considered rationalist and deductive thinkers, observe that

particular moral judgments in hard cases almost always require that we specify and balance norms, not merely that we bring a particular instance under a covering rule or principle. The abstract rules and principles in moral theories are extensively indeterminate; that is, the content of these rules and principles is too abstract to determine the acts that we should perform. In the process of specifying and balancing norms and in making particular judgments, we often must take into account factual beliefs about the world, cultural expectations, judgments of likely outcome, and precedents previously encountered to help fill out and give weight to rules, principles, and theories. (Beauchamp and Childress 2001)

Therefore, even if ethical knowledge is not reducible to empirical knowledge, this does not imply that bioethics can be autonomous, at least not in a strong sense. In a pluralistic society, bioethics can only with difficulty count on a priori moral norms deduced from pure human abstract reasoning. Furthermore, this challenge suggests the importance, for positions rejecting antinaturalism, of opening moral discourse to include the discussion of realities of stakeholders involved in ethical problems (Moreno 1999). Another challenge to the autonomous status of bioethics is based on the fact that metaethics is not just a conceptual task but can benefit from empirical research. As Beauchamp and Childress state, "Descriptive ethics and metaethics are grouped together as *nonnormative* because their objective is to establish what factually or conceptually *is* the case, not what ethically *ought to be* the case" (Beauchamp and Childress 2001).

Strong and Moderate (Pragmatic) Naturalism

My presentation of antinaturalism has served the purpose of showing that, in general, bioethics has implicitly taken some distance from most antinaturalistic epistemological commitments. However, this is still a step away from acknowledging and formalizing the epistemological naturalistic commitments of bioethics. Naturalism is a controversial stance because it is customary to view ethics and bioethics as normative and prescriptive fields and therefore different from empirical sciences, which are descriptive and explicative (Callahan 1996). Yet the hesitation to acknowledge naturalistic commitments can impede methodological and empirical progress in bioethics and in neuroethics in tackling pressing issues.

To further explore and discuss the naturalistic commitments of bioethics, I now follow the writings of Fagot-Largeault and Moreno and distinguish broadly between strong naturalism, which reduces morality to biology, and a more moderate form of naturalism inspired by pragmatism, which connects ethics to empirical research without reductionist intents (Fagot-Largeault 1993; Moreno 1999).

Strong naturalism (SN) is characterized by the following epistemological commitments:

(SN$_1$) There is no distinction between "is" and "ought."

(SN$_2$) Ethical predicates are natural properties.

(SN$_3$) Ethical knowledge is an outgrowth of empirical knowledge.

(SN$_4$) Ethical norms are natural laws.

(SN$_5$) Ethical norms stem a posteriori and from experience and observation.

(SN$_6$) Bioethics is an heteronomous discipline.

(SN$_7$) Normative ethics and metaethics are empirical.

Moderate pragmatic naturalism (MN) is characterized by the following epistemological commitments:

(MN$_1$)   The distinction between "is" and "ought" is granted with qualifications.

(MN$_2$)   Ethical predicates are properties that cannot be reduced to natural properties but are best understood within a fact-value continuum.

(MN$_3$)   Empirical knowledge does not bring ethical justification of ethical norms, but ethical knowledge must take into account human capacities. "Is" does not imply "ought," but "ought" implies "can."

(MN$_4$)   Ethical norms are not natural laws but are norms and rules proper to human social life. There are no natural moral laws as such, but moral rules can be better understood from a factual point of view that takes into consideration constraints to moral agency.

(MN$_5$)   Ethical norms do not simply follow from reason or experience but from their interaction, for example, reflective equilibrium.

(MN$_6$)   Bioethics is neither autonomous nor heteronomous but best described as an interdisciplinary field with practical goals such as creating new forms of wisdom in the delivery of healthcare and the pursuit of health.

(MN$_7$)   Normative ethics remains prescriptive but metaethics is both empirical and conceptual.

Given the proposed distinction between strong and moderate forms of naturalism, Potter's naturalism, generally speaking, is typically considered an example of strong naturalism; however, it is probably more accurately a combination of both moderate and strong naturalistic commitment. On the one hand, Potter sustains that ethics must be grounded in biology: biological knowledge directly justifies ethical obligations. It is according to this stronger sense that Potter claims that bioethics is a new branch of biology, a holistic biology or a humanistic biology that is truly interdisciplinary (Potter 1971). This also explains why Potter gives such importance to biological concepts of adaptation, evolution, and feedback in his cybernetic anthropology to which he sometimes straightforwardly assimilates ethics. For example, Potter states, "I propose to describe man as an information-processing, decision-making, cybernetic machine whose value systems are built up by feedback processes from his environment" (Potter

1971). Moreover, the primary aim of bioethics is the survival of the human species (Potter 1971), but this aim is not carefully justified in his writings and becomes a sort of "biological imperative," blurring the distinction between "is" and "ought" (SN_1). Biological laws therefore unduly become norms for the conduct of human affairs (SN_4). This form of strong naturalism that grounds moral norms in biological explanations is controversial and problematic for obvious reasons and explains the reluctance of moderate naturalists to go as far (MN_4).

On the other hand, Potter's concept of bioethics is sometimes based on a more moderate form of naturalism that closely relates the humanities and the biological sciences. The goal is only to bridge the two cultures to secure the future of humanity (Potter 1971). Another related and moderately naturalistic commitment can be found in Potter's view on the input of science in ethics. Even if he does distinguish science from wisdom, Potter upholds that the scientific method is useful for ethics. In this sense, there are no biological moral laws, but ethical norms can be better understood from a factual standpoint in order to grasp the moral constraints bearing on moral agents (MN_2 and MN_4): "Science is not wisdom, but we can use the scientific method to seek wisdom. Wisdom is the knowledge of how to use knowledge to better the human condition, and it is the most important knowledge of all" (Potter 1971).

Within a strong naturalistic epistemology, normative knowledge ("ought") directly follows from descriptive knowledge ("is") (SN_1). Consequently, Potter sometimes commits the naturalistic fallacy. Moderate naturalism refrains from this fallacy: it recognizes that "is" does not imply "ought," contrarily to strong naturalism, but acknowledges that "ought" implies "can" (MN_1) (Callahan 1996). For example, we can promote respect for autonomy as a fundamental normative requirement, but we also have the obligation to better understand the context of such normative goals in different institutional and cultural contexts (MN_2). Potter himself is closer to moderate naturalism when he argues that biological sciences introduce a factual point of view that one cannot escape from, a realistic perspective, indicating the limits and constraints of human agency: "Science cannot substitute for Nature's bounty when Nature's bounty has been raped and despoiled. The idea that man's survival is a problem in economics and political science is a myth that assumes that man is free or could be free from the forces of Nature. These disciplines help to tell us what men *want*, but it may require biology to tell what man *can have*" (Potter 1971; emphasis is mine).

Strong naturalism sustains that ethics predicates are natural properties and therefore that facts are both necessary and sufficient for the justification of ethical norms, as in Potter's survival imperative (SN_2). Moderate naturalism grants that ethical predicates are properties that cannot be reduced to natural properties but are best understood within a fact-value continuum (Dewey 1922; Norton 1996); therefore, facts are necessary but insufficient in bioethics (MN_2). In a certain sense, bioethics as a whole is committed to this latter thesis. In many decision-making processes, we need to take into account facts to contextualize and understand the issues at stake, a point of view put forward by many influential writers in bioethics (Beauchamp and Childress 2001; Jonsen, Siegler, and Winslade 1998). Bioethics has come to recognize and integrate the need to understand the concrete experience of stakeholders in various levels of ethical analysis, ranging from clinical cases to biomedical policy. The American philosopher Dewey upheld such a naturalistic commitment (and an implicit critique of its antinaturalistic counterpart) in which ethics had to be grounded in experience. The following quote well illustrates Dewey's line of thought and a moderately naturalistic stance:

But in fact morals is the most humane of all subjects. It is that which is closest to human nature; it is ineradicably empirical, not theological nor metaphysical nor mathematical. Since it directly concerns human nature, everything that can be known of the human mind and body in physiology, medicine, anthropology, and psychology is pertinent to moral inquiry. Human nature exists and operates in an environment. . . . Moral science is not something with a separate province. It is physical, biological and historic knowledge placed in a human context where it illuminates and guides the activities of men. (Dewey 1922)

The diverging commitments of strong and moderate naturalism on the nature of moral knowledge translate into different consequences on opinions regarding the origins of ethical norms and the disciplinary status of bioethics. For strong naturalism, ethical norms stem principally from experience (inductive approach) and are found a posteriori in the natural world (SN_5). Ethics becomes a subdiscipline of biology. Therefore, ethics is heteronomous and relies on the authority of biological knowledge, as Potter sometimes argues (SN_6). Following strong naturalism, normative ethics and metaethics are descriptive and empirical (SN$_7$). Science could explain what we ought to do based on empirical inquiry. Hence, the differences between the normative and the descriptive domains are suppressed.

The opposite is true for moderate pragmatic naturalism. Ethical norms fall neither from reason nor from biological observation and experience but from the interaction between ethical reasoning and context, such as in the method of reflective equilibrium (MN$_5$) (Beauchamp and Childress 2001). Hence, ethical norms are not preexisting biological *laws* but are *rules* created by human social activity. In a pluralistic society, the engagement of multiple perspectives and stakeholders becomes crucial to enrich the creation of ethical norms and rules and to ensure their validity (Habermas 1999; Racine 2003). It follows that bioethics is neither an autonomous nor a heteronomous discipline. Bioethics is fundamentally an interdisciplinary, practical, and theoretical endeavor open to various discourses and perspectives (MN$_6$). These various positions contribute to and enrich the pursuit of goals such as the creation of new forms of wisdom in the delivery of individual healthcare and in the pursuit of collective health. Moderate naturalism acknowledges that empirical knowledge is useful to shed light on metaethical issues (MN$_7$). Indeed, through interdisciplinary discourse and empirical research, views on fundamental ethical concepts such as personhood and autonomy can be enriched and elaborated.

The epistemological commitments of moderate pragmatic naturalism best describe what bioethics has become in order to respond to the challenges presented by scientific advances and new healthcare situations. Moderate pragmatic naturalism expresses some of the commitments required for the flourishing of new forms of wisdom for the delivery of healthcare and the pursuit of health. I believe that acknowledging these theoretical commitments can help pave the way for further clarification and discussion regarding the goals that should be pursued in bioethics and neuroethics individually and by the collectivity of scholars, practitioners, and various users of this knowledge.

Conclusion

I have presented three possible epistemological stances for bioethics and argued that moderate pragmatic naturalism provides the best account of what bioethics is and what it is increasingly becoming, especially with the "empirical turn" in bioethics (Borry, Schotsmans, and Dierickx 2005). Through the presentation of antinaturalism and the discussion of both strong and moderate forms of naturalism, I also hope to have highlighted some of the main reasons why bioethics has evolved and developed into a distinct field of scholarship and practice. Generally speaking, traditional philosophical antinaturalistic commitments do not correspond to the practice of bioethics and the emerging understanding of what bioethicists believe they are doing as individuals and as a community (Andre 2002). Nonetheless, taking up all commitments of strong naturalism leads to pitfalls as great as those of antinaturalism. Moderate pragmatic naturalism appears to best reflect the implicit commitments of bioethics and neuroethics practice and scholarship. The following chapter, based on this view, tackles a number of critiques addressed to neuroethics and clarifies the nature of pragmatic neuroethics.

4

Neuroethics: Exploring the Implications of Pragmatic Naturalism

Overview

We saw in chapters 1 and 2 that neuroethics is a nascent interdisciplinary field host to many different perspectives emphasizing distinct ethical issues and aspects of bioethics scholarship and practice. The previous chapter introduced a specific view of bioethics called pragmatic naturalism, which stresses the interdisciplinary and practical nature of bioethics. The present chapter explores the implications of pragmatic naturalism for neuroethics by addressing a number of controversies surrounding the field. It also highlights some traits of pragmatic neuroethics, such as the integration of pluralism as well as bottom-up research and practical approaches.

In chapter 2, I present some of the lively discussions on the nature of the new field of neuroethics. Some of these discussions were sparked by a paper that my colleague Judy Illes and I published in the *American Journal of Bioethics* in 2005 (Illes and Racine 2005a). Though not the intent of the paper, it was viewed by some as a proposal to define the field of neuroethics and argue for some of its basic characteristics. (The goal was rather to identify the challenges that functional neuroimaging carries in terms of both scientific and sociocultural interpretations, a theme I come back to in chapters 5 and 9.) In response to this paper, some colleagues argued that the parallel drawn between genetic testing and functional neuroimaging was an interesting comparison that could further ethical reflection on neuroimaging (Doucet 2005; Kennedy 2005), while others argued that genetics was an inadequate model to start with given the unique impact of neuroscience on the self and personhood (Reid and Baylis 2005). Finally, others criticized the idea of creating a new subfield dedicated to basic and clinical neuroscience. For example, Wilfond and Magnuson seriously questioned why there should be what they dubbed "a proliferation of bioethics sub-disciplines" by drawing parallels between neuroethics and genethics (Wilfond and Magnuson 2005). Others contended that Illes and I had argued for the uniqueness of the brain and had employed dubious mind–body metaphysics based on the view that we were arguing for the specific status of the brain in bioethics (Buford and Allhoff 2005).

Additional discussions on the nature of neuroethics occurred later in a special issue of the European Molecular Biology Organization (*EMBO Reports*) published in 2007. This special issue featured a number of different perspectives on neuroethics, highlighting the value of empirical research in neuroethics (Illes 2007a) and the importance of philosophical and theoretical issues in neuroethics (Evers 2007b). Others in this issue warned that neuroethics may rely on several assumptions, such as unwarranted enthusiasm for neurotechnology, somewhat like genethics, which has been criticized for being too optimistic regarding the potentials of genetics and gene-based technologies (Parens and Johnston 2007). A more recent paper by Joseph Fins on the historical aspects of neuroethics and its connections to healthcare again raised some questions and controversies about the nature of neuroethics, especially its connection to clinical care and its interdisciplinary nature (Fins 2008a; Jones 2008; Racine 2008c).

Based on these discussions of the nature of neuroethics found in previous chapters, this chapter examines six of the most salient controversies raised about the field from a pragmatic naturalistic standpoint. These controversies include debates over the specialization of neuroethics, the relationship between neuroethics and genethics, the connection between neuroethics and general bioethics, the disciplinary configuration of neuroethics, and the issue of mind–body reductionism in neuroethics. Most criticisms addressed to the field under these headings are based on legitimate concerns and should not be ignored or dismissed. As the field of neuroethics moves forward, it is bound to commit some errors and redirect itself based on constructive criticisms that help build it into a field of self-reflection and openness to a diversity of perspectives. Such criticism should be welcomed because those involved can learn much from the perspectives of colleagues who bring attention to concerns that insiders can become blind to. However, many current criticisms call for further clarification and discussion to fully capture the field as a community endeavor. In my attempt to bring clarifications in response to criticisms addressed to the field, I highlight several misunderstandings that plague current debates, including common assumptions that neuroethics exclusively focuses on science-driven issues to the detriment of healthcare concerns and that the specialized field of neuroethics jeopardizes fundamental goals of bioethics. Based on the distinctive features of a pragmatic naturalism, I argue that neuroethics is an unprecedented opportunity to focus on ethical issues that specific patient populations face (in addition to neuroscience-oriented issues) and that the concerted and interdisciplinary effort that neuroethics captures represents a step further in the development of a meaningful contribution of ethics and the humanities to broader healthcare perspectives and public debates. Indeed, pragmatic naturalism is an approach to bioethics that emphasizes the value of pluralism and the need to develop frameworks allowing for the integration of both theoretical and practical research to improve patient care. Some of the characteristics of pragmatic neuroethics follow from the discussion in chapter 3. Accordingly, from a pragmatic perspective, advances in neuroethics should

• be the vehicle of careful and thoughtful "specialization" supported obviously by an interest for patients and the public and not only by an interest for the organ of the brain. By the same token, there must be room in bioethics for specialized areas of research and practice like neuroethics that push the field forward; otherwise, if there is no room for specialization, we will not avoid a potentially self-fulfilling prophecy that new fields tend to grow in isolation.

• be critical about neuroethics' own goals and engage various voices and stakeholders to avoid being solely driven by neuroscience's research agenda; however, the many meanings and goals of neuroethics need to be acknowledged to avoid straw man arguments based on the view that neuroethics is only concerned with scientific advances and new technologies.

• make good use of precedent by taking what is valuable in our various scholarly and practical *traditions* while not hesitating to generate *innovation* if contexts differ in ways that support the need for additional research; accordingly, neuroethics should be considered an area or a field of bioethics and not a new discipline.

• value both theoretical and practical work as legitimate goals since neuroethics, as a community-level effort, will gain much from openness to distinct views and perspectives.

• separate the issue of the theoretical novelty of the objects of neuroethics from the practical importance of addressing longstanding issues. Medicine did not invent the illnesses it strives to alleviate; rather, medicine is a response to health challenges humanity faces. *Ibidem* with neuroethics, which does not need to create new ethical and social problems or devote vast amounts of energy on defending the uniqueness of certain issues; there are enough challenges plaguing healthcare in neurology and psychiatry to keep busy a community of practitioners and scholars. As discussed below, the value of working on longstanding issues must coexist with more novel objects of research.

• reinvigorate bioethics' tradition of dialogue between the humanities and the biomedical sciences; we can learn from the biological sciences on the nature of ethics (e.g., neuroscience of ethics) as long as this line of work avoids stark reductionism that is in essence contrary to the holistic perspectives and respect for the person dear to ethics.

First Critique: Neuroethics Introduces Detrimental Specialization in Biomedical Ethics

I was once bluntly asked by a senior and distinguished colleague that if there is a neuroethics, why would not a liver ethics, a lung ethics, or even a heart ethics be developed? This question was meant of course to highlight the allegedly absurd nature of bioethics specialization, especially specialization grounded in the specific structure and function of organs such as the brain, or the nervous system more generally speaking. Similarly, some perceive in the movement of bioethics specialization a phenomenon of "hyphenated ethics" that jeopardizes the goals of bioethics, such as promoting broad interdisciplinary perspectives (Parens and Johnston 2006). A related and perhaps more serious criticism regarding the specialization of bioethics is that the specialty field of neuroethics could replicate a form of reductionism found too often in biomedicine where, to caricature, the organs are treated but not the patient as a person (or even as a complex biological system). As chapter 2 describes, an analogous argument is often put forward to justify the field of neuroethics, that is, an argument based on the unique nature and role of the brain. If bioethics were to become specialized to the point of introducing such reductionism, then it would run bluntly amok. Indeed, one of the key historical and contemporary goals of bioethics was and still is the respect of the person as a whole (Callahan 1976). To orient bioethics in a contrary direction would indeed be detrimental to the endeavor of bioethics.

Others fear, not illegitimately, that specialty fields will lose connection with bioethics in general and, hence, diminish the ability to provide broad views on bioethical problems (Wilfond and Magnuson 2005; Parens and Johnston 2007). This concern may seem trivial since scholarship can be equated with specialization of interest and focus, but I think many bioethicists agree that bioethics is still rather loosely defined and that the standards for recognition of bioethics scholarship and the status of bioethicists are still evolving (Andre 2002). What this context means in practice is that bioethics is prone to being inclusive and interdisciplinary (likely good things), but there is risk that newcomers lack proper training or too quickly recognize themselves as bioethicists (likely bad things). The creation of subfields could encourage newcomers to bioethics to circumvent proper training. The result would be poorer scholarship and potentially weaker capabilities to offer sound advice to researchers, policy makers and clinicians. There is also a good case to make for an increased sense of community and collaboration within the world of bioethics that the creation of bioethics subfields would hinder by isolating different communities of interest (Andre 2002).

Response to the Detrimental Specialization Critique
The arguments suggesting that neuroethics induces undue specialization point to the need for a number of clarifications and caveats. First, few people if anyone really believe that neuroethics is an ethics of the brain per se. While some view it as a technology-driven field, defined by the issues related to neuroscience-based technologies (Wolpe 2004), others view neuroethics as a field that could address the needs of specific patient populations (not a specific organ) and that should be driven by clinical concerns (Fins 2008a; Racine and Illes 2008). Viewed this latter way, neuroethics has perhaps more in common with a field like pediatric ethics or geriatric ethics than a more technology-oriented field such as nanoethics

Pragmatic + Pluralistic approach

or genethics. There is no a priori reason to believe that a focus on specific patient populations would introduce a reductionist stance on the social and ethical issues those patients would face. On the contrary, perhaps a concerted and interdisciplinary effort to examine those issues could translate into a better appreciation of the specific needs of neurological and psychiatric patients as a whole. Clearly no one really considers neuroethics to be focusing solely on an organ, and many view this field as a patient-centered endeavor (Fins 2005a; Glannon 2007; Racine and Illes 2008). It is also important to note that the process of specialization can also mean many different things, ranging from the creation of full-blown experts to the more modest goal of sustaining a community of interests in a specific area. This latter definition is the approach that I argue for and that best fits with pragmatism and the sheer lack of proper delimitation of the boundaries of bioethics itself. Although it is a common place reference in debates, it is far easier to imagine rhetorically sub-bioethics experts disconnected from the broader field of bioethics than to actually find them in reality.

Concerns about the impact of specialties and specialization on the sense of community within bioethics are more difficult to define and address, although their relevance is clear. There are different possible approaches to this issue. Some think that the field of neuroethics is leading astray the discussion on ethics in neuroscience and related clinical care. However, on the contrary, perhaps the field of neuroethics has evolved in its current form because topics related to neuroethics were not considered legitimate topics of inquiry by the bioethics community just a few years ago. Having seen firsthand the contemporary field of neuroethics evolve and develop to its current state, I feel that the second scenario corresponds much more to the motivation of the community of interest that clusters around neuroethics. It also better reflects the historically slow response of bioethics to acknowledge that neuroscience and neurological and psychiatric patient populations deserve full attention. Historically, this view also broadly corresponds to the original characteristics of neuroethics identified by pioneers such as Pontius (1973, 1993) and Cranford (1989), and for which Bernat argues in the latest edition of the landmark *Ethical Issues in Neurology* (Bernat 2008). These authors all share the concern of approaching patients as persons.

When examining the "detrimental specialization" argument, one of the greatest risks I identify is the emergence of a defensive or reactive stance in the bioethics community regarding new fields of scholarship and practice such as neuroethics. If this tendency materializes or gathers momentum, we can expect as a consequence that further distinct communities will still take shape but will evolve outside mainstream bioethics, leading to a self-fulfilling prophecy that specialty fields disconnect from previous bioethics scholarship and practices. This will perhaps be not the *reason* or the justification for these communities emerging but the *cause* related to the lack of acceptance of different perspectives. By saying this, I want to emphasize that the inclusion of topical concerns, approaches, and objects of research within a field are not impersonal choices and decisions. They reflect what a community, or perhaps more accurately what some in a community, decide to pursue and see as legitimate within their self-understanding of what their field is about and should engage in. Bioethics itself is no stranger to those issues; its history has been shaped by struggles for interdisciplinary and inclusive approaches in healthcare, for the recognition that context matters in dealing with ethical issues, and for resisting narrow mindedness and rigid top-down approaches. There is no reason to think that neuroethics differs in that respect. Neuroethics is a new field of bioethics scholarship and practice that also attempts to foster broad perspectives of patients as persons and individuals as democratic citizens.

Second Critique: Neuroethics has a Narrow Focus, Driven by the Neuroscience Research Agenda

Some respected bioethics scholars have argued that neuroethics risks developing a narrow agenda by focusing on neuroscience and being seduced by the hype and hope surrounding neuroscience research. For example, Parens and Johnston have argued that some researchers involved in bioethics and genetics research promised too much to funders and that their own work was influenced by "genohype" (Parens and Johnston 2007). They argued correctly that individuals involved in neuroethics are not immune to a similar phenomenon of "neurohype." Neuroethics scholarship could therefore lead to ethical recommendations unduly influenced by the enthusiasm for neuroscience and its potential benefits. Parens, Johnston, and others have made an important point, and no one can pretend to be truly independent from social contexts. The position of bioethics as a field, of bioethicists, and of bioethics output (e.g., policies and recommendations stemming from consultations) can surely be affected by this—hence, it is a serious concern, and bioethicists (and others) can easily deceive themselves about their own objectivity and their distance from the phenomenon they are considering. This is the reason genethics and various bioethics efforts responding to genetic research and genetic engineering technologies have been criticized notably for engaging in scholarship that is driven by research imperatives that threaten the integrity of bioethics research. This could have reduced bioethics to "thin" or legalistic considerations and have submitted the bioethics community to a narrow research agenda (Andre 2002; Evans 2002; Turner 2003; examining the extent to which such claims regarding genethics are true or false is beyond the realm of this book).

Response to the Narrow Focus Critique
It is important to acknowledge that the discussion of ethical and social issues related to genetics and genetic engineering are constitutive of the history of bioethics. Very early on, as seen in landmark events (e.g., Asilomar conference) and early publications on the topic (e.g., early issues of the *Hastings Center Report* and the *Kennedy Institute of Ethics Journal*), ethical concerns about genetics began to be examined. This statement could to some extent be true for the ethics of neurology and psychiatry in the 1970s with the work of the Belmont Report, the Harvard ad hoc committee on the determination of death, and early publications in neurological and psychiatric ethics. However, the tremendous growth of scholarship related to genetics in the 1990s and early 2000s partly reflected the increased investments that governmental agencies were injecting in this area. For example, the U.S. Department of Energy (DOE) and the National Institutes of Health devoted 3–5 percent of their annual budget for the Human Genome Project to support research on the ethical, legal, and social issues (ELSI) of genomic research. The DOE claims that this investment constitutes "the world's largest bioethics program, which has become a model for ELSI programs around the world" (Department of Energy 2009). This organizational and financial impetus led to several

beneficial outcomes, including the development of scholarship and university training programs. But some critics have highlighted the potential drawbacks of this form of support, inferring that the bioethics research agenda could have been driven by the need to dampen public fears and to allow genetics research to carry on (Turner 2003).

At this stage, there is no reason to believe—to the disappointment of some (Greely 2007)—that neuroethics will benefit from the significant financial support associated with a large-scale neuroscience or neurotechnology initiative. Perhaps a lack of attention from the bioethics community—and the great focus on genetics—has led to the creation by default of a neuroethics community. Hence, despite first-glance beliefs, some of the forces leading to genethics and the ELSI programs for genetics and genomics in the 1990s do not correspond to the development of neuroethics thus far, which is mostly accomplished through the typical peer review grant systems of governmental funding agencies (e.g., in the United States, Canada, and the UK—with the notable exception of support from the Dana Foundation in the United States for neuroethics events and research).

In addition, most of the authors arguing for the similarities between genethics and neuroethics presuppose that neuroethics (and perhaps genethics too) is almost exclusively narrowly focused on new neurotechnology, that neuroethics is somehow addressing only ethical issues associated with technological developments. This view certainly refers to some of the goals captured by the umbrella term of neuroethics, but as illustrated by figure 4.1, neuroethics—as a community-level endeavor—is more complex, with many other meanings and goals. Neuroethics captures multifaceted and international communities of scholars and practitioners. It is also clear from looking at the various contemporary definitions of the field reviewed in chapter 2 (Roskies 2002; Wolpe 2004; Racine and Illes 2008) that there is pluralism. The literature displays a wide range of focuses, from philosophical (Evers 2007b) to empirical aspects (Illes 2007a), which are typically reflected in collective contributions in neuroethics (Illes 2006; Illes and Racine 2007). For example, mainstream bioethics' lack of attention to advances in neuroscience is one of the reasons, historically, that a slightly distinct community emerged to approach ethics in neuroscience. If bioethics had been as attentive to neuroscience as it was to genetics, perhaps history would be different. For other scholars,

Consolidating ethical perspectives across clinical neuro-specialties	Tackling challenges created by advances in neuroscience and neurotechnology	Sustaining interdisciplinary ethical approaches in basic and clinical neuroscience	Responding to public awareness of neuroscience and promoting public dialogue
Responding to bioethics' lack of attention to basic and clinical neuroscience	Attending to the unique role of the central nervous system, basis for sensory, motor, affective, and cognitive functions	Reflecting on the interdisciplinary evolution of neuroscience and changing views on "human nature"	Addressing basic healthcare needs and lingering ethical problems for specific patient populations

Figure 4.1
Various goals and views of neuroethics. First appeared in *EMBO Reports* (Racine 2008a).

interventions in the central nervous system, the basis of sensory, affective, and cognitive functions, create challenges that must be addressed in their own right (figure 4.1). Some see yet another goal in neuroethics: the potential renewal of bioethics' commitment to public dialogue on biomedical science (Doucet 2005).

Further, some of the first occurrences of the term "neuroethics" expressed a call by clinicians to pay more attention to the needs of neurological and psychiatric patients, particularly the need to protect them from potentially harmful novel healthcare interventions (Pontius 1973; Cranford 1989; Pontius 1993). This suggests that although the "narrow focus" critique is legitimate, it is partly based on a narrow understanding of what neuroethics is. As a pragmatist, my own personal view is that the single most important integrative goal underlying neuroethics is a practical one—the need to improve patient care for specific patient populations (Racine and Illes 2008). Technological advances should always be discussed in light of their potential contribution to the good of patients and the public. The narrower and somewhat reductive view of neuroethics often taken up by critics reflects inadequately the broad range of goals and perspectives that have contributed to the international evolution of neuroethics thus far (Illes 2006; Illes and Racine 2007). The thematic and analytic overviews I present in chapters 1 and 2 suggest that the critiques have targeted a common view of neuroethics—neuroethics as depicted in the media—without taking into account the diversity of the peer review literature. In many respects, this is a straw man argument, a simplified representation of the literature, which I will address at the end of this chapter. I will grant, however, that historical precedent alone will not ensure that neuroethics will yield a balanced assessment of the potentials of neuroscience research and develop a broad view from its object, and especially that this historical connection is not often acknowledged.

Third Critique: Neuroethics Is "Reinventing the Bioethics Wheel" and "Squanders Scarce Resources" by Ignoring Precedent

A concern expressed regarding neuroethics, which is connected to the two critiques already discussed, bears on the relationship of neuroethics to precedent scholarship. For example, Parens and Johnston have stated that neuroethics contributes to "carving up bioethics into ever more specialized subfields" and to "squandering scarce resources" (Parens and Johnston 2007). This concern relates partly to the use of precedent in neuroethics. Bioethics has been tackling so many areas of biomedical research and practice (e.g., reproductive technologies, stem cells, genetics and genomics) that there is bound to be overlap with neuroethical issues. Further, some topics appear, at least at first glance, to be basically the same. For example, there has been sustained scholarly discussion about the potentials for humans to enhance normal function beyond ordinary or average capacities with the help of genetic engineering and stem cell–based technologies (Harris 1992, 2007; Parens 1998). This has lead some to wonder what would be the difference between these interventions and the use of neuroscience-based technologies. Others have argued, on the contrary, against the use of precedent in neuroethics (e.g., previous scholarship about the ethical issue of genetics) because it may actually misguide neuroethics. For example, Françoise Baylis and Lynette Reid have argued (regarding neuroimaging) that "it is not at all clear that attention to ethical issues in genetics is a useful, let alone a legitimate starting point for tackling issues in neuroimaging" (Reid and Baylis 2005). They find that personal identity is much more intimately connected to the brain than genes are. Hence, interventions on the brain interact directly with personal narratives and identities to an unprecedented extent. Finally, others have proposed a balanced perspective for the use of precedent while highlighting the need to be open to the discovery of new issues in a new context that call for further attention. This is the view expressed by Jocelyn Downie and Michael Hadskis. They consider, for example, that some issues play out differently in neuroimaging than in genetics, such as the risk for physical harm (e.g., radioactive exposure in PET scan) and the assessment of cognitive function (Downie and Hadskis 2005). In this regard, analysis of how neuroimaging is perceived in the public domain has shown that neuroimaging can bias judgments about the scientific plausibility of psychological explanations (Racine, Bar-Ilan, and Illes 2005, 2006), a bias that can take the forms of neuroessentialism, neurorealism, and neuropolicy and that may need more attention. Subsequent psychological research examining this phenomenon further supports the thesis that neuroimages can lead to misleading overinterpretations (McCabe and Castel 2008; Weisberg et al. 2008). In sum, three positions can be found in the literature regarding neuroethics' relationship to precedent scholarship: those who think precedent is unduly ignored; those who believe that precedent, without being totally ignored, could be misleading; and those who believe precedent can be a useful starting point.

Response to the "Bioethics Wheel" and Squandered Resources Argument
I have myself been engaged in debates about the use of precedent scholarship in neuroethics and the continuity and discontinuity between bioethics and neuroethics. In one response to colleagues in the *American Journal of Bioethics* written with my colleague Judy Illes, I underscored how neuroethics is a dialogue between tradition and innovation (Illes and Racine 2005b), that neuroethics is a form of innovation based on tradition. The basic meaning of those terms is crucial since both are often misinterpreted based on vernacular meanings. Previous work in bioethics (and other fields) constitutes a tradition from the Latin *traditio*, meaning what is handed down to us, not at all signifying something that is worthless, obsolete, or *dépassé*. Neuroethics is a form of social and moral innovation (like bioethics). It is grounded in the fact that we are collectively facing new decision-making contexts and need to make contextually informed decisions knowledgeable of the science and clinical circumstances that shapes cases and contexts. This is precisely the meaning of

innovation, which comes from the Latin *innovatio*, meaning the renewal and alteration resulting from arts and craft and by no means signaling a form of unconnected creation, that is, *creatio ex nihilo*.

The current discussion of ethical, legal, and social issues in neuroethics (chapter 2) is consistent with this analysis. Some common issues bear on limitations and risks of current neurotechnologies and the impact of these limitations on the technologies' ethical use. These risks can be informed by precedent research, but their specificity must be understood. A second cluster of issues extends previous bioethics discussion to the context of neuroscience (e.g., enhancement and medicalization; public involvement and understanding). The examination of these issues does not make much sense without considering the tradition of previous scholarship. Finally, bioethics must be ready for a dose of innovation in the consideration of "traditional" bioethics issues that could take specific meanings in the context of current neuroethics discussion (e.g., consent, autonomy, and decision-making capacity; responsibility and free will; identity, personhood, and spirituality). Often this is needed, as I indicated earlier, because the brain is viewed as partly defining who we are, and hence, neuroscience is viewed as being able to access aspects of our personal lives and experiences.

The fears that neuroethics is disconnecting from precedent are strikingly exaggerated. Just by looking at key references in even some of the first contemporary neuroethics papers (Farah 2002; Roskies 2002), one can easily see that there is little reinventing of the bioethics wheel. Such claims lack substantial evidence. One also has to believe that *creatio ex nihilo* is possible in scholarship. In some circumstances, neuroethics as an interdisciplinary endeavor and a community, will gain much from looking at the history of bioethics scholarship as well as the history of neuroscience itself—intertwined with the history of research ethics (e.g., Nazi neuroscience experiments and the Nuremberg Trial; psychosurgery and the *Belmont Report*; Racine and Illes 2006). However, in some specific contexts, we will need to thoroughly examine an issue before we can identify good decisions and approaches. For example, prior discussion on enhancement in genetics and stem cells—an example often cited— may actually both help and mislead some of the discussions regarding the impact of neuroscience research. As I present in the first chapter, epidemiological data show that neuropharmaceuticals (e.g., analgesics, antidepressants, stimulants) are among the fastest-increasing segment of nonmedically used prescription drugs. They are also among the most abused classes of drugs (National Institute on Drug Abuse 2005). The abuse rates of prescription stimulants like methylphenidate (Ritalin) for performance enhancement specifically range from 3.7 to 11 percent among American college students (Racine and Forlini 2008). Other examples of lifestyle use of prescription drugs abound: Provigil to fight jet lag and antidepressants to enhance mood (Flower 2004). From 2002 to 2004, over 11 million Americans abused prescription drugs. This situation of lifestyle, or enhancement, use, called misuse or abuse in the public health context, is very different from futuristic uses of stems cells, gene therapy, or other forms of genetic engineering. It is commonplace and spreading, not based on expensive or innovative technologies; it involves healthcare providers and stakeholders on a daily basis; and it is already enshrined in some current social practices and contexts. These contexts and the stakeholders involved, as well as the beliefs held by those who misuse drugs, may differ considerably from prior discussion on genetic or stem-cell enhancements. Theoretically, there could be similarities, but concretely, socially informed approaches to this problem will likely differ. For example, the challenge of regulating limited investigational uses of stem cell research is strikingly different than tackling underground use of pharmaceuticals widely available through doctors. The fact that some social phenomena, such as the misuse of pharmaceuticals, have been so poorly examined in bioethics is surprising, but the precedent focus on futuristic technologies has certainly not fully prepared society and academia to deal with such emerging uses of neuropharmaceuticals. The argument that more sustained attention to new forms of cognitive enhancement may lead to squandering resources is therefore not convincing (Parens and Johnston 2007). Indeed, the converse to the "squandering of resources" view is that neuroethics is bringing new ethical perspectives and contexts to consider in their own right with the help of new colleagues and trainees. For example, some neuroscientists have taken a leading role in bringing broader attention to ethical issues in neuroscience. Neuroethics has also provided a vehicle through which interested communities can participate and individuals can work together to further their engagement and put a name on their common and genuine efforts. Some critics of neuroethics will still not be convinced, but we should collectively remember some of the reasons bioethics emerged historically, and we should be disquieted about overly rigid and disciplinary views of bioethics implicit in some of these critiques. Such views could create additional obstacles to the formation of interdisciplinary approaches and the inclusion of different ethical perspectives to address issues within specific healthcare contexts (Callahan 1976).

In the future, we should be equally open to the possibility that neuroethics will experience some failures and some successes, but understand that this will take time and not approach problems by presuming they are the same as those we have encountered but make sure we understand in some detail the specifics of contexts where decisions need to be made before drawing this conclusion (Jonsen, Siegler, and Winslade 1998). At this time, critiques that neuroethics squanders scarce resources are vague and poorly grounded.

Fourth Critique: "Neuroethics Is Too Philosophical" *and* "Neuroethics Is Not Philosophical Enough"

The field of neuroethics has prompted various reactions regarding, on the one hand, its relationship to healthcare and healthcare-related disciplines and, on the other, its relationship to "established" moral theory and philosophy. Some scholars have argued that the field of neuroethics is still only loosely connected to healthcare concerns and would benefit from further healthcare perspectives. Physician and bioethicist Joe Fins, for example, has expressed concerns that bioethics has contributed to eroding medical ethics by introducing "strangers at the bedside," such as philosophers and theologians. He argues further that current neuroethics is "worrisome" and is taking the form of a "speculative philosophy." Fins also contends that the lack of inclusion of physicians in neuroethics limits its constructive impact on healthcare delivery. In this respect, concerns about cognitive enhancement, for example, would be the quasi-exclusive purview of philosophers, according to him (Fins 2008a). In contrast, others have made the case for an interdisciplinary neuroethics that would not neglect theoretical and philosophical approaches, but unlike Fins, they are not calling for the primacy of one discipline over another. For example, the Swedish philosopher and bioethicist Kathinka Evers has argued that neuroethics could be an opportunity to integrate some of the philosophical literature on the mind–body problem in biomedical ethics (Evers 2005, 2007b). Roskies has also defined the field in a way that promotes the introduction of the neuroscience of ethics into neuroethics scholarship (Roskies 2002).

Response to the Disciplinary Primacy Argument

Fins argues that current neuroethics should include more medical perspectives and ensure a better connection with the concerns of patients. His point is well taken, and I share his enthusiasm for patient-centered ethics as well as his sympathies for pragmatism (Fins, Bacchetta, and Miller 1997; Racine 2008c, 2008d). Nonetheless, I strongly resist his urge to conclude hastily that neuroethics is a speculative and worrisome field of research. It is true that media reports and Web sites have emphasized the philosophical aspects of neuroethics (see table 2.1). I also agree with Fins that improving understanding and treatment for neurological and psychiatric patients should be a key goal. Nonetheless, Fins's provocative statements about current neuroethics do not do justice to the community of plural interests underlying the emergence of this field. For example, Roskies has already presented neuroethics as a new bridge between the humanities and the biological sciences (Roskies 2002). Others see in neuroethics, in addition to the patient-oriented view, an opportunity to broaden approaches to include additional stakeholders, the voices of whom are not always welcomed in mainstream healthcare (Racine, Bar-Ilan, and Illes 2005). Reminiscent of early views on neuroethics (Pontius 1973; Cranford 1989; Pontius 1993), "palliative neuroethics" for patients with DOC has been proposed by Fins himself to ensure neuroethics' connection to patient concerns (Fins 2005a). However, although compelling and crucial, this patient-oriented view of neuroethics reflects only some of the many goals of the field as a community endeavor, where a multitude of perspectives and goals coexist (Racine 2008a). As shown in the tables and figures in chapter 2, the peer review neuroethics literature is quite rich and includes perspectives that highlight the clinical role of neuroethics. These different but potentially complementing views contribute to shaping a community of plural interests that can help improve understanding of neurological and psychiatric disorders and enrich our perspectives on patient care.

In addition, if the divergence of disciplinary perspectives is emphasized, in particular between medicine and philosophy, this risks introducing caricatures that—I would argue—we should be working to dispel. Fins contends that "cognitive enhancement" is speculative and dismisses it as philosophical (Fins 2008a). Such cursory analyses can lead one astray, however, and have the unintended consequences of slowing interdisciplinary collaborations where we need them. Physicians and biomedical scientists have collaborated in bringing attention to the lifestyle uses of neuropharmaceuticals (Young 2003; Chatterjee 2004). This phenomenon is not only a philosophical issue but now represents a real and serious public health concern. Prescription drug misuse data in recent years show new, disquieting levels and inadequate healthcare approaches to tackle this problem (McCarthy 2007). Neuropharmaceuticals used to treat pain, anxiety, sleep disorders, and attention-deficit/hyperactivity disorder are among the most frequently abused prescription drugs, thereby making timely the focus on appropriate approaches and responses to misuse. The topic has been important enough to warrant the attention of the British Medical Association, which convened an interdisciplinary work group to consider ethical issues related to cognitive enhancement and published a discussion paper conveying key points for furthering public debate (British Medical Association 2007). Hence, the interdisciplinary discussion surrounding the abuse of prescription neuropharmaceuticals illustrates the need and potential value of such dialogue, not the irrelevance of it. This is certainly consistent with one of the tenets of pragmatism as viewed by John Dewey, that disciplinary reductionism must be superseded (Dewey 1922).

Regarding the disciplinary primacy argument, it is much too early to dismiss any disciplinary perspectives in neuroethics, including both clinical and philosophical ones. We need to avoid depicting monolithic pictures of current or historical neuroethics and instead acknowledge pluralism of perspectives and disciplines. If we are truly committed to clinical perspectives, we need to not only reinforce the role of physicians in neuroethics, as suggested by Fins, but also value the contributions of other healthcare providers (e.g., nurses, social workers) as well as the broad interdisciplinary approaches to promoting the healthcare dimensions of neuroethics (Racine 2008c).

Fifth Critique: Neuroethics Is a New Field and Deals with Novel ELSI *and* Neuroethics Is Not and Does Not

Some debate has surfaced over the novelty of neuroethics. Part of the discussion concerns the novelty of the field as such and its disciplinary status: Is neuroethics a "new discipline," a "new field," a "division of bioethics," or an "area where bioethics and neuroethics intersect"? As seen in chapter 2, there are diverging perspectives on the attributes of neuroethics in the peer review literature. For example, some early papers in neuroethics described it as a "new discipline" (Illes and Raffin 2002). However, others reacted against such claims, arguing that neuroethics is not or should not be a new discipline (Wilfond and Magnuson 2005). The other part of this argument concerns the novelty of the issues neuroethics tackles: Are they novel issues or similar issues to those we have been facing in different research contexts, such as genetics, or with other patient populations, as in oncology? Some have argued that the issue is basically the same regardless of context (Wilfond and Magnuson 2005; Parens and Johnston 2007). Others have contended that some neuroethical topics are novel (Reid and Baylis 2005). Because the specificity of neuroethics is often founded in the (well-grounded) belief that the brain is the biological basis of affect, cognition, and motor behavior (uniqueness of the brain), brain interventions are typically viewed as tampering with basic aspects of who we are as humans—our personality, personal narrative, and identity.

Response to the Critiques about the Novelty of Neuroethics

First, let's examine the disciplinary status of neuroethics. The common understanding is that an academic discipline possesses distinct methodologies, training programs, and a recognized corpus of scholarly work to build upon. This is clearly not the current status of neuroethics, and even after close to forty years of scholarship, it is probably only becoming true of bioethics, which seems to be moving toward a disciplinary and departmental structure, with positive and negative consequences. The disciplinary status of bioethics is still an area of debate and controversy related to issues of professionalization in the field (e.g., standards of competency, codes of ethics for bioethicists). The disciplinary evolution of bioethics is a challenging one since bioethics is most often defined as an interdisciplinary endeavor. There are presumably trade-offs when an "interdiscipline" like bioethics becomes a discipline. For example, it may mean that bioethics is becoming better defined and rigorous but also less open to genuine interdisciplinary input. The longstanding debates on the (still uncertain) disciplinary status of bioethics and, in contrast, the early state of neuroethics development clearly suggests some challenges in arguing that neuroethics is a discipline. In fact, most scholars use the term "neuroethics" to designate a new field, not a new discipline. Now, this says nothing of the reasons neuroethics would be a new field, even if granted that it is not a new discipline *stricto sensu*.

Most authors in favor of the field of neuroethics have argued that it deals with novel issues and that this is the basis for its specificity and uniqueness. This has lead to additional critiques. Some have contended that certain neuroethical topics are novel (Reid and Baylis 2005); others have rejected this and criticized the proliferation of new bioethics "subdisciplines" (but implying that bioethics is a discipline, not an "interdiscipline"; Wilfond and Magnuson 2005; Parens and Johnston 2007). And if neuroethics is not dealing with new issues, why speak of it as a new discipline or even a new field of scholarship? First, this common argument holds at least one implicit assumption, that a new field must deal essentially with novel issues. Second, it tends to lead to a second belief, that bioethics should be pursuing or be driven by only novel theoretical objects without concern for their practical salience. Both assumptions are problematic from a pragmatic perspective.

A fundamental question is how an issue would be considered unique or truly novel. Some colleagues have argued that neuroethics addresses novel issues that we have rarely encountered or discussed. What would make an ethical issue unique or what criteria would determine uniqueness must be clarified. Then one should also explain why bioethics emerged and give good examples of what fundamentally new issues it dealt with. Concerns about futility of care and the meaning of medicine surfaced long before ventilators appeared in the 1940s and 1950s. Respect for patient autonomy emerged before the 1960s and bioethics. Perhaps bioethics itself was dealing with truly novel issues, but I have my own doubts and reservations. I prefer to think that bioethics built on historical forces to generate a new approach and method of dealing with some longstanding ethical issues based on dialogue, the need to act concretely, and the value of various perspectives in describing problems and identifying solutions. In the mid-twentieth century, social values were transformed, stakeholders changed, and medical and scientific knowledge evolved. In this respect, neuroethics continues to extend bioethics by carrying forth this vision of humanism and interdisciplinarity captured historically in the intents of bioethics.

The second part of the argument is that if a topic is not novel, then bioethics should not be examining it or dedicating attention to it. However, this is grounded in a quite theoretical and scholarly view of bioethics and one that potentially considers bioethics to be a response to high-profile media coverage and controversies that are depicted as novel and groundbreaking. But many common and important bioethical issues bear little novelty, such as justice and access to mental healthcare; respect for vulnerable patients; and stigma in mental health. These concerns are unfortunately (much too) familiar. Should bioethics be dealing with them, or should it dismiss them because they are not novel? Should the bioethicist care? My answer is an emphatic yes, partly because I view bioethics—as others do (Andre 2002)—as both a theoretical and a practical field. Somewhat analogous to healthcare professions like medicine and nursing, bioethics is a mixture of scholarly and basic work as well as concrete practices (e.g., policy writing, clinical ethics consultation). Accordingly, there is no need for bioethics to seek only novel or sensational objects of research. There are enough significant challenges in the daily life of ordinary people and within the evolution of current biomedical science to keep bioethics busy. Unfortunately, some of the comments I reported may reflect the bias of academic institutions to seek new research agendas and programs while the needs of society may also be served by more grounded and down-to-earth approaches. Interestingly, those that argue that neuroethics is technology driven also contend that neuroethics does not discuss novel issues. One then wonders what should be the appropriate driver of bioethics. If we insist that new fields of bioethics be driven by novel issues, we risk falling prey to bioethics being driven by the research and media agenda and, consequently, leave aside lingering healthcare and health-related ethical and social challenges.

Recent developments in bioethics may have reinforced hype surrounding novel technologies such as stem cells, pharmacology, and genetic technologies to the detriment of social determinants of health and nonbiological or nontechnological interventions. Bioethics should not simply be in service of science, just paving the way for a smoother transfer of knowledge and technology. But at the same time, I don't think bioethics should systematically oppose all forms of scientific and technological advances based on unfounded fears or dogmatic criticism. We need balanced approaches. As a pragmatist, I feel that the needs of patients and the public should be reiterated by bioethics and neuroethics, and that this should be the key driver of what we do. Judith Andre has eloquently pleaded for such a view of bioethics as an interdisciplinary field composed of both practices and scholarship. Bioethics has evolved differently than philosophical and theological ethics to become more practical and to deal with concrete clinical situations and health problems. Sometimes much of a bioethics discussion will revolve around clarifying facts (not ethical principles) to identify the best path to follow. Although this view may not be shared by all bioethicists, I believe that the field of bioethics has become a form of practice, which in association with allied healthcare professions strives to improve healthcare, including public health. Hence, whether neuroethics features novel or unique issues should be secondary to the social and ethical relevance of the challenges that individuals with neurological and psychiatric disorders face, such as stigma, discrimination, and misunderstanding of developmental disabilities. We are not in a situation where we can contend that neuropsychiatric disorders receive their share of public attention and resources. For example, we have not in reality gone beyond the disquieting belief that depression is a problem for high-income countries. A new vehicle like neuroethics could allow scholars and various stakeholders to work together to find concrete solutions. Medicine does not need to invent diseases. It is busy tackling existing healthcare problems and developing collaborations and approaches to handle them. *Ibidem* for neuroethics.

Sixth Critique: Neuroethics Implies a Reductionist Take on the Nature of the Mind and on Research Approaches

Some scholars have argued that neuroethics relies on reductionist assumptions about the mind, that neuroethics implies that "we are our brains" and rests on the belief that contemporary neuroscience can provide fairly complete and convincing explanations of who and what we are. This belief is sometimes called neuroessentialism since it implies a strong form of reductionism—analogous to the genetic essentialism that surfaced in the eighties (Roskies 2002; Racine, Bar-Ilan, and Illes 2005). Indeed, neuro-essentialist beliefs that we are our brains are reminiscent of beliefs that "we are our genomes" and rely on similar forms of metaphysical interpretations of the biological sciences (Mauron 2003)—although essentialist statements are arguably harder to dismiss in the context of neuroscience for reasons that I cannot examine in detail here (Illes and Racine 2005a). Strangely, such uncritical and sweeping essentialist statements and ontological reductionism have been interpreted by some as fundamental epistemological commitments of neuroethics itself (Schick 2005). Another form of reductionism, more methodological or disciplinary in nature—but not necessarily unconnected to the first one—has been identified and criticized. Ilina Singh, for example, contends that neuroethics does not take into account the social aspects of the evolution of neuroscience or the social aspects of mental health (Singh 2005). This methodological reductionism concerns less the mind–body problem itself and more broadly the relationship between what I describe as the mind-brain, on the one hand, and its relationship to environmental and social factors that shape the mind-brain, on the other hand. Hence, methodological reductionism concerns the methodologies and approaches used to understand the mind-brain relationship and tackle neuroethical issues. However, both forms of reductionism (ontological reductionism and methodological reductionism) can reinforce each other because if the mind-brain (and related medical and behavioral problems) is considered in a reductive way, we are likely to be convinced that reductionist research and interventional approaches will be sufficient to understand and treat the mind-brain.

Response to the Reductionism Critique

Some critiques quickly came to the conclusion that neuroethics is based on a form of naïve ontological reductionism and essentialism (Schick 2005). It is true that some proponents have argued that neuroethics is special or novel because it deals with interventions in the brain; that the brain is the biological basis of identity, the self, and personality; and that accordingly, interventions in the brain could impact self-identity and personality. If neuroethics is grounded on such strong beliefs, then it could carry forward a form of neuroessentialism or reductionism. However, because of a lack of precision and the need for further clarification, such statements have been conflated with strong forms of reductionism. The reality is that many scholars are actually exploring openly the relationship between mind and brain and are not committed to a form of crude and unsophisticated reductionism. There are clearly several important reasons why reductionism is ethically problematic (Stent 1990; Racine and Illes 2009). Bioethics is largely viewed as an attempt to consider and promote the patient as a person and an interdisciplinary endeavor to avoid disciplinary reductionisms (Callahan 1976). But this is exactly why some neuroethics scholars like me and other colleagues have critically examined phenomena like neuroessentialism. Neuroessentialism is a common fallacy in the popular interpretations of neuroscience research, and it could support practices that are based on questionable assumptions about neuroscience and the brain (Racine, Bar-Ilan, and Illes 2005). Obviously, a strong neuroessentialist belief that we are our brain could misguide neuroethics also. How would bioethics remain critical and provide a balanced assessment of the potentials of neuroscience research and bring to the forefront concerns of patients (Racine and Illes 2009)? The problem is that this is essentially a straw man argument against neuroethics.

Debates regarding ontological reductionism are also of vital importance in discussions surrounding the potential input of neuroscience in our views of ethics, what is often called the "neuroscience of ethics" (Roskies 2002), a topic that is discussed further in chapter 9 of this book. I will not present formal arguments on this topic at this point; however, it is reasonable to believe that no neuroessentialism or neuroexceptionalism must be postulated for neuroethics to benefit from emerging neuroscience research that could affect views on ethics. If we grant that empirical research can be useful for bioethics, then it follows that many forms of empirical research can contribute, including neuroscience and psychological research. As long as neuroscience research is not seen as the ultimate discourse revealing the final biological foundations of morality, then this input along with that of other empirical disciplines such as moral psychology, qualitative research, and the sociology of ethics can inform research and practices related to ethical decision making (Racine 2007). Of course, disciplinary reductionism can be a threat, and neuroscience may seem to convey more authority than qualitative research.

However, such reductionism can plague both the biological sciences and the humanities; in the search for ultimate and self-standing explanation of moral behavior, scholars in both areas of study can be seduced by scholarly ideologies that limit explanatory variables—either biological or social in nature—to be considered. Based on those caveats, and the pragmatic naturalism discussed in the previous chapter, neuroscience can be seen as one of the contributing disciplines to the mounting body of empirical research in bioethics (Racine 2007). As such, establishing a two-way relationship between bioethics and the biological sciences does not represent an entirely new project for bioethics.

However, the contribution of neuroscience to bioethics needs much clarification and many qualifications. Some authors have argued that the neuroscience of ethics and the ethics of neuroscience should be considered two distinct endeavors (Farah and Wolpe 2004), while others, including some arguing for this point, have contributed to the scholarship in the neuroscience of ethics (Farah and Heberlein 2007). This just exemplifies the level of confusion surrounding the neuroscience of ethics and its relationship to other aspects of neuroethics.

The second part of the argument concerns a harder issue to address and points to a longstanding challenge in bioethics: the inclusion of the social science disciplines and empirical research in bioethics (De Vries 2005). Singh and others have identified several excellent reasons to integrate such perspectives in neuroethics (Singh 2005) in addition to those already identified in bioethics at large to support a strong role for empirical research (Borry, Schotsmans, and Dierickx 2005; Solomon 2005; Racine 2008d). In addition, mental health is one area where reductionist methodological approaches and methodologies can poorly resist rigorous scientific and ethical scrutiny. Behavioral and psychiatric disorders are caused by both environmental factors (e.g., work or school environment) and biological factors. It is important to note that some tenets of social approaches—perhaps as radical as some tenets of biological approaches—seem to be on a quest to reject any form of biological understanding of these phenomena. Unfortunately, discussions have again been plagued with confusing inconsistencies, with some scholars suggesting that sociological realities are examined in neuroethics (De Vries 2005) while arguing that neuroethics does not carefully examine those realities (De Vries 2007). I think that one of the challenges in this area will be to sustain neuroethics approaches that are broad enough to foster the inclusiveness required by the field's goals. Reductionism is not unidirectional; both social and biological understandings of moral and social behavior can lead to academic ideologies suggesting that one factor or one variable explains all. An antidote to reductionism is to acknowledge the limitations of existing approaches and to be open to different kinds of scholarly and practical contributions.

Conclusion

Advances in neuroscience along with longstanding concerns for neurological and psychiatric patients have carried forward the field of neuroethics. The goals of neuroethics are substantial and likely to create diverging expectations that need to be examined and clarified. In this chapter, I have highlighted the value of critically examining neuroethics, but in doing so, I recognize that the complex and pluralistic nature of this subfield, its historical underpinnings, and its promise to create dialogues that articulate both tradition and innovation, will move forward (Illes and Racine 2005b). Most of the views discussed above fall short of acknowledging that not only is neuroethics a scholarly endeavor concerned with the sheer novelty of neuroscience developments or the ethical issues associated with these developments but that it is also a practical endeavor with practical goals.

Whatever one's position on neuroethics, examining the critiques of neuroethics shows the importance and value of choosing practical and scholarly projects well and carefully to avoid some of the pitfalls identified so far. Judith Andre has highlighted in the post-ELSI of genetics bioethics how important it is for bioethics as a community to define the goals worth pursuing and the environment needed to support collegial bioethics practices and scholarship (Andre 2002). The overall challenge for neuroethics and bioethics as a collective endeavor is to balance a willingness to help the medical and scientific communities with a fundamental commitment to the good of patients and the general public. Neuroethics is not an exception and can benefit from a wide range of goals, scholarship, and practices. At the same time, I have observed that several controversies surrounding the birth and evolution of neuroethics are based on some straightforward misunderstandings and caricatures, while others

serve as cautions for greater reflection and thinking. With its commitment to integrating several goals and views of neuroethics, pragmatic
neuroethics helps reflect that neuroethics is a community endeavor. It
builds on the field being defined by goals that are larger than those of
individuals pursuing specific research or practical objectives, goals such as
fostering broader healthcare perspectives based on bottom-up approaches,
interdisciplinary collaboration, creative thinking and problem solving,
and engaging patients and public stakeholders in bioethics reflection and
decisions. It is in this spirit that the next part of this book, inspired by
pragmatic naturalism, explores various important neuroethical topics.

5

Public Understanding of Neuroscience Innovation and Emerging Interpretations of Neuroscience Research

Overview

From a pragmatic perspective, it is crucial not only to consider expert opinions about ethics in neuroscience but also to attend to public concerns as well as emerging lay interpretations of neuroscience research. Lay beliefs about neuroscience could fuel expectations and potential misuses of neurotechnology while also shaping the landscape of public debate on neuroscience innovation. This chapter discusses salient aspects of media coverage of neuroscience innovation in its various forms, including emerging expectations regarding neuroscience.

In a paper coauthored with Judy Illes, I argued that ethical, legal, and social challenges in neuroscience research, especially in functional neuroimaging, are intertwined with epistemological issues. In the use of such technologies, determining what could be their proper ethical use (ethics) is fundamentally tied to what we believe neuroscience data mean (epistemology; Illes and Racine 2005a). Given the relationships between brain and personhood, as well as the many scientific uncertainties surrounding our current understanding of the brain, critically examining the link between ethics and epistemology becomes essential. The attribution of both scientific and social meaning to neuroscience research results can be viewed as one of the major challenges inherent to the ethical use of neuroscience. Such concerns are particularly relevant given that neuroimaging techniques can give, in the words of Donald Kennedy, "an unjustified sense of precision" (Kennedy 2005).

First, at the scientific level, the ethico-epistemological challenge relates to the simplicity of the visual format of neuroimages (Beaulieu 2002), a

simplicity that can mask the complex scientific and technological processes underlying the constructions of such images (Beaulieu 2001). Brain
activation maps depicting brain function in task performance are much
more complicated than the commonly used metaphor of a "window into
the brain" suggests. Numerous constraints, such as number of subjects,
cultural variations and statistical analysis prevent any such general sim-
plification (Illes, Racine, and Kirschen 2006). Second, at the social and
cultural level, the meaning of some of the concepts currently investigated
by neuroimaging (e.g., violence, empathy, moral emotions, deception) is
culturally laden and difficult to define authoritatively. Hence, the challenge of deriving meaning from diverse neurophysiologic signals is coupled with perennial philosophical debates about the relationship between
the mind and the brain and the various cultural perspectives on this problem (Dumit 2004). My point is that the ethical uses of this technique
necessarily summon epistemological questions, and these questions are
themselves shaped by cultural and social context.

This chapter reviews salient aspects of media coverage neuroscience
innovation, including emerging expectations regarding neuroscience as
one strategy to examine the cultural aspects of the ethico-epistemological
challenge of functional neuroimaging (Racine, Bar-Ilan, and Illes 2005;
Racine, Waldman, and Illes 2005; Illes, Racine, and Kirschen 2006;
Racine, DuRousseau, and Illes 2007; Racine, Waldman, Palmour, et al.
2007). I highlight and discuss the impact of media portrayal of neuroscience on our self-understanding given marked enthusiasm for neurotechnology as well as the need for public engagement regarding neuroscience
advances. I identify the lay understanding of neuroscience innovation
and suggest avenues to explore based on pragmatism's commitment to
public dialogue and the inclusion of various perspectives noted in chapters 3 and 4.

Neuroscience in the Media

To gain further insights into media coverage of neuroscience innovation
and its implications for society, I draw on a large-scale content analysis
of 1,256 newspaper articles retrieved using the LexisNexis Academic
database (Racine, Waldman, and Illes 2005). This sample is composed of
335 articles featuring positron emission tomography (PET) or single

photon-emission computerized tomography (SPECT); 284 for electroencephalography (EEG); 235 for neurostimulation techniques such as deep brain stimulation (DBS) and transcranial magnetic stimulation (TMS); 223 for functional magnetic resonance imaging (fMRI); and 179 for neurogenetic testing for neurological and neuropsychiatric disorders and personality traits. In this sample of articles published in major English-language United States (US) and United Kingdom (UK) news sources, 875 (70%) originated from the US and 381 (30%) from the UK. The vast majority of articles ($n = 1,233$; 98%) reported the use of neurotechnology in humans. Headlines focused on scientific breakthroughs, new diagnostic methods, and new treatments based on neuroscience, with an emphasis on the mind-reading potentials of neuroscience innovation to reveal the biological basis of disease, identity, and personality (see figure 5.1). These promises are conveyed in various claims regarding the potential for neurotechnology to create breakthroughs, powerful new diagnostic methods for neurological and psychiatric illness, and new forms of treatments, and even to decipher the healthy mind.

Figure 5.2 shows that tone varied in the coverage of the different neurotechnologies examined, with more frequent balanced ($p \leq 0.001$) and critical articles ($p \leq 0.001$) in coverage of neurogenetic testing. However, the tone of media coverage was mostly optimistic (featuring benefits of research and its applications) or neutral (no benefits and no risks or issues). Overall, 68 percent of articles ($n = 853$) presented at least one benefit (clinical or nonclinical) and 28 percent of articles ($n = 352$) presented one issue (scientific or ethical; Racine, Waldman, and Illes 2005).

Media coverage discussed some of the scientific and medical challenges related to neuroscience innovation (figure 5.3). These included notably issues of reliability, validity, and proper understanding of technology to avoid misinterpretation in the use of neuroimaging for lie detection or marketing. Risks and side effects were a key concern for neurostimulation techniques, while issues related to the interpretation of data were crucial in the discussion of neuroimaging techniques (fMRI, PET, EEG).

Discussion of ethical, legal and social issues included a broad range of topics (figure 5.4) such as commercialization and conflict of interest (the most frequent issue encountered); discrimination and stigma; and the broad meaning of neuroscience research on beliefs and values. Consistent

"Scientific breakthrough" headline (*n* = 162; 12.9%)

"Pulsing magnets offer new method of mapping brain" (Blakeslee 1996).

"Answers to alcoholism become clearer: Both environment and genetics appear to play significant roles in the risk of developing the disease" (Foreman 2004).

"What's on baby's mind? Researchers studying how an infant's brain develops are intrigued by what's going on in the heads of their tiny subjects. Their efforts, they hope, will not only teach us more about babies, but also how to make better adults" (Cummins 1997).

"New diagnosis" headline (*n* = 113; 9.0%)

"Genetic test may identify boys who will grow up to be violent" (Connor 2002).

"Brain scans search for Alzheimer's before it strikes" (Elias 2000).

"Not knowing can be as hard as knowing; As Kristin LaVine considers whether to be tested for Huntington's, uncertainty is never far away" (Schmickle 2000).

"New treatment" headline (*n* = 66; 5.3%)

"Magnetic appeal. New therapy that fights depression sparks a current of optimism"(Blake 2001).

"Keeping pace with Parkinson's doctors can't prevent or cure the disease, but they're working to alleviate the worst symptoms" (Thomas 1997).

"Their every move is electric. With pacemaker-sized stimulators and tiny computers, researchers are bypassing spines and nerves and giving paralysis and stroke victims some function" (McIntyre and Mazzolini 1997).

Figure 5.1
Most frequent headline themes in print media coverage of neuroscience innovation. $N = 1,256$.

with the analysis presented in chapter 2 regarding neuroethics, the unique biological nature of the brain and its relationship with the mind again colored discussions. For example, discussion of individual autonomy included concerns about undermining autonomous choice by direct brain intervention. Generally, neurogenetic testing was more frequently associated with ethical issues (46%) than other types of neurotechnologies examined ($p < .001$), such as PET scan (15%), neurostimulation techniques (14%), EEG (12%), and fMRI (9%).

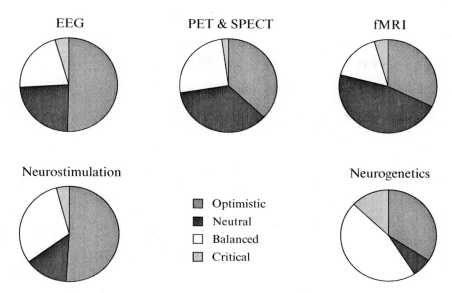

Figure 5.2
Tone of media coverage of neuroscience innovation (1995–2004)

Emerging Interpretations of Neuroscience Research

Based on a previous study of fMRI in the media (Racine, Bar-Ilan, and Illes 2005), it was possible to identify emerging interpretations of neuroscience using the concepts of neuroessentialism, neurorealism, and neuropolicy. These interpretations were found respectively in 9 percent, 9 percent, and 5 percent of articles featuring neuroimaging techniques (EEG, PET, fMRI); none were found in articles about neurogenetic testing or neurostimulation techniques (Racine, Waldman, and Illes 2005; Racine, Waldman, Palmour, et al. 2007).

Neuroessentialism

The concept of neuroessentialism identifies interpretations proposing that the brain is the self-defining essence of a person, a secular equivalent to the soul. The brain thus becomes shorthand for concepts (e.g., the person, the self) that may express other features of the individual not ordinarily found in the concept of the brain. In print media, neuroessentialism is a combination of biological reductionism and enthusiasm for

Validity ($n = 95$; 7.6%): Risks and concerns related to appropriate research design

"Critics note that the companies that sell the gene testing services do not have to give details to consumers about tests' validity in predicting disease" (Freundlich 2004).

"The tests are not yet ready for widespread use because most are not refined enough to differentiate disease from normal individual variations. In addition, the tests pick up changes that result for reasons other than Alzheimer's" (December 2004).

Misunderstanding of the technology ($n = 68$; 5.4%): Risks and concerns related to the interpretation of findings by the public and researchers

"Dr. Steven Quartz, a neuroscientist at the California Institute of Technology in Pasadena, California, said Mr. Ruskin's comments represented 'gross misunderstandings and distortions of both the power of brain imaging technology and its use in marketing'" (Blakeslee 2004).

"'The interpretation of [electroencephalogram, or EEG results] is an area of some controversy and some disagreement among neurologists,' Kline said under cross-examination" (Shaver 1998).

Safety, side effects, and discomfort ($n = 58$; 4.6%): Risks and concerns related to unintended negative physical and psychological consequences of a procedure

"Three quarters experienced mild to moderate discomfort at the site of stimulation. Two patients who experienced severe pain in the treatment dropped out of the study" (Trueland 1999).

"TMS is highly experimental and if used incorrectly can induce brain seizures in healthy people" (Blakeslee 1996).

Readiness ($n = 31$; 2.5%): Risks and concerns related to premature application of a neurotechnology

"Officially, the Alzheimer's Association says brain scans are not mature enough to be used for pre-symptomatic screening" (Torassa 2002).

Reliability ($n = 25$; 2%): Risks and concerns related to reproducibility of results and sustainability of technology

"Is the technique reliable? Too early to tell, says Faro. 'We have just begun to understand the potential of fMRI in studying deceptive behaviour'" (Anonymous 2004).

"Current electrode arrays, he said, can be jarred out of place and lose the signal" (Eisenberg 2002).

Figure 5.3
Examples of qualitative content in media coverage of scientific and medical issues. $N = 1,256$.

Commercialization and conflict of interest (n = 72; 5.7%): Concerns about the relationship between neuroscience research and the private sector (e.g., patenting, conflict of interest, and ownership of research results) and abuse stemming from the high cost of neurotechnology

"Cost is a significant barrier as the equipment and the operation to insert it can amount to Pounds 40,000" (Hawkes 2002).

"Another neurosurgeon without connection to the company will monitor the procedure to ensure that financial interests do not indicate proceeding with surgery if it is not safe" (Pollack 2004).

"It is mostly the rapid commercialization of the tests that has alarmed the experts. Some of the genes have been discovered only recently, yet already the genetic tests are being advertised to doctors, and at least one network of physicians will offer them to patients shortly" (*New York Times* 1995).

Discrimination and stigma (n = 60; 4.8%): Concerns about prejudice or damage caused by segregation, exclusion, or negative labeling

"A number of genetic discrimination cases have come to light in recent years. . . . More difficult issues include a comprehensive ban on genetic discrimination in employment, possible restriction on the use of genetic tests in life insurance underwriting and stricter regulation of the genetic testing industry" (R. Wise 1997).

Meaning of research (n = 48; 3.8%): Concerns about the meaning and direction of neuroscience research; about neuroscience threatening morals and ethics, or social, cultural, familial, and religious values; and about determinism and reductionism

"There definitely are dangers, and we do tend to address them imperfectly, so there is some possibility that this will fail" (Fixmer 1999).

"Nevertheless, the techniques have proved controversial. In America protest groups have questioned whether some of research breaks medical ethics rules, while other scientists fear neuromarketing could lead to a sinister form of consumer mind control. Commercial Alert, the American 'anti-commercialism' group, has also attracked neuromarketing on the grounds that it is 'wrong to use medical technology for marketing, not healing'"(Leighton 2004).

Privacy and confidentiality (n = 41; 3.3%): Risks and concerns related to disclosure of confidential information

"By scanning a brain into a database, a person's most private thoughts and memories would be vulnerable to intrusions by hackers" (Fixmer 1999).

Figure 5.4
Examples of qualitative content in media coverage of ethical, legal, and social issues. N = 1,256.

"Tension between patients' demand for privacy and genetic researchers' need for specimens is raising serious questions about whether science's voracious appetite for the human genome is outpacing society's ethical and legal protections" (Austin 2000).

Consent and autonomy (n = 33; 2.6%): Risks and concerns related to recruitment of research subjects, the process of informed consent, respect of individual decision-making capacity, and protection of subjects enrolled in protocols

"It is clearly a technique that if applied to humans would have huge legal, moral and ethical ramifications . . . to undermine the autonomy of an individual decision maker"(Anonymous 2002).

"While Fins discussed the ethical knots of performing surgery on people too brain damaged to give consent, Barbara Juknialis also listened intently" (Long 2002).

Justice and resource allocation (n = 17; 1.4%): Concerns related to equal treatment of persons, equal access to technology and healthcare, and fair distribution of risks to study populations

"PET (positron emission tomography) scans can give a diagnosis that is about 97 percent accurate, but the $1,200 cost, usually not covered by insurance, puts them out of reach to most people" (Peterson 2001).

Duty and responsibility (n = 13; 1%): Concerns related to the exercise of a duty or fulfilling responsibilities

"What responsibility will be perceived by, or assigned to, parents if they are held responsible for giving birth to people who develop mental illness?" (Baird 1997).

Policy and public involvement (n = 12; 1%): Concerns about government control over and management of research; about nonexistent or insufficient legislation; and about "public autonomy" and public responsibility, such as lack of public consultation, absence of public debate, manipulation of public opinion, and undemocratic process

"The Government's commitment to the moratorium on the use of genetic information for insurance purposes must be robustly enforced. It should even consider an outright ban to ensure the protection of vulnerable and disadvantaged consumers" (Griffiths 2001).

Dignity and integrity (n = 7; 0.6%): Concerns related to the treatment of humans as mere means and not ends in themselves; the sanctity of life; mischievous uses; inhumane or cruel uses; and uses that jeopardize human dignity

Figure 5.4
(continued)

"Prenatal testing for Huntington's is even more fraught. If the foetus proves to be carrying the gene, then it means that the at-risk parent also certainly carries the gene and will get the disease. 'If you decided to abort', Dr Green pointed out, 'it's in effect aborting yourself—it's a statement about the value of your own life'" (Wilkie 1996).

Enhancement (*n* = 6; 0.5%): Concerns related to the improvement of brain function

"What about the whole question of artificial intelligence and the enhancement of human abilities by means of neural implants?" (McGinn 2002).

Artificial selection and eugenics (*n* = 6; 0.5%): Concerns about the selection of embryos for desired characteristics or the desire to improve humans through genetic selection

"It is inevitable that once genetic information is available some people will want to use it for eugenic purposes" (J. Wise 1997).

Animal rights (*n* = 5; 0.4%): Concerns for animal rights and welfare; respectful and ethical treatment of animals in research

"The number of primates used in medical research is small compared with the number of mice and rats, but it is much more controversial because monkeys are so similar to humans. About 3000 monkeys are used in medical research in the UK every year. Primates are the only animal model for neurodegenerative diseases" (Firn 2003).

Figure 5.4
(continued)

neuroscience research. The reductionist component takes various forms, such as equating brain and personhood; localizing personality traits or illness; or subtly personifying the brain. Various types of neuroessentialist statements presented in the media relate to the impact of neuroimaging on self-identity:

• *Neuroscience reveals our "essence," who we are:*   "With more powerful imaging devices and new genetic information, scientists are exploring the secrets of the organ that makes humans unique" (Colburn 1999).
• *Neuroscience reveals the neuronal basis of personality traits or illness:*   "If your child has trouble reading, the problem may indeed be all in his head" (Hall 1999).

• *The brain implicitly becomes a grammatical subject*: "As any good movie director or roller coaster designer knows, people love surprises. Now, it seems, at the most basic level, the brain does too" (Nagourney 2001).

Closely associated with these various forms of neuroessentialism, enthusiasm is found for neuroscience research and the "secrets" that neuroscience can reveal about ourselves. For example, according to print media, neuroimaging technologies allow for the exploration of "the secret, uncharted areas of the brain" and the identification of "the individual sources of all our thoughts, actions and behaviour" (Dobson 1997). Neuroscience will therefore reveal "life's ultimate mystery: our conscious inner selves" (Connor 1995) and is presented as science "gone in search of the soul" (Hellmore 1998).

Neurorealism
The concept of neurorealism suggests that neuroimaging research yields direct data on brain function. Observed brain activation patterns can accordingly become the ultimate proof that a phenomenon is real, objective, and effective (e.g., in the case of health interventions such as hypnosis and acupuncture), despite the complexities of data acquisition and image processing involved. Hence, neurorealism reflects the uncritical way in which an fMRI investigation can be taken as a validation or invalidation of our ordinary view of cognitive phenomena. Neurorealism is grounded in the opinion that fMRI enables us to seize a simple "visual proof" of brain activity, despite the enormous complexities of data acquisition and processing. Again, neurorealist interpretations are found in the media, portraying neuroimaging technology using various metaphors:

• *Neuroimaging as "mind reading"*: "Hi-tech hairnet that reads minds" (Macdermid 1997).

• *Neuroimaging provides a "visual proof" or reveals the true nature of cognitive phenomena*: "But the fact that pain, like blood pressure or body temperature, can now be measured . . . will help convince doctors that patients' pain is very real" (Noble 1999).

• *Neuroimaging provides a "window into the brain," through pictures or movies of the "brain in action"*: "The fMRI gives us a window into the human brain" (Fackelmann 2001).

Neuropolicy

Neuropolicy describes attempts to use fMRI results for promoting political and personal agendas, as in the case of interest groups that uphold the investigation of social problems using fMRI. For example, the Lighted Candle Society, a Utah-based nonprofit organization dedicated to the enhancement of moral values, espouses the use of fMRI to prove that pornography is addictive (Bacon 2004). Another example of neuropolicy is reported by a neuroscientist who has received queries from "both sides of the current California debate on bilingual education" (Hall 1998). Two forms of neuropolicy were identified in media coverage:

• *Neuroimaging results inform policies and social practices:* "Zak says fMRI stands to make a big impact in what has been dubbed 'neuromarketing.' As an example of how fMRI might be used, Zak proposes a company that wants to increase its sales of milk. One way it might is to gather a group of people who like milk and scan them as they drink a glass. Some of the regions of the brain that buzz with activity might be triggered by any drink, but others may be triggered only by milk" (Sample and Adam 2003).

• *Neuroimaging informs lifestyle and everyday activities, providing a new wisdom in the conduct of one's life:* "Serious scientific research efforts have been going on in this area for many years now, and recent successes may have enormous implications for the lifestyle of the future" (Mcnaught 1996).

I have presented qualitative and quantitative data from a large-scale content analysis of U.S. and UK print media coverage of neuroscience innovation such as fMRI and PET scan. Some of the key findings are the emergence of neuroessentialism, neurorealism, and neuropolicy within print media; the infrequent presence of scientific or ethical discussion of challenges; and headlines and body content that put forward the mind-reading potential of neuroscience innovation. Accordingly, print media coverage of neurotechnology was generally optimistic about the potential benefits of neuroscience to improve diagnostic procedures and treatments. As will be seen, these facets of public understanding interact with self-identity and commercialization and illustrate the need for public dialogue and avenues for broader ethical and social debates on neuroscience.

Neuroscience's Impact on our Self-Understanding

The emergence of neurorealist and neuroessentialist interpretations of neuroscience research brings into the foreground the interaction between *lay* understandings and *scientific*, or expert, understandings of health and human behavior—what philosopher Wilfred Sellars called, respectively, the "manifest" and the "scientific" images of the world (Sellars 1963). On the one hand, the manifest image of the world reflects a commonsensical view of humankind, that is, the way we see ourselves in ordinary life based on beliefs in free will and other commonsense assumptions. So far, the investigation of these phenomena has largely been the prerogative of the humanities, although this is rapidly changing. On the other hand, the scientific image of the world reflects the scientific understanding of humankind, that is, the way we see humankind and human behavior based on scientific knowledge. The manifest and scientific images can interact in various ways. The manifest image can be largely consistent with the scientific image or both images can conflict. Accordingly, varying interpretations of this relationship have been put forward. Paul and Patricia Churchland have argued at length and since the early eighties that the scientific image will eliminate our manifest image given that "folk psychology" is bluntly a false theory (P. M. Churchland 1981; P. S. Churchland 1986, 2002). In shorthand, the scientific image will replace the manifest image of man and moral reasoning. The Churchlands are enthusiastic about this prospect since, according to them, humankind would gain a more accurate self-understanding. Others, however, view this type of interpretation of the relationship between scientific and manifest images as a potential threat to ethics (Stent 1990). Such fears have also been voiced outside academia and have found a home in interest groups (*Nature Neuroscience* 1998). Finally, others have developed a more moderate view of the integration of scientific and manifest images and have proposed noneliminative forms of reductionism (Bickle 1992; Racine 2007; Racine and Illes 2009).

It is no surprise that neuroscience's impact on our self-understanding is so intensely debated. At stake are our common intuitions about humankind, health and behavior, and self-identity, which could potentially be replaced or revised by the scientific image of the brain and human behavior. The debate on the impact of neuroscience on our self-identity and manifest image is also fueled by emerging research in "affective neuro-science" (Dalgleish 2004), "social neuroscience" (Cacioppo et al. 2000), and "neurophilosophy" (P. S. Churchland 1986), with the integrity of commonsensical concepts such as free will and responsibility being argued based on neuroscience research. The media portrayal of scientific breakthroughs is not without impact on these debates, and this chapter's review of media content clearly shows how neuroimaging in particular has nourished current discussions by yielding neuroessentialist and neu-rorealist beliefs.

Another face of the emerging neuroessentialist and neurorealist inter-pretations of neuroscience innovation is their interaction with the long-standing debate on the nature of psychiatry, which can be viewed as a brain-based discipline, a mind-based discipline, or a combination of both. The relationship between the manifest image and the scientific image here translates into the debate about the centrality of the mind or the brain (or both) for psychiatry. Nobel laureate Erik Kandel has presented a constructive framework in which both biological and nonbiological approaches complement each other (Kandel 1998). In contrast to such a moderate perspective defended by Kandel and many others, there are media claims for clinical benefits of neurotechnology, which could strongly support biological approaches (which do not by definition imply neuro-essentialism). Hence, neuroessentialist and neurorealist interpretations in the media could undermine a balanced view of the complementary roles of biological and social and humanities-based approaches to behavior and disease. A phenomenon akin to geneticization, the uncritical accep-tance of genetics-centered views of health and disease (Lippman 1991, 1992), could shape the evolution of attitudes in psychiatry, favoring a biology-based approach and deterring a mind-based approach. At stake is ultimately a fair appreciation of nonbiological understandings and approaches to mental and behavioral disorders, and an appreciation of the limitations of current approaches to our self-understanding.

Enthusiasm for Neurotechnology and Commercialization of Research

Coverage of neuroscience innovation is generally optimistic or at least does not frequently discuss the risks and issues. The percentage of articles with ethics content in non-genetics-related neurotechnology (e.g., EEG,

PET, fMRI, and neurostimulation) is lower than the percentage with ethics content in genomics and genetics, where figures around 40 percent have been reported (Craig 2000; Conrad 2001; Petersen 2001; Racine et al. 2006). Consistent with these previous studies, the data I review illustrate that ethics content was three times more frequent regarding neurogenetic testing than any of the nongenetic technologies. These results and others (Racine, Bar-Ilan, and Illes 2005; Illes, Racine, and Kirschen 2006) support the point of view that the issues of neuroscience have not yet been brought to the public eye as forcefully as issues of genomics, in spite of the considerable advances and growing applications of neuroscience (Wolpe 2002; Illes and Racine 2005a).

Despite the diverging proportions of articles with ethical content, genetics and neuroscience media articles seem to predominantly feature issues of commercialization and conflicts of interest. This has been observed in media studies of science and technology (Nelkin 2001; Tambor et al. 2002; Smart 2003; Kua, Reder, and Grossel 2004; Racine et al. 2006). Media coverage of these issues provides an interesting window on scientific integrity within the construction of scientific knowledge.

It is now well established that commercial involvement of investigators can affect data interpretation and research design (Krimsky et al. 1996; Bodenheimer 2000; Friedman and Richter 2004). In the late 1990s, such observations led the *New England Journal of Medicine* to search for truly independent physicians and scientists to write review articles. In 2002, the journal relaxed its conflict of interest policies in light of the extent and scope of scientists' and physicians' commercial involvements and the impracticality of finding suitable independent authors. Commercial and other broad pressures on science are also suspected of being major causes of professional misconduct in research (Martinson, Anderson, and De Vries 2005). The emergence of direct-to-consumer advertising (DTCA) of healthcare products and services adds another layer of complexity to the impact of the commercialization of biomedical research products. Through targeted strategies, DTCA brings patients to clinicians, including patients with chronic illnesses in psychiatry and neurology, with well-defined expectations about which treatment and brand is best suited for them (Hollon 2004; Racine, Van der Loos, and Illes 2007). Commercialization has become one of the greatest ethical and social issues for science and society.

The close relationships between commercial interests and biomedical research create a context where commercial pressures on this research have perhaps never been so great. As a result of these pressures, some could expect the media to channel knowledge to the public to gather general support for basic research. Other expectations from the public and policy makers for efficient transfer of basic research into concrete applications can be fueled by this attitude toward the media. Part of the problem of justifying research based on its deliverables, however, lies in the difficulty of predicting how and when basic research will translate into applications. Accordingly, Timothy Caulfield writes, "Commercial influence on public representations of science has the potential to create a skewed picture of biomedical research—a picture that emphasizes benefits over risks, and predictions of unrealistic breakthroughs over a tempered explanation of the incremental nature of the advancement of scientific knowledge" (Caulfield 2004). Current science reporting practices, including those for neuroscience innovation, provide a basis for concern, especially since, once published, media articles become publicly available sources of information that are used to support claims and practices that inform patient and consumer behaviors. News reports feed back into commercial activities and practices such as DTCA. Together with colleagues at Stanford University, I found that some neuroimaging facilities that sell brain scans directly (without physician referral) via Web sites and companies that promote dietary neurosupplements use favorable media coverage to support their marketing strategies (Racine, Van der Loos, and Illes 2007). Going further, Zuckerman has specifically identified and analyzed cases where research is not intended to expand knowledge per se, or even benefit humanity, but is undertaken to support the sale of products to the public. He concludes, "Much of the media coverage of health news stories is based on public relations efforts on behalf of the companies that sell the products, including pharmaceutical companies, diet clinics, or doctors selling new techniques" (Zuckerman 2003). Some of these practices involve paying physicians and other experts to speak favorably about the featured product. This situation has been judged serious enough by the Ethics, Law, and Humanities Committee of the American Academy of Neurology to warrant the development of a specific practice guideline on physician involvement in DTCA in 2001.

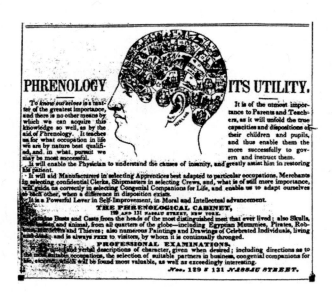

PHRENOLOGY – ITS UTILITY

Left side:

To know ourselves is a matter of greatest importance and there is no other means by which we can acquire this knowledge so well, as by the aid of Phrenology. It teaches us for what occupation in life we are by nature best qualified, and in what pursuit we may be most successful.

Right side:

It is of the utmost importance to Parents and Teachers, as it will unfold the true capacities and dispositions of their children and pupils, and thus enable them the more successfully to govern and instruct them.

Below skull:

It will enable the Physician to understand the causes of insanity, and greatly assist him in restoring his patient.

It will aid Manufacturers in selecting Apprentices best adapted to particular occupations, Merchants in selecting confidential Clerks, Shipmasters in selecting Crews, and, what is of still more importance, will guide us correctly in selecting Congenital Companions for Life, and enable us to adapt ourselves to each other, when a difference in disposition exists.

It is a Powerful Lever in Self-Improvement, in Moral and Intellectual advancement.

THE PHRENOLOGICAL CABINET,

129 and 131 Nassau Street, New York.

Contains Busts and Casts from the heads of the most distinguished men that ever lived: also Skulls from [unreadable] and animal, from all quarters of the globe— including Egyptian Mummies, Pirates, Robbers, Murderers and Thieves; also numerous Paintings and Drawings of Celebrated Individuals, living and dead; and is always FREE to visitors, by whom it is continually thronged.

PROFESSIONAL EXAMINATIONS,

With written and verbal descriptions of character, given when desired; including directions as to the most suitable occupations, the selection of suitable partners in business, congenital companions for life, [unreadable] which will be found most valuable, as well as exceedingly interesting.

Nos. 129 & 131 NASSAU STREET.

Contemporary neuroimaging has been compared with historical phrenology (Kennedy 2005). There are actually interesting phrenological counterparts to current pressures of commercialization on neuroimaging as well as to the relationship between those pressures and neuroessentialism, neurorealism, and neuropolicy. The founders of phrenology, Gall and Spurzheim, were renowned neuroanatomists. They made remarkable contributions to the integrative understanding of the central nervous system based on comparative anatomy and pre-Darwin evolutionary principles (Clarke and Jacyna 1987). However, their writings were largely popularized and disseminated in the United States by the Fowler brothers, who had keen business flair. Orson and Lorenzo Fowler promoted phrenology as a self-improvement practice that would allow individuals to overcome "mental shortcomings." As an example of early neuropolicy, figure 5.5 presents an advertisement for their phrenological "cabinet," lauding the merits of phrenology in healthcare, child rearing, mind reading, and vocational guidance. The article "Phrenology Made Easy," published in the literary *Knickerbocker Magazine* (June 2, 1838), defended phrenology as a practical approach to understanding and reforming negative character traits and argued for its wide application to child rearing, education, and marriage choices. In *Familiar Lessons on Physiology Designed for the Use of Children and Youth in Schools and Families*, Lydia Folger Fowler (Mrs. Lorenzo Fowler) argued that "a correct knowledge of the laws and principles of physiology and phrenology is undoubtedly the most effectual medium for children 'to know themselves,' mentally and physically" (Fowler 1855). Phrenologists also used popular magazines such as *Ladies Magazine* and the *New Yorker* to laud and disseminate the merits of their approach.

Contemporary examples of neuropolicy are subtler than those of phrenology but tap into surprisingly similar popular interpretations about brain function, the power of neurotechnology, and the *prima facie* authority of science. For example, the use of neuroimages in the context

Figure 5.5
1850 advertisement for the phrenological cabinet of Orson and Lorenzo Fowler on Nassau Street, New York. Published in the 1850 guide of the then famous Barnum's American Museum. The phrenological cabinet of the Fowler brothers combined a publishing house, mailorder business, and museum. Used by permission of the Lost Museum project. *Source:* http://chnm.gmu.edu/lostmuseum/lm/88.

of childhood policies or education has given rise to unrealistic expectations conveyed in the media, particularly regarding so-called brain-based education (Bruer 1998; Thompson and Nelson 2001). In the United States, some centers are already offering SPECT scans to help diagnose attention deficit/hyperactivity disorder and Alzheimer's disease (Illes and Kirschen 2003). Whole-body and brain scans are offered on the Internet even though their clinical value is questionable (Illes et al. 2003; Racine, Van der Loos, and Illes 2007). Other products (e.g., toys) or educational intervention strategies, in particular for low-achieving children, are marketed as being supported by brain-based neuroimaging research (e.g., showing seductive before-and-after scans) and feed into the general culture of self-help tools and resources (Johnson 2008).

A sad reminder of previous public enthusiasm for neuroscience innovation is the unhappy legacy of psychosurgery (Gostin 1980), which can serve as an extreme and dramatic warning of the responsibilities of neuroscientists. Finding enthusiasm in media coverage in the 1930s and 1940s, Diefenbach and colleagues wrote, "Indeed perhaps a cautionary lesson can be learned from the history of lobotomy" (Diefenbach et al. 1999). These authors concluded that media coverage "may have been a factor influencing the quick and widespread adoption of lobotomy as a psychiatric treatment."

Fostering Communication and Broader Debate about Neuroscience

This chapter identifies several features of media coverage of neuroscience innovation. Salient characteristics included enthusiasm and high expectations regarding neurotechnology, infrequent discussion of ethical issues related to nongenetic neuroscience research, emerging neuroessentialist and neurorealist interpretations revealing the profound impact of neuroscience on our self-identity and our manifest image, and healthcare that relies on a full appreciation of the complex nature of the mind-brain. These observations suggest the importance of broadening perspectives and promoting discussion concerning the use of neuroscience innovation. These features of media coverage exist within a distinct scientific context that is still in many respects overwhelmed by the complexity of the brain and our still limited understanding of its normal and pathological functioning and its relationship to consciousness and self-identity. To paraphrase the neurobiologist Yadin Dudai, the danger is that "we will think that we have understood it all" (Dudai 2004) and act prematurely based on this scientific and social belief.

Other aspects of media coverage of neuroscience innovation shed light on the nature of science communication by displaying the inadequacy of unidirectional communication approaches. Traditionally, communication has been thought of as a one-way process, where scientists are considered the experts on the topic they are researching (Racine, Bar-Ilan, and Illes 2005). Accordingly, science communication is viewed as the process of using an appropriate medium to transmit clearly, accurately, and without distortion the objective knowledge yielded by research. Hence, this unidirectional model suggests that researchers are in control of media content and are the primary gatekeepers of scientific knowledge. Additional assumptions inherent in the model include the belief that science is primarily driven by value-free and rational knowledge emerging from an intersubjective scientific community that validates its worthiness, that is, the scientificity of knowledge (Rose 2003).

The unidirectional model of science communication has been criticized in the political science literature as well as in communication studies and bioethics. Major criticisms include the removal of science from its political and social context, such as political and ideological pressures, in line with Weber's classic analysis of rationalization processes in modernity (Habermas 1968), as well as the lack of attention to the complexity of emitter-transceiver interactions in a multicultural context (van Djick 2003). These critiques reinforce doubts that the traditional model could adequately support ethical approaches to science communication and public involvement (Goggin and Blanpied 1986; Joss and Durant 1995), especially that this model fosters strong expert-nonexpert dualism in biomedical policy (Reiser 1991; Racine 2003). Such a model accordingly fails to recognize possible input of citizens in science policy and dismisses considerations such as those voiced in public discourse that at first glance are apparently not grounded in "value-free science" (Jennings 1990; Gutmann and Thompson 1997).

Research into media coverage of neuroscience innovation supports a broadened multidirectional approach to the understanding and practice of science communication (see second column of table 5.1). When research moves from the lab to the headline, findings are not simply transmitted

but translated. Language literally changes, as do the meanings ascribed
to the research and the fundamental goals of science communication. For
example, in a previous study about the media coverage of brain-machine
interfaces in rats (Talwar et al. 2002), the concluding section of the original paper containing predictions and speculation on real-world applications became the primary focus in print media lead paragraphs (Racine,
DuRousseau, and Illes 2007). Instead of knowledge driving the communication process, fascination for application in clinical and real-world
use dominated press coverage. Far from an act described as *transmission*,
the communication process became a phenomenon that can be described
as a *translation*.

Table 5.1
From unidirectional to multidirectional communication: insights from emerging
research on media coverage of neuroscience

Assumptions of the expertise model of science communication	Emerging insights informing multidirectional science communication
Science is a discourse of experts.	Science is a social discourse.
Science is driven by knowledge.	Applications lead interest in science.
Science is a community.	Media tend to emphasize scientific controversies and debates between researchers.
Science is rational and free of value.	Science includes applications and values sustaining them.
	Science brings reactions based on personal belief and culture.
Communication is initiated by individual researchers.	Communication leads to involvement of multiple actors.
Researchers are experts.	Researchers make comments as ordinary people do.
Distortion of message should be avoided.	Some distortion is unavoidable.
Scientists control content.	Scientists are one source of information.
Communication is unidirectional.	Flow of information is multidirectional.

Source: Adapted from Racine, DuRousseau, and Illes 2007.

Other assumptions of the traditional model of science communication found in table 5.1 can be seriously questioned. The communication process is typically only partly controlled by researchers. For example, historical events and previous news coverage and scientific reports can influence media coverage. Dissenting scientific voices and various stakeholders can provide divergent appreciations of neuroscience research, thus showing the multifaceted aspects of science communication and dispelling the image of a monolithic scientific community. In addition, the *act* of communicating can perhaps better be framed as an *interaction,* where researchers are brought to respond and comment on the expectations and concerns of journalists and stakeholders. Researchers also make "ordinary people" comments on the value of their research implications and the applications it could propel. Consequently, these observations dissipate ideals of scientist control over media content and suggest that some distortion of messages is unavoidable, given the number and diversity of sources for quotations as well as the highlighted translation effects. Overall, it is more realistic to view science communication as a multidirectional process.

Multidirectional Approaches to Neuroethical Debates

Given that the scientific complexity of the brain is overwhelming and that its implication for self-identity should be part of a wider debate (Racine, Bar-Ilan, and Illes 2005), approaches to science communication will need to be adjusted accordingly. In this respect, neuroscience can be a model for further exploring principles of multicultural communication (van Djick 2003) and mechanisms that foster open science communication. From the public's point of view, when publicized research results concern personality and concepts related to self-identity, they are bound to interact with the various cultural, religious, and secular sources of our self-identity (Taylor 1989). As a 1998 *Nature Neuroscience* editorial stated, discussing the relationship between neuroscience and emerging public concerns, neuroscientists "should recognize that their work may be construed as having deep and possibly disturbing implications" (*Nature Neuroscience* 1998), including on the nature of morality and identity (Racine, Bar-Ilan, and Illes 2006).

Indeed, the issues raised by neuroscience create a need for a broad and inclusive outlook on the social implications of scientific epistemology

(Leshner 2005). The need for careful and thoughtful dissemination and application of results as well as relevant interdisciplinary dialogue on and input in the design and interpretation of neuroscience research are some of the ethical lessons that can follow from the current context marked by some unbridled enthusiasm for neuroscience innovation and overinterpretations regarding self-identity. Research supports a broadened multidirectional approach to the understanding and practice of such science communication. However, traditionally, science communication has been thought of as a unidirectional process, where scientists are considered experts and where communication is viewed as the process of using an appropriate medium to transmit clearly, accurately, and without distortion the objective knowledge yielded by research (Racine, Bar-Ilan, and Illes 2005). The falsity of the assumption that science is primarily driven by value-free and rational knowledge validated by an intersubjective scientific community (Rose 2003) only underscores the need for a paradigm shift in the public communication of science.

Conclusion

This chapter shows, using print media coverage of neuroscience innovation, that unidirectional views on communication cannot acknowledge the complexity and various sources of ethical concerns. The sheer complexity of the brain and the many unknowns that populate the scientific and medical understanding of common neurological and psychiatric conditions shape the challenge of using neuroscience research and neurotechnology ethically. Media coverage can (but does not need to) contribute to reductionist views of the brain and related disorders by conveying beliefs of neuroessentialism, neurorealism, and neuropolicy. In such cases, one of the crucial tasks of bioethics and neuroethics can be to unveil different forms of reductionism and bring awareness to the inherent complexity of research and patient care.

The participation of nonscientists in public dialogue could help broaden perspectives and ensure that a balanced appreciation of the complexity of the brain accompanies the introduction of innovative neuroscience-based technologies and approaches in broader society. Supplementing traditional models of science communication is necessary, and recognizing the multidirectional nature of the communication process affects the practice of science communication, especially the strategies that can be used to tackle ethical issues. A number of multidirectional approaches have now been used to foster more direct interactions and communication between scientists and lay audiences, ranging from neuroscience exposition fairs that introduce children to neuroscience principles (Zardetto-Smith et al. 2002) to citizen's conferences and other deliberative public involvement mechanisms to launch public debates.

6

Enhancement of Performance with Neuropharmaceuticals: Pragmatism and the Culture Wars

Overview

We are witnessing a context of increasing prevalence and salience of non-medical uses of neuropharmaceuticals for performance enhancement. While prescription misuse is generally on the rise, expectations that we will one day have genuine cognitive enhancers is sparking debates. Diverging moral-political approaches have stemmed from liberal and conservative perspectives, although many aspects of this emerging phenomenon are still left unattended. This chapter examines critically some of the assumptions behind the conservative and liberal moral-political approaches to this issue. I make the case, from a pragmatic standpoint, for the relevance of a moderate liberal approach. This approach recognizes pluralism and seeks approaches that minimize harm and promote autonomy while urging for full considerations of the impact of "cognitive enhancers" on the public good and on healthcare systems.

In the United States, the emergence of radical moral-political divisions in the public domain has been dubbed the "culture wars" by the sociologist James Davison Hunter (1992). Hunter proposed that American politics and public debates reflect fundamental disagreements between liberal and conservative moral views on crucial and wide-ranging issues such as drug prohibition, family values, homosexuality, privacy, and women in combat. The impact of the culture wars is also felt specifically on several important bioethical issues, such as stem cell research; end-of-life decision making, including withdrawal of life support (e.g., Schiavo case); reproductive rights; and teenage sexuality. Even abortion resurfaced as a topic of American public debate in the past years.

Although not the dominant major public controversy in the culture wars context, the misuse of prescription drugs to fulfill lifestyle choices, often called "enhancement" in the bioethics literature, has been hotly debated (President's Council on Bioethics 2003). The prospect of improving cognitive and motor performance as well as mood in otherwise healthy individuals has gathered in the last years a sizeable amount of public interest and media attention. Specific areas where the practice of such prescription misuse have been identified range from prescription stimulants to enhance concentration and improve academic performance (Racine and Forlini 2008; Wilens et al. 2008) to antisleep medications, typically used to treat narcolepsy, being used to fight jet lag (Vastag 2004; Sahakian and Morein-Zamir 2007), and even to antidepressants used as mood enhancers (Kramer 2000). Many other drugs are also explored for lifestyle fulfillment (Lexchin 2001; Farah et al. 2004; Flower 2004). A survey published in *Nature* in spring 2008 reported that 20 percent ($n = 288$) of the 1,427 respondents admitted to using prescription drugs for cognitive enhancement purposes. Most of these (62%) had misused methylphenidate (Ritalin), and almost half of these respondents (49%; $n = 116$; $N = 238$) were using drugs for nonmedical reasons on a weekly or daily basis. Overall, the majority of respondents to the survey (69%; $n = 873$; $N = 1,258$ who responded to this question) thought that it would be acceptable to "boost" their "brain power by taking a cognitive enhancing drug" if it would have a "normal risk of mild side effects" (Maher 2008). With advances in neuroscience, many enhancement opportunities are expected to surface. For example, memory enhancers (Lynch 2002; Rose 2002; Yesavage et al. 2003) and suppressors of traumatic memories are being researched to treat Alzheimer's disease and post-traumatic stress disorder respectively (Pitman et al. 2002; Glannon 2006b). Other applications could bear on social relationships (Savulescu and Sandberg 2008) and work productivity (Appel 2008; Warren et al. 2008).

Millions of Americans misuse prescription drugs each year for medical and nonmedical reasons including enhancement (National Institute on Drug Abuse 2005). The culture wars legacy has yielded two basic moral-political positions advocated in the bioethics literature regarding this topic: (1) the liberal acceptance of lifestyle fulfillment based on individual rights and freedom to "enhance" cognitive function by the means available, including prescription drugs (Caplan 2003); and (2) the conservative rejection of lifestyle fulfillment based on concerns for the integrity of human nature, the unnaturalness of enhancement, and fear of hubris (President's Council on Bioethics 2003; Sandel 2004). This chapter approaches the issue of prescription misuse for lifestyle purposes in the culture wars context. It examines critically some of the assumptions behind the conservative and liberal moral-political approaches to this issue and argues from a pragmatic standpoint for the recognition of pluralism and the need for practical solutions.

Enhancement and Two Concepts of Morality

Debates about the nonmedical lifestyle use of prescription drugs have gained prominence in the past years. Debates about the role of science in improving quality of life, however, are constitutive of Western civilization at least since post-Renaissance modernity. For example, Francis Bacon wrote in the *Meditationes Sacræ: De Hæresibus* (1597), "*Ipsa Scientia Potestas Est*" (Knowledge is power), a fundamental tenet of modern science, philosophy, and culture as a whole. This commitment to the improvement of healthcare and living conditions through technology represents one current of modernity and modern science and contrasts with François Rabelais's equally famous statement in *Pentagruel* (1532): "Science sans conscience n'est que ruine de l'âme" (Knowledge without moral conscience leads to the loss of one's self). These are just reminders that such debates about the ethical use of technology and science have long been part of our scientific and cultural history, and that we need to also take a historical perspective on the current discussions.

Similarly, current bioethical debates also bring contrasting moral-political views on how to use the power to enhance ourselves individually and collectively (Doucet 2007). On the one hand, enhancement is viewed as the achievement of humankind, the pinnacle of modern self-transformation and self-creation. Proponents of this view believe that individuals should have the right to enhance themselves and to pursue goals they freely define as good to pursue. On the other hand, some contend that enhancement threatens our very humanity and the essential conditions of current forms of being.

Closer analysis of the existing positions and debate reveals that two general underlying meanings to the question of enhancement's ethics can be distinguished: (1) Is enhancement moral or ethical in the sense of *moral acceptability?* and (2) Is enhancement moral or ethical in the sense of *moral praiseworthiness?* In the first sense, performance enhancement can be acceptable if it conforms to usual standards governing the introduction of technology (e.g., effectiveness and safety, respect for autonomy). Moral acceptance captures some of the basic commitments of the liberal view. In the second sense, performance enhancement raises issues that are in some respects beyond those typical of current regulation of technology (e.g., altering the biological and social conditions of human existence) and that directly confront views on moral achievement and moral excellence. Moral praiseworthiness reflects the "thicker" considerations found in the conservative view. Hence, the current disagreement on the ethics of enhancement reflected in the culture wars partly lies on a more fundamental one, the nature of ethics itself and the requirements that need to be fulfilled before performance enhancement use of pharmaceuticals could be considered moral, that is, right or good.

The concepts of moral acceptability and moral praiseworthiness that I am elucidating are reminiscent of Isaiah Berlin's distinction in political philosophy between "freedom from" (negative liberty) and "freedom to" (positive liberty; Berlin 2002). And just like Berlin, I intend the concepts to be complementary. In my view, and contrary to the sometimes acrimonious tone of current bioethics debates, both moral acceptability and moral praiseworthiness are genuine views that together help express the complex nature of moral thought and moral behavior (see table 6.1).

First, let's start with moral acceptability. The concept of moral acceptability relies heavily on the moral principle of not doing harm to others, nonmaleficence, and other negative obligations that do not entail positive requirements of action from the moral agent. When striving for moral acceptability, we seek permission to do something within an existing framework while respecting social and legal obligations. Hence, sources of moral acceptability typically lie in extrinsic, or outside, sources such as the law and social consensus or socially accepted norms. Moral acceptability yields what some call a minimal or thin form of morality. Accordingly, if I can legally do something without hurting others and respecting their freedom, I can pursue action; it is morally acceptable. Moral acceptability is also consistent with a procedural view of the public good and commitments to liberal individual rights. These commitments of liberal moral-political thought usually constitute the main argument advanced by proponents of lifestyle fulfillment and are likely, in combination with liberal economic forces and product marketing, to be key ingredients of any proenhancement position. For example, Arthur Caplan, a proponent of liberalism in bioethics, stresses that in current American society, "the answer is not prohibiting improvement. It is ensuring that enhancements always be done by choice, not dictated by others" (Caplan 2003).

Now let's look at moral praiseworthiness. Moral praiseworthiness questions if we should morally and ideally pursue cognitive enhancement regardless of whether it fulfills moral acceptability conditions. It relies on some of the moral insights captured in the ethical principle of beneficence and other positive obligations that entail prosocial behavior. When searching for moral praiseworthiness, we seek to fulfill responsibilities and duties toward others. Hence, the sources of moral praiseworthiness typically lie in intrinsic, or inner, sources of morality, such as empathy and self-reflection, and are beyond the requirements of most normative obligations found in legal documents and other forms of social agreement or social consensus. In comparison to moral acceptability's "minimal morality," moral praiseworthiness yields a "morality of ideals." A good illustration of this commitment is Eric Cohen's statement, "at stake [in human enhancement] is the very meaning and nature of human excellence and human happiness" (Cohen 2006).

From a moral praiseworthiness standpoint, moral acceptability can be viewed as a necessary but insufficient condition. Surely, before actively seeking to promote a particular vision of the good (moral praiseworthiness), we must ask ourselves if we are not causing any harm or hindering anyone's freedom (moral acceptability). However, it should be clear that moral praiseworthiness implies further considerations based on a substantial view of morality (in opposition to a "thin" liberal view), committed to the analysis of the impact of lifestyle fulfillment on relationships, community, human nature, and moral motivations. These points have been eloquently put forward by Sandel in his discussion of enhancement and related hubris and in his work in political philosophy.

Table 6.1
Two complementary concepts of morality

	Moral acceptability	Moral praiseworthiness
Reformulations	Can we (morally) do this? Minimal morality	Should we (morally) do this? Morality of ideals
Inspiring principles	Nonmaleficence	Beneficence
Obligations	Negative obligations	Positive obligations
Sources	Extrinsic sources of morality Regulations and obligations	Intrinsic sources of morality Ideals and responsibilities

I do not think the main problem with enhancement and genetic engineering is that they undermine effort and erode human agency. The deeper danger is that they represent a kind of hyperagency—a Promethean aspiration to remake nature, including human nature, to serve our purposes and satisfy our desires. The problem is not the drift to mechanism but the drive of mastery. And what the drive to mastery misses and may even destroy is an appreciation of the gifted character of human powers and achievements (Sandel 2004).

Generally speaking, bioethics seeks clinical and research practices that at least fulfill moral acceptability conditions and strives to identify and promote moral praiseworthiness, that is, forms of moral excellence. Anything that does not hurt others can in principle be done (in the moral acceptability sense), but anything that can be done without hurting others should not necessarily be done (in the moral praiseworthiness sense). I therefore propose that both perspectives should be seen as complementing each other and discuss the implications of this in the following pages.

Two Moral Tests for Cognitive Enhancement

Based on the above distinction between moral acceptability and moral praiseworthiness, I now consider under which conditions enhancement is ethical. Based on the two concepts of morality, I propose that there are two concomitant tests: the moral acceptability test and the moral praiseworthiness test.

In the moral acceptability test, even though the concept of moral acceptability on which it is based seems to imply complete openness to performance enhancement technologies, there are many serious issues to consider.
The *necessary* conditions enhancement must fulfill can be divided according to various sets of issues. Table 6.2, based on an overview of topics discussed in the literature, should be considered a starting point for further
exploration and discussion about the moral acceptability of enhancement.

The moral praiseworthiness test requires that the necessary conditions
of the moral acceptability test be first fulfilled. Since moral praiseworthiness is an effort to realize more substantial views of the good, additional
questions need to be addressed. Conditions for the moral acceptability
test can take the form of criteria that can or not be fulfilled (e.g., safe or not
safe); those of the moral praiseworthiness test appeal to ideals somewhat

Table 6.2
Moral acceptability test: Under which conditions would enhancement be ethically acceptable?

Scientific and medical conditions	Ethical and legal conditions	Cultural and social conditions	Policy and regulatory conditions
Reliance on scientific data	Prevention of coercion; promotion of autonomy	Identification of and response to potential public health issues	Justification of how enhancement fits in priorities for research funding
Establishment of safety, risks, and side effects	Respect for privacy and acceptance of differing views about enhancement	Definition of just and fair resource allocation	Development of regulation and monitoring mechanisms for approbation, commercialization, and marketing
Determination of neurotechnology readiness and relevance	Mitigation of discrimination	Assessment and response to the impact of enhancement on health coverage	Adoption of democratic forms of governance and development of strategies for public involvement in the regulatory and policy process

Table 6.3
Moral praiseworthiness test: Following which moral ideals would enhancement be ethically praiseworthy?

Scientific and medical ideals	Ethical and legal ideals	Cultural and social ideals	Policy and regulatory ideals
Advancement of science and technology to address critical medical needs	Promotion of authentic self-realization	Promotion of cultural achievement	Promotion of democratic decision processes
Development of therapies in the general interest of humankind	Pursuit of moral growth and self-reflection	Pursuit of equality and social justice	Achievement of a shared view of public good

harder to define and that we can never be sure of attaining. Again, the content of table 6.3 should be seen as a starting point for further discussion and definition of what should be included in a moral praiseworthiness test for enhancement.

Policy Implications of Moral Tests

There are four distinct sets of answers to the two moral tests (table 6.4). I rule out one possibility (morally praiseworthy but not morally acceptable) a priori as being illogical because moral praiseworthiness implies the necessary conditions of the moral acceptability test. Therefore, the three remaining logical possibilities correspond grossly speaking to the well-known moral-political philosophies of liberalism, conservatism, and moderate liberalism.

Strong liberalism, or libertarianism, accepts enhancement based on the promotion of individual autonomy and often rejects the need to address the moral ideals under the umbrella concept of moral praiseworthiness. The main reason is that in modern societies, no consensus can be achieved on fundamental views of a shared public good, and we should not expect human social interactions to reflect such thick moral commitments. Our societies are too diverse. To paraphrase Berlin, there are risks that the realization of positive liberty inherent to the pursuit of a common good jeopardizes the negative liberty of individuals.

Table 6.4
Possible logical answers to moral tests for enhancement

		Moral praiseworthiness test	
		Morally praiseworthy	Not morally praiseworthy
Moral acceptability test	Morally acceptable	*Liberalism*	*Moderate liberalism*
	Not morally acceptable		*Conservatism*

In my opinion, the conditions of the moral acceptability test for enhancement are far from being fulfilled, and our ability to do so is sometimes overestimated. For example, what are the risks and side effects of cognitive enhancers? Are current practices supported by sound science? Should we even use the somewhat misleading term "cognitive enhancement" (akin to gene "therapy" or "therapeutic" cloning) if we do not yet have a well-informed sense of the effectiveness and risks involved in enhancement uses of prescription drugs or dietary supplements? Even though some argue that enhancement is in principle morally acceptable, there is considerable need for evidence showing that it does not have major negative impacts on individuals and society, that is, *primum non nocere.*

Conservatism (especially social conservatism) questions the morality of cognitive enhancement based on the inviolability of human nature, human dignity, sanctity of life, or the value of human culture. Practically speaking, however, radical forms of conservatism do not acknowledge the ongoing practices of enhancement already taking place by other means with the use of common technology (e.g., computers) that allow us to increase our capacity to work and learn (and even nonbiological and nontechnological forms of self-improvement such as discipline and hard work). For Western civilizations, part of the contemporary confidence in the abilities of humans to rule themselves individually and collectively with technology and based on the culture of reason in the form of modern science is a legacy of the Enlightenment (traces of this stream of thought can also be found earlier in the Renaissance). Our contemporary hope and search for improving the quality of our lives through reason and technology are related to this constitutive scientific and philosophical movement. In this sense, strong forms of conservatism are reactionary, propel pessimism, and express no confidence in humanity and the power of understanding. It is therefore no surprise that one of the major problems with conservatism is that its extreme form does not reflect the social and political dynamics of democratic societies, which are culturally diverse, based on liberal economies, and value individual rights and freedoms as well as a public sphere informed by reasonable discourse. More bluntly, conservatism seems to reject some of the tenets of modern medicine and science expressed by early thinkers of modernity (Taylor 1989) such as Bacon and Locke. Keep in mind, however, that conservatism has the merit of taking seriously an important set of moral ideals captured in the praiseworthiness test, which are sometimes washed out in the thin forms of liberalism. Conservatism attempts to provide a fuller view of the many deeper sources of morality that involve community (and other forms of) relationships while insisting on the search for excellence and virtue in the conduct of human affairs.

Moderate liberalism is the middle-ground view that I believe best reflects the dual nature of morality I have highlighted (the combined search for moral acceptability and moral praiseworthiness) and makes possible the integration of both liberalism and conservatism thinking. In this perspective, cognitive enhancement could be morally acceptable, but we need more evidence to fulfill the conditions of the moral acceptability test, preferably with a combination of evidence-based general guidelines and case-by-case judgments. The autonomy of individuals would therefore be respected and the possible positive value of enhancement for individuals and society recognized. This being said, however, considerations for the public good, that is, something that is more than the addition of individually defined goods, remain. This is a striking challenge given the predicted broad implications of enhancement for society, culture, and policy. However, this public good cannot be solely defined based on traditional views, as conservatism advocates. Contemporary societies are too diverse to find the foundation of public good and shared values in a single tradition (e.g., Judeo-Christian ethics). In addition to being an ethical infringement on the negative liberties of individuals, this would likely represent a highly unstable, potentially explosive, solution. From a pragmatic perspective, the potential for moral innovation and moral growth created by social diversity and open dialogue would also be lost. But the modern challenges of pursuing a public good absolutely do not render obsolete the need for the pursuit of it and of shared values. As I will try to explain, new shared commitments to a common good must be created according to deliberation and collective self-reflection. I have in mind here "creative liberty in thinking" (Alexander 1949), a hallmark of democracy highlighted by the Nuremberg commissioner Leo Alexander.

Moderate Liberalism, Pragmatism, and Public Deliberation

An interesting venue for rethinking the public good and the requirements of both moral acceptability and moral praiseworthiness (consistent with pragmatism and the current pluralistic social contexts) comes from the literature on deliberative democracy and discourse ethics (Racine 2003). This area of scholarship is wide-ranging, and I will rely in this chapter on the view presented by the pragmatic thinking of German philosopher Jürgen Habermas, especially his later work. In his monumental *Between Facts and Norms*, Habermas provides an insightful perspective on the complementary nature of individual autonomy (liberalism) and public autonomy (republicanism or conservatism) based on concepts akin to moral acceptability and moral praiseworthiness. I believe the account provided by the discourse ethics of Habermas constitutes a very powerful way to capture the requirements of moral acceptability and moral praiseworthiness.

Habermas's thinking is helpful insofar as it captures the tension between individual autonomy and public autonomy and recognizes that both are necessary. He identifies in Kant's thinking the need to respect individual rights and freedoms. Although Kant's thinking is complex, and I would argue that Habermas's account does not fully capture Kant's commitment to dignity and intuitions beyond individual rights, Habermas's rendition is shared by others, and his views of Kant can help us think through the challenges we currently face. Kant emphasized individual autonomy, and this is the basis of his practical philosophy expressed in the different formulations of the categorical imperative (e.g., "Act only that maxim through which you can at the same time will that it should become a universal law" and "Act in such a way that you treat humanity, whether in your own person or in the person of any other, always at the same time as an end and never merely as a means to an end"; Kant 2002). Hence this view of moral law maps well with moral acceptability and captures much of its essence as described above. Nonetheless, the challenge has always been to figure out how moral praiseworthiness and the public good could emerge and develop within a moral-political culture that cherishes individual rights and autonomy. Only some basic conditions of the public good are yielded by individual rights, that the search and realization of moral praiseworthiness should not impede the individual rights of others and need to be contained within the framework of sovereign individuals (Habermas 1997).

However, Habermas understands the limitations of moral-political philosophies emphasizing almost exclusively individual rights and autonomy. His thinking also reflects the need to capture the importance of public autonomy and the need to contemplate and realize a public good. Historically, Jean-Jacques Rousseau was a key proponent of the public good. In contrast to Kant, Rousseau started sketching his moral-political philosophy with public autonomy, not individual autonomy. According to Rousseau, the general will is that which is wanted by all for everyone; it is the united will of all, and it transforms individuals into citizens through a social contract. For Rousseau, individuals are fully realized as citizens. Contrary to Kant's perspective, individual rights are subsequent to public autonomy; public autonomy protects individual rights because the general will should always express itself as general and universal moral laws. In its exercise, public autonomy filters out nonuniversalizable interests because only universal laws can guarantee individual rights to all. Individual rights are therefore enshrined in the exercise of public autonomy. In contrast to Kant, Rousseau's reasonable will is formed in a kind of macro-subject, not the individual subject. This means that legislative action, the political gesture par excellence, must be formulated according to a form of Kantian universalization. The general will has to apply to everyone and be consistent with the search for the common good.

Habermas points out rightly that Rousseau's confidence in the articulation of the general will by a collective body of individuals does not fit the practical reality of modern pluralistic societies. As I mentioned earlier, it is extremely hard if not impossible in contemporary societies to derive moral-political approaches from existing moral traditions and views of the public good without giving the impression of infringing on individual

rights. Further, Rousseau's idealistic depiction of the legis
ticism that an elite group will impose its view of the genera
too great a risk that the enactment of the public good wiḷ
vidual rights, and the protections offered by Rousseau are noṭ
speaking, strongly grounded. Even though Rousseau wrote exte   on
political culture and democratic education (Rousseau 1819), nis confidence in defining a priori the nature of the general will is too great for
complex and culturally diversified modern democracies and contemporary biomedical issues. However, Habermas also correctly identifies how
the Kantian tradition and today's sometimes dogmatic adhesion to individual autonomy and individual rights create challenges for Rousseau's
view of the general will and contemporary attempts to achieve any common good beyond individual choices. In addition, moral agents, even if
they submit their individual moral maxims to a universalization test à la
Kant, will never be able to truly determine whether their actions are morally justified or not in reality. Kant's categorical imperative does not make
explicit the need to take into account the other person in concrete reality
and complexity.

In a nutshell, Habermas's solution consists of applying his theory of
communicative action and his work in linguistic pragmatics to ethics.
At least three important and basic aspects of this approach need to be
underscored here. First, this approach relies on the pragmatic conditions
that regulate the search for the best argument; second, the communicative
model will be the one used to assess the universal validity of norms; third,
language as an act of intercomprehension (in opposition to mere strate-
gic action) unites will and reason (Habermas 1997). Accordingly, Habermas introduces a universalization principle consistent with Kant's view
of individual autonomy:

(U) All affected can accept the consequences and the side effects its general
acceptance can be anticipated to have for the satisfaction of everyone's interests
(and these consequences are preferred to those of known alternative possibilities
for regulation). (Habermas 1991)

However, Habermas (and his colleague Karl-Otto Apel) also bril-
liantly introduce the discussion principle to reconcile public autonomy
with individual autonomy: "Just those action norms are valid to which all
possibly affected persons could agree as participants in rational discourse"
(Habermas 1997). To accept a norm as valid, the discussion principle, or

(D), states, "Only those norms can claim to be valid that meet (or could meet) with the approval of all affected in their capacity as participants in a practical discourse" (Habermas 1991). Accordingly, the validity of an ethical norm must be verified in the course of discussion. In other words, concrete discussion is needed to determine if the norm has intersubjective validity and if it therefore truly respects the universalization principle, or (U). In this sense, discourse ethics is an ethics for pluralistic societies where diverse conceptions of the "good" exist and where solutions must be found to ethical challenges through the elaboration of valid and accepted ethical norms.

The discussion principle allows for the elucidation of a general moral view point (similar to Kant's formulation of the categorical imperative); unites both individual and public autonomy; and, finally, grounds norms in reason beyond religious and metaphysical references and frameworks (Habermas 1997). The discussions needed to enact the discussion principle must include all participants concerned by the consequences of a norm's application and be conducted without external constraints (to prevent the rule of force).

Following the thinking laid out by Habermas, I suggest that the validity of norms, especially those that strive to reach moral excellence and moral praiseworthiness, must be tested in actual open and democratic discourse. Moral praiseworthiness and the search for a common good and other moral ideals must be enacted in ways that are consistent with a commitment to both individual autonomy and public autonomy. What is yielded according to Habermas is a moderate form of liberalism that encapsulates the ethical obligation to respect individual rights while acknowledging that the public good and shared intersubjective norms are needed. Ethics begins with individual autonomy but does not end there; the ability to exercise one's rights can be an opportunity to take part in realizations that surpass those of individual choices.

Pragmatism and Moral Innovation through Deliberation

So far, in this chapter, I have explored some of pragmatic naturalism's commitments toward interdisciplinary scholarship and approaches and highlighted some of the pitfalls of current frameworks to approach the performance enhancement uses of neuropharmaceuticals. I have tackled some of the associated ethical challenges by illustrating how competing normative approaches have led to a difficult dialogue in bioethics given the culture wars context. My starting point, in the current context, is that given the evolution of medicine and society, we should (1) work toward middle-ground approaches and not dismiss commercial and social pressures for the general acceptance and use of cognitive enhancers; and (2) explore the philosophical underpinnings of various moral-political philosophies and enhancement and their commitments to broader views of the public good and governance. My analysis showed the complementary nature of conservative and liberal views on enhancement in a cultural war context in which arguments sometimes have sharp rhetorical overtones that make dialogue and the search for innovative solutions difficult (Callahan 2005).

In the culture wars context, it is important to acknowledge that both liberal views (individual autonomy) and conservative views (public autonomy) are reasonable moral-political philosophies and express distinct views of ethics. The pragmatic form of moderate liberalism argued for in this chapter builds on the strength of both. It suggests that we need to answer the moral acceptability test, debate moral praiseworthiness openly, promote inclusive democratic policy making, and provide opportunities for researchers to reflect as a community on the effects of science and the use of lifestyle drugs on a global scale. Moderate liberalism also highlights some pitfalls of an extreme politicization of bioethics and suggests the importance of bridging moral political divides to find innovative solutions. Erik Parens has made a similar point using a different terminology, that is, the "gratitude framework" and the "creativity framework," noting that some moral intuitions in the debate need to be captured using broader and more inclusive approaches (Parens 2005).

From the gratitude framework, the first impulse is to speak of letting things be. The first worry is that the intervention compromises authenticity, that it might separate us from what is most our own. From the creativity framework, the first impulse is to speak on behalf of the liberating authenticity-promoting potential of the intervention. . . . The hope of settling down and becoming comfortable in just one framework may be quintessentially human, but it is the foe of thinking. (Parens 2006)

The polarization of contemporary bioethics is understandable but must be surmounted. On the one hand, bioethics has evolved more closely to

decisional circles and governmental politics. In a certain sense, this
reflects that bioethics is becoming engaged in what Edmund Pellegrino
has called "big P politics" and reflects that many bioethical issues raise
questions about the public good. (In his 2006 address to the American
Society for Bioethics and Humanities, Edmund Pellegrino distinguished
"big P politics," the pursuit of the public good and common interests,
from "small p politics," partisan politics that divide the community and
embitter the climate of bioethics itself; Pellegrino 2006.) The fact that
social and commercial interests appear to be factors in the emergence of
cognitive enhancement (Atkinson 2002) gives credibility to the view that
enhancement calls for such public considerations. In this sense, the ethics
of cognitive enhancement is not only a *stricto sensu* individual autonomy–
related ethical dilemma, narrowly defined as a conflict of values or ethical principles, but also a broad social and political issue on which there
must be a correspondingly broad moral-political outlook incorporating
concerns for the public good (Callahan 1994).

On the other hand, bioethics may have become contaminated by partisan politics and the way that American politics have unfolded in the past
fifteen years. Daniel Callahan has highlighted the pitfalls of the polarized
and tense climate surrounding the evolution of bioethics scholarship. By
focusing on divisions and emphasizing them, culture wars bioethics can
fuel partisan "small p" political views instead of examining the underlying moral values and principles that support different moral-political
views on bioethical issues. Some of the negative consequences of the culture wars on bioethics include the further radicalization of moral-political positions; the transformation of bioethics into an "advocacy forum";
and the creation of additional obstacles to formulating an environment
that fosters identifying innovative solutions that are in the public's general interest. Bioethics and neuroethics cannot be fruitful if they become
simply an advocacy forum for polarized views. Consequently, Callahan
argues that bioethics must develop approaches that will take into account
the complexity of moral decision making, especially by taking into account
and building on pluralism.

The inclusion of bioethics in the culture wars hardly represents moral progress
for the field. . . . Yet if bioethics is to retain its vitality and be taken seriously, it
will have to find a way to extricate itself from the culture wars. . . . The present
situation is one in which there is practically no serious interchange between liberals

and conservatives. They live and write in increasingly separate worlds. A healthy bioethics should expect and welcome struggles between opposing viewpoints. (Callahan 2005)

Now, where does moderate liberalism lead us in comparison to stronger forms of liberalism and conservatism? This question is highly relevant given the political polarization observed in bioethics (Cohen 2006; Macklin 2006) and that no clear-cut yes or no answers are yielded by a pragmatic and moderate liberal approach. One might think here that citizen deliberations and deliberative democracy are useful in creating new forms of agreements and shared visions of public good that are adapted to today's environment (Fishkin 1991; Gutmann and Thompson 1997; Racine 2003). Citizens' juries and conferences have had some success in this respect, but they need to be further evaluated and their merits qualified (Rowe and Frewer 2000; Abelson et al. 2003). In addition, researchers as a community dedicated to the advancement of knowledge need to reflect on the nature of their actions and their involvement in research as it pertains to opportunities of enhancement (Racine and Illes 2006). Finally, perhaps the greatest challenge is to initiate and sustain forms of collective existence and shared agreements that strike a constructive balance between individual rights and freedoms and the search for a shared understanding of a public good and its ensuing requirements of all of us individually and collectively (Callahan 1994).

Conclusion

Despite its limitations, the pragmatic framework of moderate liberalism, as I have laid it out, suggests that the culture wars context can only be a dead end for bioethics and hinders the search for open discourse through deliberation. Worse, the further radicalization of existing moral-political positions could transform bioethics into an advocacy forum, where the emphasis is on defining positions rather than examining their underpinnings. Another way to state this point is that current debates are geared toward arguing what is *right* and *wrong* instead of seeking what is the *good* or *best thing to do*. The state of affairs described by Callahan as cited above can only make more difficult the search for the best ethical approaches that integrate a wide range of concerns and perspectives beyond the belief in objective moral absolutes. This does not mean that we need to reach a soft consensus, a compromise between the liberal and conservative extremes. In this respect, Aristotle rightfully distinguished the simple mathematical middle from the golden mean and the various forms of moral excellence, or virtues. The golden mean is not simply what is halfway between two extremes or options. Aristotle's illustration was that of a baby's need being only, for example, a teacup full of food and the adult's need being four cups; the golden mean is not halfway between both quantities. And I am less concerned here about the specific virtues Aristotle identified (e.g., courage, truthfulness), which can seem somewhat out of touch and outdated in contemporary contexts. However, his approach to moral reasoning and his quest for moral praiseworthiness can inspire us to engage in open dialogue and reflection to help in identifying contemporary golden means through deliberation. Aristotle's way of approaching ethics—not inconsistent with Dewey's pragmatic naturalism—can help us to generate wisdom adapted to current contexts and social and medical goals and to nourish a dialogue between tradition and innovation that I believe to be constitutive of moral reasoning (Illes and Racine 2005b). I want to conclude by stressing that there could be a wide range of solutions and ideas to help bioethics move beyond polarization and the current culture wars. The key to this deadlock, however, may be less in the specific outcome of the process than in the conditions required to engage in a constructive dialogue, such as open mindedness, acceptance of diverging views as legitimate, and acknowledgment of the value of different points of view.

7

Disorders of Consciousness in an Evolving Neuroscience Context

Overview

In this chapter, I review the basic medical understanding of disorders of consciousness (DOC) with a focus on the persistent vegetative state (PVS) and the minimally conscious state (MCS). I also review the evolving neuroscience context using neuroimaging results and their impact on clinical care and the understanding of the diagnosis and prognosis of PVS and MCS.

Clinical and scientific discussions regarding the nature of coma and vegetative states have a long, complex, and fascinating history. Historically, physicians have tried distinguishing between different forms of coma and establishing diagnostic criteria and tests to properly identify the prognoses of coma patients. For almost three centuries, however, the understanding and diagnosis of DOC remained crude and the evidence base rather thin (Koehler and Wijdicks 2008). Different terminologies and classification systems distinguishing types of comas (e.g., coma, stupor, or partial loss of consciousness) emerged in the eighteenth and nineteenth centuries, but the causes of coma (damage to the ascending reticular activation system, or ARAS) remained elusive until the first half of the twentieth century. Today, contemporary medical practice as well as legal and bioethics discussions distinguish between different DOC such as coma, PVS, and MCS (Bernat 2006a). (Brain death, or death defined by neurological criteria, stands in a category by itself because it is considered the equivalent of death and does not constitute a DOC.)

The past decades have yielded advances in neurology and intensive care that allow for a more accurate and rigorous description of different states of coma and unresponsiveness of the neurological patient. Yet our understanding of these disorders is still incomplete and evolving. In this context, debates have surfaced about the impact of neuroscience research like functional neuroimaging in changing the basic understandings of DOC and improving diagnostic and prognostication practices (Fins et al. 2008). This context of emerging scientific advances yields questions about traditional understandings of the vegetative state (VS) and other DOC, notably regarding the ability of these patients to process (or not) language and pain stimuli (Coleman et al. 2007; Boly et al. 2008; Owen and Coleman 2008). Some intensively discussed findings have suggested that vegetative patients actually understand far more than typically suggested by standard neurological guidelines (e.g., the guidelines of the American Academy of Neurology [1989], the Royal College of Physicians in the UK [2003], and the Multi-Society Task Force on PVS [1994]). Owen suggested that his patient was aware and processing language as evident in functional magnetic resonance imaging (fMRI) and positron emission tomography (PET) scan results (Owen et al. 2006; Owen and Coleman 2008). These strong interpretations have provoked discussions on what we consider an actual and accurate understanding of DOC to be (Fins et al. 2008). Another challenge is the clinical and public understanding issues related to this area of research (Racine and Bell 2008). Ethical and medical questions raised by this mode of inquiry include the refinement of neuroimaging research to maximize chances that improvements in diagnosis will be achieved as well as balanced transfer of knowledge to the public and stakeholders to avoid fueling expectations of early clinical translation.

In this chapter, I first review some basic terminology and history about brain death and DOC. This is important to comprehend how neuroscience innovation regarding the understanding of DOC interacts with longstanding challenges, and in some cases neglect, of these conditions. After, I briefly present some recent advances in neuroscience research on DOC to highlight the type of research conducted and how both researchers and the public (through the print media) have interpreted these findings. These two sections of this chapter provide the background for the subsequent part of the chapter, which discusses how current medical and ethical practices in the context of severe brain injury shape challenges of clinical and public understanding of DOC.

Disorders of Consciousness and Brain Death

There has been an enduring medical interest in patients who do not recover from severe brain injury and remain in an apparent state of deep sleep, or coma. The existence of coma was acknowledged early on in Western medicine; famous physicians of antiquity such as Hippocrates and Galen described forms of coma. Physicians from the seventeenth century onward tried distinguishing between different forms of coma to establish diagnostic criteria and tests to properly identify those states and their related prognoses. Their efforts were frustrated by the natural scarcity of coma cases, lack of knowledge about brain function, and the absence of technology to assist them in their task. Although different terminologies and classification systems distinguishing types of comas, such as coma, stupor, or partial loss of consciousness, emerged in the eighteenth and nineteenth centuries, the causes of coma remained elusive for a long time. This situation began to change when the ARAS responsible for arousal of the human brain started to be better understood in the late 1940s and early 1950s. In 1949, a study entitled "Brain Stem Reticular Formation and Activation of the EEG [electroencephalography]," by Giuseppe Moruzzi (1910–1986) and Horace Magoun (1907–1991) examined the impact of stimulating the reticular formation in cats and proposed a major role of the ARAS in arousal and wakefulness (Moruzzi and Magoun 1949). Today, the existence of distinct DOC is acknowledged by physicians worldwide, and a quick tour of these concepts is necessary to understand the subsequent discussion on the evolving neuroscience context and related challenges.

It is also important to understand that the clinical approach to consciousness as a neurological concept is different from how most philosophical and religious traditions have discussed the nature of consciousness. Based largely on the work of neurologists Fred Plum and Jerome Posner (*The Diagnosis of Stupor and Coma*), clinical approaches to consciousness typically consider it a two-fold concept defined by wakefulness and awareness (Bernat 2006a). First, wakefulness is basically equated to arousal; wakefulness consists of mechanisms that keep "the patient awake and which relate[s] to the physical manifestations of awakening from sleep" (Cartlidge 2001). Second, awareness refers to "the content of consciousness or the awareness of self and environment," including psychological functions such as emotions, thoughts, and sensory experience (Cartlidge 2001). In a nutshell, wakefulness and arousal depend on the integrity of the ARAS and its projection to the thalamus, while awareness of self and the environment requires that the thalamus, cortex, and their white matter connections be functional (Bernat 2006a). Clinicians rely on observable behaviors and responses to determine if a patient is awake or aware. This reliance on clinical observations creates its own challenges and leads to misconceptions outside the clinical environment because of the indirect nature of this inference and the distinct "conceptual domains" (e.g., anatomy, awareness, behavior) that constitute consciousness (Shewmon 2004). Before describing different DOC, I will first say a few words on brain death since brain death is often conflated with DOC even though brain death is not a DOC.

Brain Death and Irreversible Coma

Brain death, or death defined by neurological criteria, is another way to establish death in addition to the cessation of respiration and heart beat, the cardio-respiratory criteria for establishing death (National Conference of Commissioners on Uniform State Laws 1980). Brain death, even though it is not considered a DOC, was referred to early on as a form of irreversible coma. In the 1940s and 1950s, advances in critical care led to an unparalleled situation where patients who would have died by cardiac or pulmonary arrest could be brought back to life with the help of life support. However, in some cases, pulmonary and cardiac activity could be reinitiated and sustained by mechanical ventilation while the patient remained in a very severe and apparently irreversible coma. This situation induced some leading critical care physicians to ask Pope Pius XII (during their World Congress in Rome in 1957) for advice on the need to maintain those patients on life support and to better define this neurological gray zone (Jonsen 2008). A few years later, in a landmark paper, two French physicians, Pierre Mollaret, a neurologist, and Maurice Goulon, an intensivist, distinguished a new type of coma, "coma dépassé," or "beyond coma," which is now called brain death (rarely do physicians speak of irreversible coma). Goulon and Mollaret also distinguished coma dépassé, or brain death, from other forms of coma. They concluded their paper by articulating an ethical question: "Do we have the right to stop life support [called then 'la réanimation'] in the name of criteria pretending to trace a valid frontier between life and death?" (The translation is mine.) Interestingly, at that point Goulon and Mollaret concluded that they had not been able to perform the *police verso*, the thumb down sign used by Roman officials to command the sacrifice of a defeated gladiator. Goulon and Mollaret believed their criteria and the current discussion to be insufficiently certain or mature to exclude any hope of recovery and clearly identify death (Jonsen 2008).

After some research and discussions in the 1960s, the form of irreversible coma discussed by Goulon, Mollaret, and others became increasingly viewed as the equivalent of death. An ad hoc committee of the Harvard Medical School was created to deliberate on the status of patients in this form of irreversible coma and on the definition of death. This committee, chaired by Henry Beecher (1904–1976; who also was a major figure in the development of research ethics in the 1960s), established that death could be declared when the brain ceased to function, that is, permanent nonfunctioning. This would be established when a number of features were exhibited: (1) unreceptivity and unresponsivity; (2) no movements or breathing; (3) no reflexes; (4) flat electroencephalogram (Ad Hoc Committee of the Harvard Medical School 1968). Brain death was described by the Harvard committee as the abolition of activity at the "cerebral, brain-stem, and often spinal levels" (Ad Hoc Committee of the Harvard Medical School 1968). The committee viewed its role as prompted by the existence of new devices that could separate the function of various biological organs in such a way that death of the brain was not coincident with the cessation of function of other organs like the heart and lungs:

> From ancient times down to the recent past it was clear that, when the respiration and heart stopped, the brain would die in a few minutes; so the obvious criterion of no heart beat as synonymous with death was sufficiently accurate. In those times the heart was considered to be the central organ of the body; it is not surprising that its failure marked the onset of death. This is no longer valid when modern resuscitative and supportive measures are used. These improved activities can now restore "life" as judged by the ancient standards of persistent respiration and continuing heart beat. (Ad Hoc Committee of the Harvard Medical School 1968)

Of course, the practical interest in establishing a definition for brain death came from the brain dead patients' potential to donate their organs. This social relevance of brain death has always created impressions for some that it jeopardizes, from the medical and social standpoints, the integrity of the concept of brain death itself as well as the clinical examinations used to ascertain it (Bernat 2008).

Today, brain death is widely viewed by the vast majority of medical associations as death defined by neurological criteria and is enshrined in the United States within the Uniform Determination of Death Act (UDDA). The UDDA established in 1980 that "an individual who has sustained either (1) irreversible cessation of circulatory and respiratory functions, or (2) irreversible cessation of all functions of the entire brain, including the brain stem, is dead. A determination of death must be made in accordance with accepted medical standards" (National Conference of Commissioners on Uniform State Laws 1980). According to this act, the specific tests and techniques to establish irreversible cessation of the entire brain are to be determined by the medical profession. The preamble of the act also clarifies that "the 'entire brain' includes the brain stem, as well as the neocortex. The concept of 'entire brain' distinguishes determination of death under this Act from 'neocortical death' or 'persistent vegetative state'" (National Conference of Commissioners on Uniform State Laws 1980). The authors of the UDDA did not deem these latter states to be valid medical or legal foundations for determining death.

The modern clinical criteria for the diagnosis of brain death in adults and children include presence of coma; apnea; absence of motor responses; and absence of brain-stem reflexes (pupillary responses to light; corneal reflexes; Wijdicks 2001). The clinical examination that ascertains neurological determination of death is supplemented by a number of tests based on cerebral angiography, electroencephalography, or other techniques. It is important to note that on some very rare occasions, clinical signs may falsely suggest preserved brain function (Wijdicks 2001). For example, some body movements (e.g., when the body is carried for retrieval of organs) can be generated by the spine, including flexing of the body at the waistline, which may make the body seem to rise. Clinicians also need to exclude potential confounders such as hypothermia, drug intoxication, and the locked-in syndrome (described below; Wijdicks 2001). In addition, brain death still attracts some controversies despite the broad medical, legal, and ethical consensus worldwide (Baron et al. 2006). Some scholars maintain that brain dead patients actually breathe (with the help of the ventilator) or could have remote chances of feeling pain

(Truog 2007). Others have questioned the global nature of the disintegration of physiological functions caused by brain death (Shewmon 2001), but proponents of brain death have rightfully, in my opinion, clarified that it is the global properties of the individual biological organism that are in cause, not all physiological processes (Bernat 2008). The term "brain death" also gives the impression that there are two types of death, death of the brain and death of the whole organism, which is an unfortunate drawback of the term brain death (Bernat 2006b). However, the UDDA makes it clear that there are two accepted methods for determining death, and more recent attempts to clarify the neurological determination of death have emphasized this (Canadian Council for Donation and Transplantation 2005).

Coma

Coma "is a state of unresponsiveness in which the patient lies with eyes closed and cannot be aroused to respond appropriately to stimuli even with vigorous stimulation" (Posner et al. 2007). Coma comes from the Greek κῶμα, which means deep sleep, and in fact, coma patients do not have sleep-wake cycles; in terms of motor function, they display only reflexes and postural responses. A patient in a coma is unable to wake up following vigorous sensorial stimulation and has no arousal and no spontaneous movements. Coma can be brought about by various causes, including metabolic disorders, intoxication, or severe brain injury. The depth of coma is typically assessed using the Glasgow Coma Scale, developed by Teasdale and Jennett in Glasgow and published in 1974 (Teasdale and Jennett 1974), which assesses visual, motor, and verbal responses, but other scales are also used to assess the depth of coma. According to experienced neurologists, true coma rarely lasts more than thirty days (Bernat 2006a). It is important to note that patients suffering from coma can awaken and improve; transition to a VS; or die (The Multi-Society Task Force on PVS 1994; Stevens and Bhardwaj 2006).

The (Persistent) Vegetative State

In an important paper, physicians Bryan Jennett and Fred Plum proposed the term "persistent vegetative state" to describe a syndrome in which patients with severe brain damage exhibit very limited responsiveness without showing signs of awareness other than primitive postural reflexes and reflex movements of the limbs (Jennett and Plum 1972). Jennett and Plum described patients that typically started to open their eyes after two or three weeks in deep coma (first only following arousing stimuli but after without provocation). They noted that in these patients, "it seems that there is wakefulness without awareness" and that a certain reflex (e.g., grasp reflex) "may look as though it was initiated by the patient and may even may be regarded as purposeful or voluntary" by inexperienced observers and family members (Jennett and Plum 1972). They used the term "persistent" instead of "irreversible," "prolonged," or "permanent" to avoid discussing the prediction of the state given the lack of data on these aspects of PVS at that time (Jennett and Plum 1972). Jennett and Plum emphasized that the term "describes behaviour" and should invite "further clinical and pathological innovation of the condition rather than giving the impression of a problem completely understood" (Jennett and Plum 1972). Further, they noted that "the essential component of this syndrome is the absence of any adaptive response to the external environment, the absence of any evidence of a *functioning mind* which is either receiving or projecting information" (Jennett and Plum 1972) and that the "immediate issue is to recognize that there is a group of patients who never show evidence of a *working mind*" (Jennett and Plum 1972; emphasis is mine). Interestingly, PVS was seen by Jennett and Plum as a useful term to "facilitate communication, between doctors or with patients' relatives or intelligent laymen, about its implications." This term was judged to be "advantageous" to avoid "the mystique of highly specialized medical jargon to describe a condition likely to be discussed widely outside the profession" (Jennett and Plum 1972). Jennett and Plum acknowledged that although "a continuum must exist between this VS and some of the others described, it seems wise to make an absolute distinction between patients who do make a consistently understandable response to those around them, whether by word or gesture, and those who never do" (Jennett and Plum 1972).

Today, PVS is largely viewed as an absence of responsive behavior and an absence of awareness and consciousness despite preserved wakefulness (sleep-wake cycles; Bernat 2006a). The diagnosis of a PVS includes unawareness of self and the environment; incapacity of interacting with others; and no sustained reproducible or purposeful voluntary behaviors in response to stimuli (Bernat 2006a). The potential behaviors of PVS patients are severely limited and include sleep-wake cycles; spontaneous breathing; utterance of sounds; swallowing saliva; reflexive crying or smiling; brief unsustained visual pursuits; facial expressions such as grimacing in response to pain; brief orientation to auditory startle; and brief visual fixation (Multi-Society Task Force on PVS 1994; Giacino et al. 2002; Bernat 2006a). Like patients in a coma, patients in a VS show no signs of awareness of self or their environment (Multi-Society Task Force on PVS 1994). A VS, by convention, is declared persistent one month after acute traumatic or nontraumatic brain injury or lasting for at least one month in patients with degenerative or metabolic disorders or developmental malformations (The Multi-Society Task Force on PVS 1994). Current evidence suggests that recovery from PVS after three months in nontraumatic brain injury (e.g., stroke) cases is very rare, and recovery after twelve months in patients with traumatic brain injury is highly unlikely (Multi-Society Task Force on PVS 1994). These different timelines for potential recovery are explained by the greater gray matter damage in nontraumatic brain injury and the greater ability of white matter tracts (usually damaged in traumatic injury) to recover after several months (Bernat 2006a). The acronym PVS is also used to refer to a "permanent vegetative state," and given the possible confusion, some authors have suggested separating the diagnosis (vegetative state) from the prognosis (persistent or permanent; Bernat 2006a). Although I acknowledge this source of confusion, I use PVS to refer to the persistent vegetative state.

Controversial aspects of PVS are occasionally debated, such as the true absence of consciousness of PVS patients, particularly the ability of clinical examinations to assess this lack of cognition (Shewmon 2004); patients' experience of pain (Boly et al. 2008); their processing of language stimuli (Owen et al. 2006; Owen and Coleman 2008); and their ability to track visual stimuli and visual fixation (Royal College of Physicians 2003). Misdiagnosis of PVS is apparently common (Childs, Mercer, and Childs 1993; Andrews et al. 1996), and the suspected causes of this call for increased professional education and training (Gill-Thwaites 2006). As I present in the second section of this chapter, in the past years, neuroimaging research on PVS patients has provoked further debates on the true absence of consciousness of PVS patients, especially the ability of PVS patients to preserve some cognitive functions despite received knowledge to the contrary and the limits of the clinical examinations (based on motor response) to reveal this.

The Minimally Conscious State (MCS)

MCS is a diagnosis that was defined and approved by a consensus recommendation of the American Academy of Neurology in 2002, following the meetings of the Aspen Neurobehavioral Conference Workgroup in the mid-1990s. MCS has a much shorter history than PVS but one that is still quite complicated. Years before 2002, healthcare professionals had started to describe a "minimally responsive state" (American Congress of Rehabilitation Medicine 1995). The term minimally responsive state is still in use and is sometimes preferred to MCS given that, as with PVS, the evidence on consciousness itself is elusive and largely based on behavioral observations (National Health and Medical Research Council 2008). Minimally conscious patients distinguish themselves from VS patients "by the presence of behaviors associated with conscious awareness" (Giacino et al. 2002). To be diagnosed as being in MCS, patients must exhibit "limited but clearly discernible evidence of self or environmental awareness" on a "reproducible or sustained basis" (Giacino et al. 2002). Such behaviors can include following simple commands and intelligibly verbalizing or behaving purposefully (e.g., appropriate smiling or crying; touching or holding objects in a manner that accommodates size and shape of the object; Giacino et al. 2002). MCS patients can exhibit one or more of these behaviors; at least one of these behaviors is required to distinguish them from PVS patients. There are few studies on the prognosis of MCS patients compared with that of PVS patients, but MCS patients are usually thought to have a better prognosis. MCS is typically viewed as one step in the process of recovery from a VS (Stevens and Bhardwaj 2006). Although very preliminary, thalamic deep brain stimulation (DBS) on an MCS patient has yielded interesting and promising results (Schiff et al. 2007). When stimulation was on, the frequency of specific cognitively mediated behaviors, limb control, and oral feeding increased, possibly because DBS compensated for the functional loss of the patient's arousal regulation mechanisms under the control of the frontal lobe. The team interpreted these results as providing "evidence that DBS can promote significant late functional recovery from severe traumatic brain injury. Our observations, years after the injury occurred, challenge the existing practice of early treatment discontinuation for patients with only inconsistent interactive behaviors and motivate further research to develop therapeutic interventions" (Schiff et al. 2007). Since the MCS may be a step in the recovery process, the withdrawal of life support decisions can be more controversial than in PVS. More research on the expected prognosis of MCS patients could help inform the decisional process and facilitate communication with family members.

Other Confounding Neurological States

DOC should not be conflated with other syndromes. For example, the "locked-in syndrome" is not a disorder of consciousness but a state of anarthria and quadriplegia where patients can sometimes communicate only through limited vertical eye movement and blinking (Giacino et al. 2002). The story of a locked-in patient has been self-reported by Jean-Dominique Bauby, a journalist who suffered a stroke (the typical cause of locked-in syndrome is a pontine stroke). Bauby wrote the book by communicating his thoughts through blinking his left eyelid. His touching book *Le scaphandre et le papillon* was published in French in 1997 (Bauby 1997) and made into a film in 2007. Another confounding state is "akinetic mutism" (also called "coma vigil"), in which patients are mute and unable to move (akinetic). This condition is often caused by lesions to the frontal lobes, and in the early stages, akinetic mutism can be difficult to distinguish from the VS since these patients also have sleep-wake cycles. There is some debate regarding the need to distinguish it from the VS (Cartlidge 2001). "Stupor" refers to a state in which individuals appear asleep but can be aroused when vigorously stimulated. This state is encountered in psychiatric patients and can be identified by the presence of normal brain activity revealed by EEG (Cartlidge 2001).

This overview of different DOC has highlighted some details about the nature of these diagnoses, their history, and the reasons they came about, but much is still unknown regarding DOC. The next section discusses how neuroscience research has started to challenge some of the common understandings of these conditions.

Disorders of Consciousness in an Evolving Neuroscience Context

Neuroscience research on PVS patients has provoked further debates on the nature of DOC. The ability of PVS patients to preserve some cognitive functions despite received knowledge to the contrary has sparked controversy, especially about clinical observations not assessing consciousness per se. In contrast, research on MCS has tended to be less controversial and bring further support to the integrity of the MCS diagnosis by substantiating the view that MCS patients have limited awareness and responses. This research has also sparked hope that more can be learned and far more done for these patients (Fins 2005b). One revealing case of the shortcomings in the care offered to some patients is that of Terry Wallis. Terry Wallis suffered traumatic brain injury (in 1984), was diagnosed with a PVS, and was refused further examination for years until he awoke and started to talk (in 2003; Fins and Schiff 2006).

As Fins, Illes, Bernat, and colleagues indicated in a Stanford-based consensus workshop paper, there is a wide range of important challenges related to the emergence of recent neuroimaging research with patients in states of disordered consciousness (Fins et al. 2008). Rightfully, this authoritative group of authors identified concerns regarding the acquisition and interpretation of the data yielded by functional neuroimaging and, in particular, its ability to reveal signs of consciousness in response to simple tasks. Perhaps functional neuroimaging could identify signs of awareness, consciousness, or meaningful response in those patients when clinical examination has not. Current practices to identify signs of awareness require careful examination by a clinician to determine if they are "simply reflex responses that do not require awareness or are cognitive or intentional responses that could be made only by an aware person" (Fins et al. 2008). I discuss and analyze these issues in more detail, but first I must describe the type of research being conducted internationally.

Functional Neuroimaging in PVS

Functional neuroimaging research on PVS has tended to examine if PVS patients are truly unconscious and unresponsive as stated in standard neurological guidelines. For example, in a comparative study of severely brain-injured MCS and VS patients, Coleman and colleagues found that three out of seven VS patients and two out of five MCS patients showed "significant temporal lobe responses in the low-level auditory contrast" (Coleman et al. 2007), a task involving a contrast between auditory stimuli and silence. The patients also "showed significant temporal lobe responses" in a mid-level speech perception contrast that involved a comparison of intelligible speech to unintelligible noise stimuli (Coleman et al. 2007). The seven other VS and MCS patients in that study showed no significant activation in this low-level auditory contrast task. The authors did not exclude the possibility that task performance issues (head movement of the patient, which interferes with fMRI data acquisition) and subthreshold activation could have been responsible for some of the lower responding patients. The authors concluded that "these results provide further evidence that some vegetative patients retain islands of preserved cognitive function and that in the absence of behavioural evidence, functional imaging provides a valuable tool to the assessment team" (Coleman et al. 2007). The authors claimed that the findings could be important for diagnosis when residual cognitive function cannot be observed because the patient is not able to produce overt motor responses. They warned that their data "do not, on their own, permit strong conclusions concerning whether those patients showing intact fMRI responses were consciously aware of speech" (Coleman et al. 2007); however, they did conclude that "these results provide further evidence that a subset of patients fulfilling the behavioural criteria for the vegetative state retain islands of preserved cognitive function" (Coleman et al. 2007).

One of the most discussed and controversial research reports was published in 2006 in *Science* by Adrian Owen (also involved in the study discussed above) and his research group, the Cognition and Brain Sciences Unit, based at the Medical Research Council in the UK. Owen and colleagues examined brain function in a twenty-three-year-old female vegetative patient who had been injured in a car accident. They established a diagnosis of VS and then presented to the patient some mental imagery tasks such as imagining playing tennis and navigating in her house. They found that her brain activation patterns were comparable to a normal healthy individual performing the tasks (Owen et al. 2006). Owen and colleagues concluded, "These results confirm that, despite fulfilling the clinical criteria for a diagnosis of VS, this patient retained the ability to understand spoken commands and to respond to them through her brain activity, rather than through speech or movement." They also suggested that the patient made a "decision to cooperate with the authors," which in their words "confirmed beyond any doubt that she was consciously aware of herself and her surroundings." The researchers envisioned that such patients could perhaps eventually use their "residual cognitive capabilities to communicate their thoughts to those around them by modulating their own neural activity" (Owen et al. 2006). This patient could have been classified as being in an MCS (Fins and Schiff 2006), but Owen and colleagues did use language suggesting awareness and volitions to describe their results.

Owen and colleagues also examined a thirty-year-old male patient who was diagnosed using PET scan and fMRI as being in PVS following a stroke. In the PET studies, the patient was presented with a language comprehension task (Owen et al. 2005). This task involved presenting to the patient English-language declarative sentences presented at three intelligibility levels (low, medium, and high; a form of distortion was used to dampen the intelligibility level for the low- and medium-level intelligibility sentences). The fMRI experiment involved high- and low-ambiguity sentences, the latter being matched for number of words and syntax. The PET studies (involving three levels of ambiguity), conducted four months and thirteen months after ictus, revealed, according to the authors, "that basic auditory processes were probably functional" (Owen et al. 2005). The comparison of low-intelligibility and high-intelligibility sentences (thirteen months after ictus) did not reveal statistically significant activation in the superior and middle temporal gyri of the left hemisphere, but the authors wrote, "these peaks are well within the region found to be activated in healthy volunteers during this same task" (Owen et al. 2005). The fMRI results (based on the high- and low-ambiguity sentences) yielded similar results to the PET examinations, namely that the bilateral middle and superior temporal gyri were activated similarly to healthy volunteers. The interpretation of these results again posed a number of challenges. For example, "there was no reliable mechanism for ensuring that the presented stimuli were actually *perceived* by the patient," even though the patient's brain activation patterns were different in the language comprehension task and the semantic ambiguity task (Owen et al. 2005). Despite this, the authors concluded that their study "yielded compelling evidence for high level residual auditory processing in the

PVS patient," and that "some of the processes involved in activating and selecting contextually appropriate word meaning may be intact in the patient, despite his clinical diagnosis of PVS" (Owen et al. 2005). The authors warned, however, that "definitive judgments regarding the 'awareness' or 'consciousness' in this and similar patients are difficult" (Owen et al. 2005). Again, perhaps this patient was not truly in PVS, or he could have been processing basic meaning of the stimuli presented to him. In spite of the controversy and ongoing discussion over these conclusions (Fins and Schiff 2006; Greenberg 2007; Nachev and Husain 2007; Fins et al. 2008), in a review paper, Owen has reiterated his belief that the female patient (Owen et al. 2006) was conscious: "despite the fact that she fulfilled all of the clinical criteria for a diagnosis of VS, the patient retained the ability to understand spoken commands and respond to them through her brain activity, confirming beyond any doubt that she was consciously aware of herself and her surroundings" (Owen and Coleman 2008).

A Chinese group led by Di conducted an examination of seven patients in the VS and four in MCS (Di et al. 2007). They examined, using fMRI, if patients would respond as healthy individuals would when hearing their own names spoken by a familiar voice versus other verbal stimuli without meaning. Two vegetative patients failed to show any significant cerebral activation; three showed activation in the primary auditory cortex (associated with basic auditory input processing) in response to their name; two vegetative patients and all four MCS patients showed activation in their primary auditory cortex and in hierarchically higher-order associative temporal areas (associated with complex auditory input processing). The authors noted that the two patients in the VS showing this higher-order activation also showed signs of clinical improvement three months after their fMRI examination. These authors concluded that "the cerebral responses to patient's own name spoken by a familiar voice as measured by fMRI might be a useful tool to preclinically distinguish minimally conscious state-like cognitive processing in some patients behaviorally classified as vegetative" (Di et al. 2007).

Figure 7.1 shows that some of these more controversial interpretations about functional neuroimaging in PVS were captured in media reports. It is important to stress that many cautionary statements can be found in the original papers, as seen from the last pages.

Sample *conclusion statement* regarding results of functional neuroimaging research on PVS in peer review literature

"Despite the fact that she fulfilled all of the clinical criteria for a diagnosis of vegetative state, the patient retained the ability to understand spoken commands and respond to them through her brain activity, confirming beyond any doubt that she was consciously aware of herself and her surroundings" (Owen and Coleman 2008).

Sample *cautionary note* regarding results of functional neuroimaging research on PVS in peer review literature

"Definitive judgments regarding the 'awareness' or 'consciousness' in this and similar patients are difficult" (Owen et al. 2005).

Sample *media statement* regarding results of functional neuroimaging research on PVS in peer review literature

"Despite the patient's very poor behavioral status, the fMRI findings indicate the existence of a rich mental life, including auditory language processing and the ability to perform mental imagery tasks. On one hand, this single case makes a strong argument for the development of fMRI and other neurophysiological tools (such as monitoring electroencephalogram brain responses to external stimuli) to evaluate cognition in such patients. On the other hand, we should not generalize from this single patient, who suffered relatively few cerebral lesions, to most other vegetative state patients, who typically have massive structural brain lesions" (Naccache 2006).

Figure 7.1
Sample conclusion statement, cautionary note, and media statement regarding results of functional neuroimaging research in persistent vegetative states (PVS).

These studies of patients in vegetative states have sparked interest and enthusiasm in the scientific community and beyond. They have reached public groups and stakeholders, including relatives of PVS patients. Would such research improve the diagnostic accuracy of PVS by clinicians? Could we now be in a position to access the "thought processes" of these patients? Are we in a position to obtain better insights into their chances of an eventual recovery? Could we eventually communicate with them to learn about their end-of-life preferences if they have sufficient "residual cognitive capabilities," and if so, would patients be able to convey simple messages to their loved ones? These questions and several others related to the potential use of neuroimaging in DOC raise important issues, especially given the vulnerability of the patients, our limited understanding of DOC, and the sometimes desperate state of parents and friends of patients. However, several important scientific challenges with ethical purport must be examined, such as standardizing task designs used to illicit brain activation, validating current procedures on a greater number of patients, and establishing guidelines for the interpretation of brain activation in the PVS and the MCS (Bernat and Rottenberg 2007). As some leading neurologists have commented, this research may not be ready for broad use and dissemination (Hopkin 2006). I will come back to this issue once I have addressed the challenges in interpreting the gaps between experts and also between experts and nonexperts (Racine and Bell 2008) in the next chapter.

Functional Neuroimaging in MCS

In comparison to research on PVS, which has tended to raise questions about the integrity of the PVS diagnosis, research bearing on the MCS has tended to support that MCS patients exhibit different responses than PVS patients. Research has therefore generally provided evidence to support the diagnosis of the MCS as well as the distinction between the MCS and the VS, because MCS patients display higher-order brain activation responses than VS patients.

For example, perceptions of pain in MCS patients resemble that of normal patients (e.g., activation of the "pain matrix," composed of the secondary somatosensory cortex, and the frontoparietal and anterior cingulate cortices; Boly et al. 2008), while responses of PVS patients appear to be much weaker and limited to the thalamus and the primary somatosensory area (Laureys et al. 2002; Boly et al. 2008). This was shown in a study comparing PET activation in five MCS patients, fifteen PVS patients, and fifteen healthy volunteers. Pain was induced by electrically stimulating the median nerves bilaterally. Brain activation responses of PVS patients to noxious stimuli also appeared isolated, while that of MCS patients was better integrated as illustrated by better preserved functional connectivity between primary and secondary areas of the cortex (Laureys et al. 2002; Boly et al. 2008). The authors conveyed this point by acknowledging that "although brain imaging is not a shortcut to subjectivity, we interpret the brain activation and functional connectivity patterns seen in patients in MCS as likely to show conscious perception of noxious stimuli" (Boly et al. 2008).

Another study published by Laureys' group examined regional blood flow using PET scans in response to auditory click stimuli in five MCS patients, fifteen PVS patients, and eighteen healthy controls (Boly et al. 2004). In comparison with PVS patients, the MCS patients showed stronger functional connectivity, in particular between secondary auditory cortex and associative cortices (temporal and prefrontal). More precisely, the MCS patients exhibited bilateral activation in the temporal gyri (Brodmann 41, 42, and 22), while the PVS patients showed activity only in areas 41 and 42. The authors concluded that "although assumptions about the level of consciousness in severely brain injured patients are difficult to make, our findings suggest that the cerebral activity observed in patients in an MCS is more likely to lead to higher-order integrative processes, thought to be necessary for the gain of conscious auditory perception" (Boly et al. 2004). They also warned that it is of "major importance to stress that our results should be used with appropriate caution regarding clinical decisions in individuals in a PVS or an MCS" (Boly et al. 2004). A case study published the same year by Laureys and colleagues showed similar results in a fifty-two-year-old male MCS patient. The study reported that "auditory stimuli with emotional valence (infant cries and the patient's own name) induced a much more widespread activation than did meaningless noise" (Laureys et al. 2004). This activation was similar to activation obtained in controls. The patient also displayed different activation in response to his own name. This stimulus activated distributed neuronal circuits in areas typically associated with self-awareness. This patient appeared to be on his way to recovery before dying unexpectedly, and accordingly, the authors cautioned, "It is important to stress that our results cannot be extended to the general MCS population. In a case like this one, MCS may be a transitional state on the route to further recovery, just like the patient's VS was a transitional state earlier in his course" (Laureys et al. 2004).

In one of the first fMRI studies examining brain activation in two MCS patients (in comparison to seven healthy individuals), neurologist Nicholas Schiff and colleagues found that "auditory stimulation with personalized narratives elicited cortical activity in the superior and middle temporal gyrus" (Schiff et al. 2005). This activation was similar between healthy volunteers and the two MCS patients. When the narratives used in the study were presented backward, however, without any linguistic content, the MCS patients showed marked reduced response, "suggesting reduced engagement for 'linguistically' meaningless stimuli" (Schiff et al. 2005; the healthy volunteers reported recognizing the reversed linguistic stimuli as speech). The study also involved tactile stimulation of the hands, which elicited very similar patterns of brain activation in both patients and healthy volunteers. The authors concluded, "these findings of active cortical networks that serve language functions suggest that some MCS patients may retain widely distributed cortical systems with potential for cognitive and sensory function despite their inability to follow simple instructions or communicate reliably" (Schiff et al. 2005). However, the authors carefully observed that, for example, "the right temporal activation observed in all subjects and the two patients could be related to voice perception irrespective of the semantic content of rudimentary right hemisphere word recognition," and noted, "The observed activation of prefrontal, parietal, and occipital regions in our patients is suggestive of awareness but potentially consistent with other interpretations" (Schiff et al. 2005). Again, this study emphasized the potential value of neuroimaging findings that reveal information not yielded by traditional clinical examination.

Consistent with these observations by Schiff and colleagues, Bekinschtein and colleagues published a case report in which an MCS patient was presented with a story read by his mother and by an age-matched control (Bekinschtein et al. 2004). The patient was a seventeen-year-old male who had suffered head trauma after being hit by a train while riding his bicycle. At the time of the study, he met the criteria for MCS (e.g., spontaneous eye opening, sleep-wake cycles, sustained visual fixation, and contingent smiling). Using fMRI, the authors observed that the mother's voice activated the amygdala (associated with emotional processing), the insula, and the inferior frontal gyrus (Bekinschtein et al. 2004). This research team concluded that the activation was perhaps acting jointly as an integration of limbic activity. They also mentioned that "although residual cerebral activity was unequivocal in our case, representing fragmentary cognitive processing, it should not be assumed that it depicts a fully integrated system required for normal levels of awareness" (Bekinschtein et al. 2004). Interestingly, the authors guarded against the impact

Sample *conclusion statement* regarding results of functional neuroimaging research on MCS in peer review literature

"These findings of active cortical networks that serve language functions suggest that some MCS patients may retain widely distributed cortical systems with potential for cognitive and sensory function despite their inability to follow simple instructions or communicate reliably" (Schiff et al. 2005).

Sample *cautionary note* regarding results of functional neuroimaging research on MCS in peer review literature

"The observed activation of prefrontal, parietal, and occipital regions in our patients is suggestive of awareness but potentially consistent with other interpretations" (Schiff et al. 2005).

Sample *media statement* regarding results of functional neuroimaging research on MCS in peer review literature

"Thousands of brain-damaged people who are treated as if they are almost completely unaware may in fact hear and register what is going on around them but be unable to respond, a new brain-imaging study suggests" (Carey 2005).

Figure 7.2
Sample conclusion statement, cautionary note, and media statement regarding results of functional neuroimaging research in minimally conscious states (MCS).

of potential careless bedside chatter given that MCS patients may understand fairly complex linguistic stimuli.

And as seen with PVS research, many cautionary statements in functional neuroimaging research in MCS were voiced, and some of them made it through the print media (see figure 7.2). Unfortunately, some commentators notoriously confused MCS with PVS and thought that MCS-related research showed that VS patients were conscious. For example, writing in the *New York Times Magazine*, one reporter stated erroneously, "New research suggests that many vegetative patients are more conscious than previously supposed—and might eventually be curable" (Zimmer 2003).

Conclusion

In this chapter, I have provided background on DOC (and brain death) to show some common assumptions now shared by medical professionals about coma, PVS, and MCS. My review of recent functional neuroimaging research into PVS and MCS illustrates how researchers drew conclusions and how they, in many cases, made cautionary warnings, which did not deter some controversial interpretations both in the scientific literature and in media reports. The next chapter examines more closely the tensions between lay and expert perspectives and between the manifest image and the scientific image of consciousness and behavior—and the challenges this creates for communication.

8

Communication of Prognosis in Di, of Consciousness and Severe Brain I. A Closer Look at Paradoxical Discou. the Clinical and Public Domains

Overview

Following the background material presented in the previous chapter, I now specifically tackle the issue of clinical and public communication in disorders of consciousness (DOC) and severe brain injury in an evolving neuroscience context. Two cases are presented to illustrate challenges previously identified by Bernat (2004), such as those related to physician bias and the use of technical jargon. The first case illustrates that clinical confusion persists given existing rates of diagnostic errors and poor understanding of DOC. Variability in opinions regarding prognosis and quality of life for patients with DOC also complicates healthcare decisions for these patients. I use a qualitative study of prognosis for a comatose patient to illustrate a number of these points. The second case demonstrates how public understanding of DOC and expectations regarding the evolving neuroscience understanding of DOC collide. The results of a large-scale media content analysis of a persistent vegetative state (PVS) patient (Terri Schiavo) illustrate this second point. I argue that there is a tension at work between, on the one hand, intuitive notions about consciousness and behavior and, on the other hand, scientific and medical understanding of consciousness and behavior. Given the staunchness with which these paradoxical perspectives have developed, clinical and research approaches will need to integrate this tension in clinical care and in communication with families and other stakeholders.

Prognostication is fundamental in the care of severely brain-injured patients; several interacting factors (Johnston 2000; Shevell 2004) give weight to this claim. Withdrawal or withholding of treatment routinely precedes death in the intensive care unit (ICU; Garros, Rosychuk, and Cox 2003; Curtis 2004). Uncertainty about patient outcome and prior wishes, however, can create considerable tensions between families and healthcare teams, thus complicating meaningful communication and respect for patient autonomy (Johnson et al. 2000). End-of-life (EOL) preferences of pediatric patients are often indirectly articulated by a proxy decision maker, typically members of the family. In addition, many ICU patients cannot express their preferences given their altered mental status (Hewitt 2002) or the presence of communication problems (Andrews et al. 2005). Physicians and bioethicists have emphasized the role of advanced directives to inform proxy decision making. However, such directives remain infrequently used, and when available, their interpretation is fraught with difficulties (Thompson, Barbour, and Schwartz 2003). These advance directives apply with additional challenges in pediatric care (Walsh-Kelly et al. 1999; Parker and Shemie 2002; Hammes et al. 2005).

Severe brain injury can lead to lifelong impairments, and thus the meaning of spending years with severe cognitive or motor disability becomes a fundamental consideration. Studies have shown that cognitive deficits weigh heavily in judgments about functional outcomes, quality of life, and EOL decision making (Mink and Pollack 1992; Masri et al. 2000; Devictor and Nguyen 2001; Cook et al. 2003; but see Garros, Rosychuk, and Cox 2003 for data suggesting otherwise). Therefore, the conditions in which EOL decisions take place, especially in the severe brain-injury context, leave a heavy burden on specialty physicians who must participate in decisions typically made on the patients' behalf. Understanding prognostication practices for severely brain-injured pediatric patients is clearly important, particularly in the context of variable brain death practices and the interacting factors that complicate EOL decision making in this population.

Chapter 7 reviews basic understandings of chronic DOC and illustrates some of the controversies surrounding recent neuroscience research that in some cases may challenge current healthcare practices and communication with families and the public. In particular, I introduce the basic terminology used in neurology to describe DOC and underscore how this terminology evolved historically and is still discussed today. This chapter will build on this background to highlight challenges in both

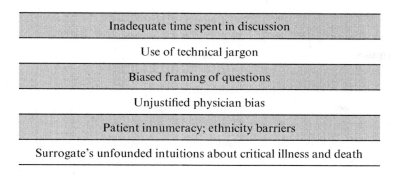

Figure 8.1
Challenges in the communication of poor neurological prognosis (identified by James Bernat; Bernat 2004)

clinical and public understanding related to the diagnosis and especially the prognosis of DOC. Two clinical cases illustrate some of the challenges created by the clinical and ethical aspects of chronic DOC. The first concerns the prognostication of outcomes by physicians for patients in a comatose state following anoxic brain injury (Racine, Lansberg, Dion, et al. 2007); the second bears on public understanding of PVS in the Terri Schiavo saga (Racine et al. 2008). While presenting these data, I also try to illustrate some of the key challenges James Bernat has identified in the communication of prognosis in severe brain injury and in the neurointensive care context (Bernat 2004). These challenges face physicians and healthcare providers as well as families and members of the public (see figure 8.1). I highlight in this chapter that the very nature of DOC and the discourse used to describe the diagnosis and prognosis create important challenges in the communication of prognosis and shared decision making.

Variability and Confusion in the Diagnosis and Prognosis of Disorders of Consciousness

First Case: Variability in Prognosis and Assessment of Quality of Life

One of the important issues regarding DOC concerns the accuracy of diagnosis and prognosis by healthcare providers, especially physicians. In particular, providers need to rely on a reasonably clear understanding of the different DOC and sound prediction of outcomes, especially in terms of level of certainty and uncertainty related to both diagnosis and prognosis. To assess potential variability regarding prognosis, in a study conducted with colleagues experienced in neurology and bioethics, I interviewed critical care physicians (intensivists) and neurologists with expertise in intensive care for neurological patients (neurointensivists) in two American academic medical centers (Racine, Lansberg, Dion, et al. 2007). The eighteen participating physicians first completed a demographic questionnaire and then read a clinical vignette featuring a comatose patient suffering from post-anoxic brain injury. The patient in the vignette was a forty-year-old male who had suffered cardiac arrest and was resuscitated. After a week, he was still comatose; his pupils were reactive, and he was overbreathing his ventilator. He had by now spontaneously opened his eyes for some parts of the day; he withdrew to pain in response to noxious stimuli; he did not follow any commands; and he had no corneal, gag, or cough reflexes (Racine, Lansberg, Dion, et al. 2007). A second questionnaire captured the physicians' prognosis and prediction of outcomes, and a semistructured interview followed to obtain qualitative perspectives on prognosis.

Interestingly, along with colleagues, I found in this study that physicians differed in their assessment of long-term outcomes for the patient described in this clinical vignette. Two main sources of prognostic variability emerged from these data. First, there was variability in predicting functional outcome along an evaluative dimension. When asked to predict the overall long-term functional outcome for the patient, responses ranged from fair/good to poor. Second, there was variability in predicting overall long-term functional outcome along a confidence dimension. Consequently, physicians could be categorized in the following prognostic quadrants: (1) physicians who considered the prognosis fair to good with relative certainty; (2) those who felt the prognosis was fair to good but were uncertain; (3) those who considered the prognosis poor with relative certainty; and (4) those who believed the prognosis was poor but were uncertain of this. Physicians most commonly fell in the fourth quadrant, expressing concern about a poor prognosis with marked uncertainty ($n = 7$; see table 8.1), but physicians representing each of the four views were identified.

Physicians were also questioned regarding outcome predictions for three specific domains (cognitive, social, and motor deficits). Considerable variability was observed in the type and degree of predicted deficits. For

Table 8.1
Prognosis for comatose patient as described by physicians (N = 18)

Fair to good (*n* = 3)	Poor (*n* = 3)
"The prognosis is probably good in terms of survival[;] as far as his functional capacity, I think it has a moderate probability of regaining excellent function. I think he is likely to have some impairment if he does recover."	"He is young but he has a number of things working against him. That the paramedics didn't arrive until 12 minutes after arrest, and after a week his GCS is 9. So I think his prognosis is poor. Likely to remain, not vegetative, but severely disabled."
Fair to good, emphasizing uncertainty (*n* = 5)	**Poor, emphasizing uncertainty** (*n* = 7)
"I would say the prognosis at six months is uncertain. He has continued to have clinical improvement through-out his hospitalization. Do I think that he'll be exactly the same as before this event occurred to him[?] I think it's unlikely, but in terms of . . . potentially his cognitive abilities; but I can't say that with all certainty."	"I think the likely outcome for this patient is probably not good, but I think good meaning . . . it's unlikely that he will return to his prior state of high functioning, I think it's probably unlikely that he will return to independent living[,] and my best estimate of where he is probably going to end up is need a lot of care, maybe a little ambulatory and have severe cognitive deficits. . . . So that is my prediction of his likely outcome, but . . . the prognosis at this time I believe is unclear."

example, while some physicians predicted quasi-inescapable motor impairments (e.g., "I would guess it'd be very unlikely that he would be able to sit up independently, and move extremities in a purposeful fashion. I think it even less likely that he'd be able to walk"), others thought the patient would likely be free of any such motor problems (e.g., "I think he would have no motor problem"; Racine, Lansberg, Dion, et al. 2007). Such variability could have important consequences on families and healthcare teams involved in the care of severely brain-injured patients; family members could be exposed to fairly wide-ranging prognoses.

Physician attitudes toward the quality of life of the hypothetical anoxic brain-injured patient also varied considerably. Variation was observed along two dimensions: an evaluative dimension (good or poor) and a "style" dimension (objective or subjective). Eight physicians expressed objective (third person) judgments about quality of life (i.e., quality of life that could be judged "objectively" poor or "objectively" fair to good). Seven physicians expressed objective statements that the patient would likely have poor quality of life. For example, one of these physicians said, "My assessment would be that his quality of life would be expected to be poor. He may have substantial neurologic impairment; he may have no substantial improvement over his current status. His current vegetative state may persist, and . . . may not improve substantially over the long term over where he is now." In stark contrast, one physician expressed an objective statement that the patient would benefit from a good quality of life: "I think his quality of life will be reasonably good. I think that he will have some degree of disability. I think that he will be able to do many of the things that he was able to do prior to this arrest." Although some expressed such "objective" statements, a majority of physicians ($n = 10$) fell into the "subjective" category. These respondents considered quality of life to be subjective, that is, they saw quality of life as a first-person matter that cannot be assessed, and hence, they refrained from any attempt to predict the patient's quality of life. For example, one physician said, "It depends on the patient. . . . I can only comment on functional status. It seems like it's the patient's job to interpret what functional status means to them in terms of their own quality of life. So quality of life is inherently value laden, and it's only for the patient to decide for a particular functional status what the quality associated with that is."

This first example clearly illustrates three of the challenges identified by Bernat (figure 8.1). First, ethical and communication issues can be created if physicians spend inadequate time in discussions with family members or if they provide conflicting messages to family members. This example shows that this can happen in difficult cases, especially if many different physicians are involved, which is not unusual in the ICU. Second, physicians can provide prognoses and responses that engage their own subjective perspective, and they must acknowledge this. Third, physicians must be careful not to bias the framing of questions, notably those that involve opinions regarding outcomes, potential recovery, and quality of life (Bernat 2004).

Second Case: Terri Schiavo and the Public Understanding of the Persistent Vegetative State

The case of Theresa (Terri) Schiavo is one of the best-known recent examples of a patient in PVS because of the unfortunate media exposure and political and legal battles this case provoked. In 1990, Schiavo suffered brain injury following severe hypoxia and evolved into PVS (Perry, Churchill, and Kirshner 2005). Many scholars suggested that the media played a negative role in creating and sustaining the controversy. For example, bioethicist George Annas wrote, "the case of Terri Schiavo . . . was being played out as a public spectacle" (Annas 2005). Neuroscientist Joy Hirsch commented that, despite all the legal and medical examinations, "public exposure of this case raised substantial doubts about her diagnosis, cognitive status, and prognosis that eroded public confidence in the medical assessment and complicated the ethical, legal, and medical considerations of the case" (Hirsch 2005). With a number of colleagues, I examined in detail the media coverage that the Schiavo case received in four American print media sources (Racine et al. 2008). I identified systematically some of the potential shortcomings that some commentators had alluded to. I was particularly interested in assessing the accuracy of the description of Schiavo's neurological condition, her behavioral repertoire, her prognosis, and the description of the withdrawal of life support. This was to my knowledge one of the first attempts to collect and analyze media coverage of such a famous clinical ethics case—after this study, there was much gained from closer scrutiny of the historical cases of Nancy Cruzan and Karen Ann Quinlan, who were both in PVS (Pence 2004).

I examined 1,141 news reports and editorials published between 1990 and 2005 (inclusively) in the four most prolific newspapers concerning this case and available through the LexisNexis Academic database (the *Tampa Tribune*, the *St. Petersburg Times*, the *New York Times*, and the *Washington Post*). This study found overall that the legal, ethical (including EOL decision making and withdrawal of life support), and political aspects of the case were featured prominently in headlines. Interestingly, I found that "persistent vegetative state" ($n = 392$; 34%) was the most frequently used term to describe Schiavo's neurological condition. Nonetheless, a plethora of other terms were also employed, such as the looser terms "brain damage" (n = 316; 28%) and "severe brain damage" (n = 145; 13%) to describe her neurological status. Importantly, 6 percent of articles (n = 71) included refutations of her PVS diagnosis, and 1 percent claimed, respectively, that she was "brain dead" (n = 12) or "minimally conscious" (n =10). Overall, explanations of chronic DOC (e.g., PVS, minimally conscious state, or MCS, and coma) and brain death were rare (found in ≤ 1% of articles for any one of these diagnoses). Less technical terms like "brain damage" were used mostly by journalists, while the term PVS was often used by cited physicians (e.g., journalists frequently attributed the technical concept to physicians, such as "doctors say she's in PVS"). Although some of the false claims regarding her diagnosis were disconcerting, they did not match, as will be seen, the confusion around Schiavo's prognosis and behavioral repertoire, where I observed frequent and substantial confusion.

This study found that 21 percent (n = 237) of articles reported statements that Schiavo "might improve" and 7 percent (n = 76) included statements that she "might recover." This was despite the evidence suggesting that recovery from PVS after three months in nontraumatic brain injury is rare, and recovery after twelve months in traumatic brain injury is highly unlikely (Multi-Society Task Force on PVS 1994). Thirteen percent (n = 143) of articles included statements that she will not improve, and 13 percent (n = 151) that she will not recover. I found that several claims about Schiavo's behavioral repertoire were clearly inconsistent (highlighted in black in figure 8.2) with the PVS diagnosis (e.g., she "responds," she "reacts"). Other claims (highlighted in gray) could seem at first glance consistent with a sound neurological description of her condition (e.g., she "smiles," she "laughs"), but they were used ambiguously (e.g., mostly by the Schindlers, but also by politicians) to reflect meaningful and purposeful behaviors instead of sheer reflexive behavior as customarily understood for PVS patients (American Academy of Neurology 1993; Bernat 2006a; Stevens and Bhardwaj 2006).

Given confusion regarding the behavioral repertoire and prognosis of Schiavo, it was not surprising (but still flabbergasting) to find depictions of Schiavo's withdrawal of life support as "murder" (n = 107; 9%), "death by starvation" (n = 46; 4%), and "euthanasia" (n = 13; 1%), those involved in the decision judged to be "playing God" (n = 8; 1%). Such language has been used in previous famous PVS cases.

Behavior	Affirmation (%)	Refutation (%)
Responds	117 (10)[1]	17 (1)
Reacts	104 (9)[2]	7 (1)
Incapacitated	63 (6)	0 (0)
Smiles	61 (5)*	10 (1)
Laughs	57 (5)*	7 (1)
Breathes	50 (4)	0 (0)
Moans	49 (4)*	7 (1)
Reflexes (has)	45 (4)	4 (0)
Cries	42 (4)*	6 (1)
Aware or alert	41 (4)[3]	56 (5)
Disabled	41 (4)*	2 (0)
Sees	40 (4)[4]	28 (2)
Moves purposefully	37 (3)[5]	54 (5)
Talks or pronounces words	30 (3)*	30 (3)
Communicates	28 (2)[6]	18 (2)
Hears	28 (2)[7]	5 (0)
Sleeps	25 (2)	0 (0)
Cognitive function (has)	19 (2)[8]	61 (5)
Conscious	18 (2)[9]	35 (3)
Discomfort (feels)	17 (1)[10]	5 (0)
Wakeful or awake	16 (1)	1 (0)
Grunts or groans	16 (1)*	2 (0)

Consistency with PVS diagnosis

- ■ Inconsistent
- □ Consistent
- ▨ Ambiguous

* Schindler party is most frequent source of affirmations for this ambiguous statement.

Most common sources of erroneous statements

1. Schindler party (N=97); doctors w/o declared allegiance (N=13); politicians (N=8)
2. Schindler party (N=92); journalists (N=7); doctors w/o declared allegiance and members of the general public (N=2 each)
3. Schindler party (N=18); doctors w/o declared allegiance (N=9); journalists (N=5)
4. Schindler party (N=29); journalists (N=4); doctors w/o declared allegiance (N=4)
5. Schindler party (N=21); doctors w/o declared allegiance (N=7); journalists (N=4)
6. Schindler party (N=24)
7. Schindler party (N=22); journalists (N=2); politicians (N=2)
8. Schindler party (N=10); advocacy groups (N=4); doctors w/o declared allegiance and Schiavo party (N=2 each)
9. Schindler party (N=11); politicians (N=4); doctors w/o declared allegiance (N=2)
10. Politicians (N=12)

Figure 8.2
Consistency of media description of Schiavo's behaviors with PVS diagnosis. First published in *Neurology* (Racine et al. 2008).

This second case example illustrates three other challenges related to the communication of poor prognosis identified by Bernat (Bernat 2004): the use of technical jargon in chronic DOC (e.g., PVS, MCS), which may have made public understanding and knowledge transfer more difficult (contrary to Jennett and Plum's intents, as reported in the previous chapter); the potential innumeracy of family members (who may not understand very poor chances of recovery in the same way as healthcare providers do); potential cultural and ethical barriers based on beliefs and traditions and unfounded intuitions about critical illness and death, especially the withdrawal of life support as it happened in the Terri Schiavo case.

These two examples of research reflect broader and more general issues in the clinical and public understanding of chronic DOC. Also, the emerging functional neuroimaging research on PVS and MCS (see chapter 7) connects to the general context of variability and confusion about DOC.

Source of Confusion and Perplexity in the Diagnosis and Prognosis of Disorders of Consciousness

Clinical Confusion and Variability in Healthcare Practices

The first example I presented on prognostication in anoxic brain injury showed the presence of considerable variability in matters of prognostication, attitudes toward quality of life, and predicted domains of impairment. This study illustrated subjective aspects to prognosis and outcome prediction. Previous research has shown that independent of patient characteristics, physician characteristics—such as specialty and subspecialty, age, experience, religious beliefs, and practice setting—influence EOL care in the ICU (Cook et al. 1995; Randolph et al. 1997; Keenan et al. 1998; Prendergast, Claessens, and Luce 1998; Asch et al. 1999; Cook et al. 1999; Marcin et al. 1999; Rebagliato et al. 2000; Marcin et al. 2004; Rocker, Cook, and Shemie 2006). For example, a European study has shown marked geographical differences in ICU EOL practices among Northern Europe (Denmark, Finland, Ireland, Netherlands, Sweden, UK), Central Europe (Austria, Belgium, Czech Republic, Germany, Switzerland), and Southern Europe (Greece, Italy, Portugal, Spain, Turkey). In short, withdrawal and withholding of life support is more frequent in Northern Europe than in Southern Europe (Sprung et al. 2003; Ganz et al. 2006). Another study has shown that compared with different European regions, Israeli EOL care includes much less withdrawal of support and far more withholding of life support (Ganz et al. 2006). A study that investigated European physician decision making toward infants with poor neurological prognoses identified the country of practice of the physician as a strong predictor of attitudes toward EOL decision making (Rebagliato et al. 2000). Variability both across and within countries was identified. This practice and setting-related variability could affect EOL practices because we live in increasingly multicultural societies, where healthcare providers and patients can hold different nationalities and entertain distinct cultural and religious beliefs.

Specialty training and healthcare professions have also been shown to influence EOL care (Randolph et al. 1997; Rocker et al. 2004). A comparative prospective study of mortality-risk estimates in the pediatric intensive care unit (PICU) has shown that critical care attending physicians, critical care fellows, pediatric residents, and nurses differ in their predictive accuracy (Marcin et al. 1999). In this study, fellows, residents, and nurses overestimated the mean mortality in PICU compared with the estimates of attending physicians, who were both more accurate and more certain of their predictions. Another study has also demonstrated that professional experience is a significant variable in the level of certainty regarding mortality predictions in critically ill children (Marcin et al. 2004). Research has also suggested an influence of religion (having no religious background) and gender on attitudes toward EOL decision making in the neonatal ICU (Rebagliato et al. 2000).

Physician characteristics such as specialty training or practice setting do not explain all the variance in EOL decision making. Physician characteristics interact with patient characteristics, such as disease severity and level of cognitive impairment (Mink and Pollack 1992; Devictor and Nguyen 2001; Cook et al. 2003). However, non-patient-related variability, for which there is general mounting evidence, interacts with existing challenges for the delivery of EOL care, particularly for severely brain-injured patients and patients with DOC. The divergence of physician opinion and prognostication practices (Shevell, Majnemer, and Miller 1999; Parker and Shemie 2002; Andrews et al. 2005) may complicate EOL decision making and complicate consistent communication with members of the family and other healthcare professionals (Tomlinson and Brody 1988; Bowman 2000; Andrews et al. 2005). In addition, since withdrawal of life support in severe brain injury commonly leads to death, available data may be based on self-fulfilling prophecies, that is, severely brain-injured patients don't improve because life support is withdrawn (Becker et al. 2001).

Based on this current research, one can foresee that families can be exposed to physicians that present different prognoses, express various levels of certainty, and have diverging approaches to quality-of-life and EOL decision making in the context of severe brain injury and DOC. This variability merits full attention given that communication with families can affect the EOL experience and the subsequent bereavement process (Jeffrey 2005). Fluctuations of opinions about prognosis, withdrawal of life support, and EOL care in severe brain injury are inescapable in some cases. However, even if some sources of variability remain hard to tackle, others are possibly amenable to discussion. For example, concerted team approaches (Doucet, Larouche, and Melchin 2001) suggest a positive role for ongoing discussion among all those involved in the delivery of care to ensure the best standards of practice and a collaborative approach to patient care and discussion with family members. More research on patient outcomes could also be helpful for physicians who are not involved in following up on their patients once they leave the hospital.

The previous chapter shows that neuroimaging research in states of disordered consciousness may change how we view and understand the vegetative state (VS) and the MCS. This research could help improve consistency in diagnosis and provide more accuracy in prognosis by allowing physicians to better distinguish PVS from MCS and identify those MCS patients who are most likely to recover. It is important to keep in mind, however, that this outcome would likely surface where there appears to be an important gap between previous neuroscience research and current healthcare perspectives. Studies have shown that a pervasive confusion exists among healthcare providers regarding the nature and diagnosis of DOC. For example, one study found that some providers conflate PVS with brain death (Youngner et al. 1989). Such confusion has been found even among neurologists and neurosurgeons (Tomlinson 1990). Diagnostic inaccuracy of patients in VS is also high (Childs, Mercer, and Childs 1993; Andrews et al. 1996). Further, there is evidence that basic clinical tools such as the Glasgow Coma Scale, a commonly used tool to assess the level of awareness in neurological ICU patients and predict prognosis, may actually be applied inaccurately and inconsistently (Buechler et al. 1998; Crossman et al. 1998). There is even well-known variability in understanding the concept of brain death and the clinical determination of death (Mejia and Pollack 1995; Bell, Moss, and Murphy 2004; Doig et al. 2006; Hornby et al. 2006; Joffe and Anton 2006).

Hence, available data suggest that previous research and common neurological perspectives on DOC have not fully penetrated general healthcare knowledge and practice. The possible reasons for this are many: lack of general healthcare education about DOC, low prevalence of DOC, lack of exposure to this patient population, or the sheer difficulty in distinguishing DOC, especially for the nonexpert in neurological, trauma, or intensive care. In this respect, neuroimaging research could help to improve the clarity and consistency of diagnosis. However, one risk given the current situation is that well-intentioned clinical translation of research could fuel further confusion about states of disordered consciousness, leading to continued inconsistencies in diagnosis and care, including EOL decision making. Hence, a balanced clinical translation approach needs to incorporate the idea of maximizing the benefits based on the novel insights of research while tackling the existing confusions to prevent harm. This would require resources and commitment from healthcare institutions and agencies to support integrative programs, recognizing the importance of accurate diagnoses of patients and the need for consistency and clarity (and the impact of the lack of it). To my knowledge, there have been few pilot studies examining how different DOC are best explained to healthcare providers. The momentum of research in neuroimaging could be an opportunity to tackle this important underlying issue, especially with the emergence of organ donation after cardiocirculatory death (Rocker, Cook, and Shemie 2006), which brings another texture to conceptual and diagnostic clarity in severe brain injury.

Family and Public Perspectives are Vulnerable to Overinterpretations and Unrealistic Expectations

Previous chapters on public information and neuroscience innovation (chapter 5) and the media depiction of neuroimaging research on DOC (chapter 7) show that the dissemination of complex scientific and medical information is a challenge. The portrayal of Schiavo's neurological condition of PVS in the media indicates a gap between lay and expert perspectives on EOL decision making. There is a similar gap regarding fundamental aspects of the PVS, such as the interpretation of behaviors and prognoses of such patients. For example, the behavioral repertoire of a patient in a PVS like Terri Schiavo can lead to irreconcilable interpretations of specific behaviors because the use of discourse (e.g., "smiles," "laughs") to describe nonpurposeful behaviors can induce family members to believe that these are in fact purposeful and meaningful behaviors (Bernat 2004). This ambiguity and confusion yields many puzzling questions for family members. How can conscious activities of a PVS patient be ruled out by physicians? What is the evidence supporting claims that PVS patients do not feel pain and no not process language? How does new evidence from neuroimaging of DOC support or refute existing medical views about the diagnosis and recovery of PVS patients? How are sheer reflexive behaviors distinguished from truly meaningful behaviors? The challenges created by potential misunderstandings and misinterpretations of nonmeaningful behaviors of PVS patients can lead to difficulties in communication with family members and fuel a climate of mistrust toward the medical team (Fins 2005b).

The divide found in the media about Terri Schiavo's prognosis is yet another aspect of the gap between lay and expert perspectives on the PVS. Even though Schiavo's chances of recovery were practically nonexistent after years in a PVS, claims that she would or might improve or recover were frequent in media coverage. This finding is consistent with results from a study that showed that more than one-fifth of families of brain dead patients still believe in the potential recovery of their loved ones (Siminoff, Mercer, and Arnold 2003). Not surprisingly, a study has also shown that mischaracterizations of the comatose patient regarding prognosis and recovery are common in popular films. Wijdicks and collaborators have shown in an innovative study how coma was generally ill described and misinterpreted in thirty popular movies (1970–2004). Most (18/30) motion pictures represented patients who woke up, even from prolonged coma, with intact cognition; only two motion pictures provided a reasonably accurate depiction of coma (E. F. Wijdicks and C. A. Wijdicks 2006). Definitional difficulties in distinguishing different neurological disorders have also been found in an examination of the depiction of coma (2001–2005) in American newspapers (E. F. Wijdicks and M. F. Wijdicks 2006). Further, as shown in chapter 5 and elsewhere, media portrayals of neuroscience innovations include strong neurorealist interpretations, which suggest that neuroimaging is a new form of mind reading (Racine, Bar-Ilan, and Illes 2005). In general, the fundamental principles of neuroimaging research design and techniques are sporadically explained (Racine, Bar-Ilan, and Illes 2005, 2006). Therefore, the lay public may be quite confused about the diagnoses as well as the prognoses and behavioral repertoire of patients in DOC. These findings resonate with comments that Terri Schiavo was "at the centre of a political, legal, and media tempest over the removal of a feeding tube" (Weijer 2005) and that "despite media saturation and intense public interest, widespread confusion lingers regarding the diagnosis of persistent vegetative state, the judicial processes involved, and the appropriateness of the ethical framework used by those entrusted with Terri Schiavo's care" (Perry, Churchill, and Kirshner 2005).

In the media in particular, the diagnosis of PVS and the realistic description of the behavioral repertoire and prognoses of PVS patients can be loosely coupled concepts. Clarification of the diagnosis of PVS or other DOC should therefore not be assumed to lead automatically to a clear understanding of neurological prognosis, especially when, for families, emotional factors and narratives constructed about specific behaviors can prevent the acceptance of a poor neurological prognosis (Bernat 2004). Consequently, there appears to be a sizeable gap between current expert medical views and public views on DOC. These observations alone send powerful messages regarding the need for active and concerted participation of the medical and bioethics communities in broader communication efforts to expose the scientific and medical underpinnings of EOL decision making in patients in PVS (and other DOC). Current public sources of information may need supplementation to support adequate translation from a neuroscience and ethics perspective. The position statement of the American Academy of Neurology on patients lacking decision-making capacity was a welcomed step in that direction given some political and legal pressures that could have jeopardized currently accepted standards and procedures for EOL decision making for patients with DOC (Bacon, Williams, and Gordon 2007). For example, because of the turmoil provoked by the Schiavo case, some state legislators have proposed bills that challenge standard proxy decision making by introducing a default presumption in favor of sustaining treatments in patients lacking capacity unless there is clear and convincing written evidence stating otherwise.

Conclusion

The future contribution of neuroscience, particularly neuroimaging of severely ill neurological patients, may generate important results to improve patient care and to yield more accurate neurological diagnoses and prognoses. Nonetheless, such neuroscience research is likely to flourish in controversial contexts and cases. There are at least two areas that need action.

First, healthcare providers need to be better informed about DOC to minimize diagnostic errors and, if prognostic certainty cannot be achieved in some cases, convey with sensitivity and empathy the uncertainty in prognosis. Future neuroimaging research and subsequent clinical translation in this area need to take this context carefully into consideration to make a meaningful contribution to the advancement of care and ethics. Hasty comments that introduce controversial interpretations based on debatable assumptions should be systematically avoided in favor of reflecting the complexity of understanding emergent properties of the brain such as consciousness, thought, and language processing. Research on prognostication in severe brain injury and coma supports the need for ongoing research for critical neurological disorders as well as further discussion on the obstacles inhibiting consistent and concerted communication of prognosis in the severe brain injury EOL context. Specific areas needing further investigation include the causes underlying differences of prognosis and EOL decision making among healthcare providers in the acute neurological setting, the discourse used to communicate to families (and its consequences), as well as an appreciation of the impact of discourse and diagnostic methods used by physicians in acute neurological care on the family's decision-making process and the global EOL experience. Current discussions have also highlighted other challenges to prognostication in modern medicine, such as the lack of emphasis in medical texts; poor mentorship; stress and unease involved in predicting outcomes; lack of experience in making predictions; and the need to recognize limitations in accurate prognostication (Christakis 1997; Christakis and Iwashyna

1998; Christakis 1999; Christakis and Lamont 2000; Rocker and Heyland 2003).

Second, the nature of DOC is difficult to convey given the structure of clinical examinations used to assess patients and the potential confusion in the discourse used to convey the neurological interpretation of the reflexes and behavioral repertoire of these patients. The analysis of print media examples revealed that the public has been provided conflicting information about medical diagnoses and prognoses, and that statements conveying false hopes for recovery were disseminated in a general absence of adequate critical examination and background information about PVS and DOC (Racine et al. 2008). Since the media and other forms of public information can shape expectations and beliefs about health, pervasive challenges in the communication of EOL decisions for patients with DOC are likely to persist in the post-Schiavo era in the absence of greater attention to the complex and multifaceted aspect of improving communication in the PVS and EOL context. The results and analysis in this chapter strongly support the need for research into communication strategies that efficiently address common misleading messages and interpretations about standard approaches to the PVS and EOL decisions.

The translation of neuroimaging research on DOC in the clinical and public domain therefore faces preexisting challenges, such as longstanding confusion regarding these states in both the clinical and the public domains. New challenges are created by the combination of two publically misunderstood areas of neuroscience (neuroimaging and DOC). There is a strong tension here at work between, on the one hand, intuitive notions about consciousness and behavior and, on the other hand, scientific understanding and medical discourse describing consciousness and behavior. Given the staunchness with which these paradoxical perspectives have developed, clinical and research approaches will need to integrate this tension in clinical care and communication with families and other stakeholders. At this point, opposing extremes need to be avoided: the lack of integration of research in clinical care but also its hasty integration in the public domain. One recommendation made by Fins, Illes, Bernat and colleagues (2008) to ensure more transparency and rigor is that an interdisciplinary panel of experts be formed to advise and guide the translation in this area of research. These authors have proposed that such a panel "could also act as a clearinghouse of information to ensure the accuracy of press coverage as needed." I agree with this suggestion, and such a panel could even have an upstream role in ensuring a community-level review of findings before they make their way through the media and public domain. This panel or a similar body could also advise institutions and stakeholders that, although highly interesting and sometimes provocative, findings in this area need peer review and discussion before widespread interpretation and utilization takes place. A similar form of concerted and interdisciplinary mechanism could support clinical translation. In this respect, initial attempts could be documented and evaluated (e.g., pilot studies) for the greater benefit of all and for the international integration of cutting-edge research. Further, more specific consideration of issues raised by the future use of neuroimaging tools in the care of patients with DOC would also be required.

9

Social Neuroscience: A Pragmatic Epistemological and Ethical Framework for the Neuroscience of Ethics

Overview

At the beginning of this book, I mentioned the possibility that neuroscience could provide powerful insights into the mechanisms underlying moral reasoning, cooperative behavior, and emotional processes such as empathy. This area of neuroethics is sometimes called the "neuroscience of ethics" and is not necessarily viewed unanimously or without controversy as an area of neuroethics scholarship. In this chapter, I provide a quick overview of this area of neuroscience research, that is, social neuroscience. This field has prompted discussions about the impact of neuroscience on humanity, society, and human behaviors as well as about the areas of scholarship traditionally dedicated to understanding these aspects of human life (the humanities, social science, and ethics). I then present some theoretical clarification to provide an epistemological and ethical pragmatic framework based on the philosophy of emergentism. This framework yields conditions and guidance for the meaningful contribution of neuroscience to ethics. This then brings me to address some of the common concerns about the neuroscience of ethics. The pragmatic multilevel emergentist framework debunks common arguments against the introduction of neuroscience research into ethics and also addresses overstated promises. I conclude with a few remarks on the necessity to address the full impact of social neuroscience on society, warfare, and humanities scholarship.

The Ethical Implications of Social Neuroscience

I was first confronted by the promises and challenges of social neuroscience around 2000, when the Vice Dean of graduate studies of the University of

Montreal, Laurent Descarries, brought to my attention the fascinating findings of a study led by Michael Meaney, a McGill professor and researcher at the Douglas Hospital. In this landmark study published in *Science*, Meaney and his colleagues showed how hereditary traits in rats could be transmitted through generations without any genomic modification (Francis et al. 1999). Based on experimental procedures that I can't review here in detail, they managed to isolate rats with a high frequency of maternal licking and grooming and arched-back nursing and to show that the offspring of these female rats had different stress responses indicated by differential expression of genes involved in stress response (e.g., increase in hippocampal glucocorticoid reception messenger RNA). By doing so, the authors found that "the expression of genes in brain regions that regulate stress reactivity can be transmitted from one generation to the next through behaviour." Whenever a female rat with high frequency of "caring maternal" behaviors took care of pups (biologically hers or sham-adopted animals), the pups were less fearful under conditions of novelty. The authors concluded that their "findings in rats may thus be relevant in understanding the importance of early intervention programs in humans" because of the potential impact of maternal care on offspring behavior. The study also suggested a possible biological impact of contextual factors on a child's development, including the development of neurological function.

Although singling out one study or one area of research (even within social neuroscience) does not convey the full scope of its potential promises, this study is a good example of the potential contribution of neuroscience to understanding human behaviors and eventually informing approaches to deal with social behaviors and social problems. I do not by any means want to suggest that the carryover from animals to humans can be simple or that such application of neuroscience is necessarily ready despite the growing self-help literature on brain-based education and other forms of neuropolicy discussed in chapter 5. However, it is important that we recognize the potential enlightenment that neuroscience research will yield and prepare for the sound integration of this research into policies and approaches to human behavior. Meaney's research, for example, shows how neuroscience could give insights into the mechanisms that underlie reactivity to stress. His paper hints at how poverty and inequalities could have important neurological consequences. Perhaps with further research related to the development of offspring, we could start to think about how new responsibilities and new humanistic obligations are created in tackling the effects of poverty and inequalities. For example, this research suggests that some behaviors are nongenetically transferred, thereby suggesting a role of socioeconomic context in the transmission of behaviors. This new knowledge can support actions that would counterbalance the effects of deprivation; however, for the evil minded, this could also lead to the reinforcement of harmful strategies to control and manipulate social behaviors.

In the past decade, social neuroscience has flourished and its scope broadened (Cacioppo and Berntson 1992). One area where this is visible, and that I focus on in this chapter, is what is called by many the "neuroscience of ethics" (Roskies 2002), which overlaps with social neuroscience, affective neuroscience and cognitive neuroscience. This is not to say that the impetus of using brain-based knowledge to approach social questions is entirely new. Interest in the impact of neuroscience on moral decision making is actually not unprecedented. Mid-nineteenth century phrenologists were keen on extrapolating their thinking to child rearing, marriage, education and teaching, and judicial processes, as seen in chapter 5. The physician and neuroscientist Paul MacLean, best known for his theory of the "triune brain," wrote with hope in 1967: "We are beginning to understand enough about the brain and behavior to realize—with a little chagrin—that we have out-lived the time when it is fashionable to put an overriding emphasis on impersonalized basic research. I say 'chagrin' because it would seem that we have been so bent on pure research as to neglect research on such basic human problems as those concerning the brain, empathy and medical education" (MacLean 1967).

Precursors of the contemporary neuroscience of ethics can also be found in the writings of the French neurobiologist Jean-Pierre Changeux (1981, 1983) and the philosophical work of Patricia Churchland (1986) and Paul Churchland (1981) in the early eighties. Only of late, however, has the neuroscience of ethics become a concerted and structured interdisciplinary endeavor.

In chapter 1, I introduce another relevant landmark study published by Joshua Greene and other colleagues from Princeton University. They used the example of the trolley problem well known by philosopher-ethicists to illustrate how traditional moral theory poorly captured the complexity of actual moral reasoning. From a theoretical perspective, it is difficult to understand why responses to the trolley dilemma and its variants would differ based solely on traditional ethical theories (utilitarian or deonto-logical). In fact, Greene and collaborators found that these dilemmas varied systematically in the extent to which they engaged emotional pro-cessing and that these variations in emotional engagement influenced moral judgment (Greene et al. 2001). Now, after several years, multiple functional magnetic resonance imaging (fMRI) studies have examined the neuroscience of moral decision making. Table 9.1 gives an overview of some of the several dozen studies published in the peer review litera-ture in 2008 and before. These recent studies have examined, for exam-ple, brain-network differences between males and females in moral decision making and tackled how different moral theories trigger specific brain activation systems. An interdisciplinary perspective that integrates knowledge from the biological sciences to inform views on ethics is con-sistent with pragmatic naturalism and the writings of Dewey and Potter. And the investigation of the biological underpinnings of ethics is gaining momentum with increased technological capabilities and new interdisci-plinary collaborations supporting social neuroscience and the neurosci-ence of ethics.

The emergence of contemporary social neuroscience and the neurosci-ence of ethics raises questions regarding the nature of ethics (e.g., is ethics only a matter of understanding neuronal networks involved in decision making?) and the potential meaningful input of neuroscience on ethics (e.g., will this change how ethics is applied in clinical practice or how ethics is taught?). It also brings about questions concerning the potential dangers and risks of such research given the potential for misuse and dual use, and the difficulty in predicting the long-term consequences (e.g., could some individuals or groups be interested in using social neurosci-ence to manipulate behaviors and restrict the opportunities available to some human populations?). Such controversies have surrounded the appli-cation of neuroscience research to inform marketing practices. For exam-ple, neuromarketing has raised the opposition of consumer protection groups ("Emory University Asked to Halt Neuromarketing Experiments" 2003; Ruskin 2004) and the scientific community to some extent (*Econ-omist* 2002; *Nature Neuroscience* 2004). Similar reactions have shaped the ways in which neuroscience could provide lie-detection measures

(Olson 2005) based on neuroimaging studies of lying and deception (Langleben et al. 2002). These areas of research and others have also sparked discussions on how neurotechnology could be commercialized in ethically sound and socially beneficial ways (Eaton and Illes 2007), but there are many potential loopholes in existing regulations for medical devices and use of neuroscience research outside academia and publicly funded institutions.

With this background in mind, this chapter focuses on how social neuroscience research, particularly research on moral decision making (the neuroscience of ethics), holds the potential to improve our understanding of ethics but also create unprecedented challenges to the respect of persons, their autonomy, and their decision-making capacity. I first articulate a framework for thinking about the controversial relationship between neuroscience and ethics. This framework is based on pragmatic thinking and emergentist philosophies of science for which higher-order properties (e.g., mind-level properties) should not be viewed as, strictly speaking, *reducible* to the language of neuroscience (e.g., neuronal properties). Rather, mind-level properties can be partly *understood* (not reduced or explained away) by neuroscience. The fuzziness of mind-level properties (in comparison to other higher-level biological properties), however, creates challenges that have fueled philosophy of mind and the literature on the so called mind–body problem. The emergentist multi-level pragmatic framework argues for the interdisciplinary understanding of ethics and, consequently, the complementary role of disciplinary approaches (e.g., biological, anthropological, psychological, and social approaches). This builds on the interdisciplinary nature of neuroscience research itself, which spans multiple levels of biological organization, such as from biophysical properties of neurons and neurotransmission to the examination of brain-network activity. Because of the complexity of the brain (itself organized into multiple levels) and the fuzziness of the language used in describing the mind, I argue for a careful research approach and cautious interpretations.

This then paves the way to the second part of this chapter, where I tackle a number of arguments that have been put forward against the neuroscience of ethics, such as semantic dualism (mind properties cannot be understood as biological properties and are completely autonomous from more basic levels of organization), the naturalistic fallacy, and the

Table 9.1
Representative examples of fMRI research on moral decision making

Study	Sample results or conclusions
"Individual Differences in Moral Judgment Competence Influence Neural Correlates of Socio-Normative Judgments"(Prehn et al. 2008)	"Participants with lower moral judgment competence recruited the left ventromedial prefrontal cortex and the left posterior superior temporal sulcus more than participants with greater competence in this domain when identifying social norm violations. Moreover, moral judgment competence scores were inversely correlated with activity in the right dorsolateral prefrontal cortex (DLPFC) during socio-normative relative to grammatical judgments. Greater activity in right DLPFC in participants with lower moral judgment competence indicates increased recruitment of rule-based knowledge and its controlled application during socio-normative judgments. *These data support current models of the neurocognition of morality according to which both emotional and cognitive components play an important role.*"
"Gender Differences in Neural Mechanisms Underlying Moral Sensitivity" (Harenski et al. 2008)	"As predicted, females showed a stronger modulatory relationship between posterior cingulate and insula activity during picture viewing and subsequent moral ratings relative to males. Males showed a stronger modulatory relationship between inferior parietal activity and moral ratings relative to females. *These results are suggestive of gender differences in strategies utilized in moral appraisals.*"
"The Influence of Prior Record on Moral Judgment" (Kliemann et al. 2008)	"We found that subjects judged actions producing negative outcomes as more 'intentional' and more 'blameworthy' when performed by unfair competitors. Although explicit mental state evaluation was not required, moral judgments in this case were accompanied by increased activation in brain regions associated with mental state reasoning, including predominantly the right temporo-parietal junction (RTPJ). The magnitude of RTPJ activation was correlated with individual subjects' behavioral responses to unfair play in the game. *These results thus provide insight for both legal theory and moral psychology.*"
"The Neural Basis of Belief Encoding and Integration in Moral Judgment" (Young and Saxe 2008)	"*The results indicate that while the medial prefrontal cortex is recruited for processing belief valence, the temporo-parietal junction and precuneus are recruited for processing beliefs in moral judgment via two distinct component processes: (1) encoding beliefs and (2) integrating beliefs with other relevant features of the action (e.g., the outcome) for moral judgment.*"

Table 9.1
(continued)

Study	Sample results or conclusions
"An Agent Harms a Victim: A Functional Magnetic Resonance Imaging Study on Specific Moral Emotions" (Kedia et al. 2008)	"Results indicated that the three emotional conditions associated with the involvement of other, either as agent or victim (guilt, other-anger, and compassion conditions), all activated structures that have been previously associated with the Theory of Mind (ToM, the attribution of mental states to others), namely, the dorsal medial prefrontal cortex, the precuneus, and the bilateral temporo-parietal junction. Moreover, the two conditions in which both the self and other were concerned by the harmful action (guilt and other-anger conditions) recruited emotional structures (i.e., the bilateral amygdala, anterior cingulate, and basal ganglia). *These results suggest that specific moral emotions induce different neural activity depending on the extent to which they involve the self and other.*"
"The Neural Processing of Moral Sensitivity to Issues of Justice and Care" (Robertson et al. 2007)	"We demonstrate that sensitivity to moral issues is associated with activation of the polar medial prefrontal cortex, dorsal posterior cingulate cortex, and posterior superior temporal sulcus (STS). These activations suggest that moral sensitivity is related to access to knowledge unique to one's self, supported by autobiographical memory retrieval and social perspective taking. We also assessed whether sensitivity to rule-based or 'justice' moral issues versus social situational or 'care' moral issues is associated with dissociable neural processing events. Sensitivity to justice issues was associated with greater activation of the left intraparietal sulcus, whereas sensitivity to care issues was associated with greater activation of the ventral posterior cingulate cortex, ventromedial and dorsolateral prefrontal cortex, and thalamus. *These results suggest a role for access to self histories and identities and social perspectives in sensitivity to moral issues, provide neural representations of the subcomponent process of moral sensitivity originally proposed by Rest, and support differing neural information processing for the interpretive recognition of justice and care moral issues.*"

Table 9.1
(continued)

Study	Sample results or conclusions
"Selective Deficit in Personal Moral Judgment Following Damage to Ventromedial Prefrontal Cortex" (Ciaramelli et al. 2007)	"Compared to normal controls, patients were more willing to judge personal moral violations as acceptable behaviors in personal moral dilemmas, and they did so more quickly. In contrast, their performance in impersonal and non-moral dilemmas was comparable to that of controls. *These results indicate that the ventromedial prefrontal cortex is necessary to oppose personal moral violations, possibly by mediating anticipatory, self-focused, emotional reactions that may exert strong influence on moral choice and behavior.*"
"Caught in the Act: The Impact of Audience on the Neural Response to Morally and Socially Inappropriate Behavior" (Finger et al. 2006)	"In line with our hypothesis, ventrolateral (BA 47) and dorsomedial (BA 8) frontal cortex showed increased BOLD responses to moral transgressions regardless of audience and to social transgressions in the presence of an audience relative to neutral situations. *These findings are consistent with the suggestion that these regions of prefrontal cortex modify behavioral responses in response to social cues.* Greater activity was observed in left temporal-parietal junction, medial prefrontal cortex and temporal poles to moral and to a lesser extent social transgressions relative to neutral stories, regardless of audience. These regions have been implicated in the representation of the mental states of others (Theory of Mind). The presence of an audience was associated with increased left amygdala activity across all conditions."
"Affective Response to One's Own Moral Violations" (Berthoz et al. 2006)	"Consistent with our hypothesis, the amygdala was activated when participants considered stories narrating their own intentional transgression of social norms. *This result suggests the amygdala is important for affective responsiveness to moral transgressions.*"
"Neural Correlates of Regulating Negative Emotions Related to Moral Violations" (Harenski and Hamann 2006)	"Passive viewing of both picture types elicited similar activations in areas related to the processing of social and emotional content, including MPFC [medial prefrontal cortex] and amygdala. During regulation, different patterns of activation in these regions were observed for moral vs. non-moral pictures. *These results suggest that the neural correlates of regulating emotional reactions are modulated by the emotional content of stimuli, such as moral violations. In addition, the current findings suggest that some brain regions previously implicated in moral processing reflect the processing of greater social and emotional content in moral stimuli.*"

Table 9.1
(continued)

Study	Sample results or conclusions
"The Moral Affiliations of Disgust: A Functional MRI Study" (Moll et al. 2005)	"Results indicated that (a) emotional stimuli may evoke pure disgust with or without indignation, (b) these different aspects of the experience of disgust could be elicited by a set of written statements, and (c) pure disgust and indignation recruited both overlapping and distinct brain regions, mainly in the frontal and temporal lobes. *This work underscores the importance of the prefrontal and orbitofrontal cortices in moral judgment and in the automatic attribution of morality to social events.* Human disgust encompasses a variety of emotional experiences that are ingrained in frontal, temporal, and limbic networks."
"Influence of Bodily Harm on Neural Correlates of Semantic and Moral Decision-Making" (Heekeren et al. 2005)	"During moral and semantic decision-making, the presence of bodily harm resulted in faster response times (RT) and weaker activity in the temporal poles relative to trials devoid of bodily harm/violence, indicating a processing advantage and reduced processing depth for violence-related linguistic stimuli. Notably, there was no increase in activity in the amygdala and the posterior cingulate cortex (PCC) in response to trials containing bodily harm. *These findings might be a correlate of limited generation of the semantic and emotional context in the anterior temporal poles during the evaluation of actions of another agent related to violence that is made with respect to the norms and values guiding our behavior in a community.*"
"Brain Activation Associated with Evaluative Processes of Guilt and Embarrassment: An fMRI Study" (Takahashi et al. 2004)	"Both guilt and embarrassment conditions commonly activated the medial prefrontal cortex (MPFC), left posterior superior temporal sulcus (STS), and visual cortex. Compared to guilt condition, embarrassment condition produced greater activation in the right temporal cortex (anterior), bilateral hippocampus, and visual cortex. Most of these regions have been implicated in the neural substrate of social cognition or Theory of Mind (ToM). *Our results support the idea that both are self-conscious emotions, which are social emotions requiring the ability to represent the mental states of others. At the same time, our functional fMRI data are in favor of the notion that evaluative process of embarrassment might be a more complex process than that of guilt.*"

Table 9.1
(continued)

Study	Sample results or conclusions
"The Neural Bases of Cognitive Conflict and Control in Moral Judgment" (Greene et al. 2004)	"The present results indicate that brain regions associated with abstract reasoning and cognitive control (including dorsolateral prefrontal cortex and anterior cingulate cortex) are recruited to resolve difficult personal moral dilemmas in which utilitarian values require "personal" moral violations, violations that have previously been associated with increased activity in emotion-related brain regions. Several regions of frontal and parietal cortex predict intertrial differences in moral judgment behavior, exhibiting greater activity for utilitarian judgments. *We speculate that the controversy surrounding utilitarian moral philosophy reflects an underlying tension between competing subsystems in the brain.*"
"An fMRI Study of Simple Ethical Decision-Making" (Heekeren et al. 2003)	"Simple moral decisions compared to semantic decisions resulted in activation of left pSTS [posterior superior temporal sulcus] and middle temporal gyrus, bilateral temporal poles, left lateral PFC [prefrontal cortex] and bilateral vmPFC [ventromedial prefrontal cortex]. *These results suggest that pSTS and vmPFC are a common neuronal substrate of decision-making about complex ethical dilemmas, processing material evocative of moral emotions and simple ethical decision-making about scenarios devoid of violence and direct bodily harm.*"
"Functional Networks in Emotional Moral and Non-moral Social Judgments" (Moll, de Oliveira-Souza, Bramati et al. 2002)	"We found that a network comprising the medial orbitofrontal cortex, the temporal pole and the superior temporal sulcus of the left hemisphere was specifically activated by moral judgments. In contrast, judgment of emotionally evocative, but non-moral statements activated the left amygdala, lingual gyri, and the lateral orbital gyrus. *These findings provide new evidence that the orbitofrontal cortex has dedicated subregions specialized in processing specific forms of social behavior.*"
"The Neural Correlates of Moral Sensitivity: A Functional Magnetic Resonance Imaging Investigation of Basic and Moral Emotions" (Moll, de Oliveira-Souza, Eslinger et al. 2002)	"We show that both basic and moral emotions activate the amygdala, thalamus, and upper midbrain. The orbital and medial prefrontal cortex and the superior temporal sulcus are also recruited by viewing scenes evocative of moral emotions. Our results indicate that the orbital and medial sectors of the prefrontal cortex and the superior temporal sulcus region, which are critical regions for social behavior and perception, play a central role in moral appraisals. *We suggest that the automatic tagging of ordinary social events with moral values may be an important mechanism for implicit social behaviors in humans.*"

Table 9.1
(continued)

Study	Sample results or conclusions
"Frontopolar and Anterior Temporal Cortex Activation in a Moral Judgment Task: Preliminary Functional MRI Results in Normal Subjects" (Moll, Eslinger, and Oliveira-Souza 2001)	"Regions activated during moral judgment included the frontopolar cortex (FPC), medial frontal gyrus, right anterior temporal cortex, lenticular nucleus, and cerebellum. Activation of FPC and medial frontal gyrus (BA 10/46 and 9) were largely independent of emotional experience and represented the largest areas of activation. *These results concur with clinical observations assigning a critical role for the frontal poles and right anterior temporal cortex in the mediation of complex judgment processes according to moral constraints.* The FPC may work in concert with the orbitofrontal and dorsolateral cortex in the regulation of human social conduct."
"An fMRI Investigation of Emotional Engagement in Moral Judgment" (Greene et al. 2001)	"Moral dilemmas vary systematically in the extent to which they engage emotional processing and that these variations in emotional engagement influence moral judgment. *These results may shed light on some puzzling patterns in moral judgment observed by contemporary philosophers.*"

Note: Emphasis is mine to indicate conclusions drawn from the studies.

potential dangers of the neuroscience of ethics. I argue that the multilevel pragmatist and emergentist framework provides an epistemologically and ethically reasonable approach to guide the contribution of neuroscience to ethics.

Pragmatic Neuroethics and Reductionism in the Neuroscience of Ethics

The mind–body problem and the relationship between so-called mind-level properties and biological (or physical) properties have been extensively discussed in the philosophical literature. My goal here is not to try to solve the numerous philosophical quandaries in this area but to delineate a pragmatic approach that (1) highlights the potential of neuroscience to shed light on the nature of moral reasoning and other mental functions of interest and (2) captures the need to move cautiously forward in interpreting the relationship between the psychological and the biological because of the longstanding academic controversies and, more importantly, the social consequences of overinterpretations that either dismiss or overly imbue the power of neuroscience to inform ethics. Before presenting in more detail a multilevel pragmatic approach based on emergentism, I briefly consider other candidate approaches (see table 9.2).

Reductionism, Holism, and Emergentism

Reductionism

Reductionism is a philosophy stating that properties of the whole are always found among the properties of their components, and knowledge of the components is both necessary and sufficient to understand the whole (Blitz 1992). Concerning the mind–body problem, this approach supports reduction of higher-order functions to the properties of the nervous system. It is, for example, Crick's astonishing hypothesis that "you, your joys and your sorrows, your memories and your ambitions, your sense of personal identity and free will, are in fact no more than the behavior of a vast assembly of nerve cells and their associated molecules" (Crick 1995). In this eliminativist variant of reductionism, ordinary-language descriptions of psychological phenomena called folk psychology or propositional attitude psychology could be eliminated and replaced by neuroscientific explanations. Proponents of eliminitavist materialism argue that these folk psychological explanations are in fact bound to disappear to the profit of a scientific view of the world (Rorty 1965; P. M. Churchland 1981, 1989, 1995; P. S. Churchland 1986).

From an ethical point of view, the implications of a strong reductionist stance are problematic. If the self is only the "detailed behavior of a set of nerve cells" (Crick 1995), then the framing of neuroethical problems becomes difficult. Can an ethically charged notion like the concept of person really translate into neurobiological concepts? What happens to ethical concepts and principles that deal with the person and autonomy if these are to be reduced to neuronal activity? What becomes of the social and normative dimensions of the concept of person and the consideration of others as persons? The prospect of eliminating propositional attitude psychology and seeing ourselves and others only as complex neuronal organisms threatens the scope and relevance of ethical concepts. Sensitivity to ethical issues raised by neurotechnologies could be jeopardized by the replacement of ordinary (manifest image) worldview ethics with neurobiological explanations (scientific image). Proponents of reductionism may argue that this is not the case, and that the elimination of folk psychology will only bring more precise ethical concepts into our cultural landscape. For example, contenders argue that by replacing our lay conceptualization and reasoning with more scientifically warranted neural network views, we might dismiss some possibly erroneous ethical perspectives (P. M. Churchland 1989, 1995; P. S. Churchland 2002). However, precedent in the history of medicine and neuroscience suggests that the power of biomedical language is great and can have unintended consequences. The case of lobotomy, for example, illustrates both disastrous consequences and the related overenthusiastic and uncritical public portrayal of the procedure (Diefenbach et al. 1999). Engelhardt's analysis of biomedical language as descriptive and etiological and, at the same time, social and evaluative (Engelhardt 1996) further highlights this problem. Replacing ordinary views with neurobiological ones could lead to hasty attempts to discredit some moral perspectives and intuitions as being erroneous based on preliminary scientific data or by not taking into account the value-laden character of scientific and medical language, especially when the public appropriates it. Hence, one can only be skeptical of explanations that depict mind–body reductionism as a neutral and harmless process.

In addition, we must be cautious in stating that neuroscience will change the way we see ourselves, particularly ethics and ethical behaviors. By overemphasizing neuroscientific revision of folk psychology, we may devalue our ordinary insights into the ethics of neuroscientific advances. In an early discussion of the ethical implications of mind-brain philosophies, Gunther Stent provided a relevant comment on Patricia Chuchland's *Neurophilosophy*, emphasizing how strong reductionist statements can be ethically problematic (Stent 1990). If we reduce ethical concepts to neurobiological explanations, we may in fact lose the ability to take some distance and look more critically at the evolution of neuroscience. Ethical discourse is complex, and reduction of ethical language may not carry this complexity forward; this is in addition to the fact that what constitutes "ethical discourse" and the moral domain is shaped by different moral views (Racine 2008b). Could globally rejecting the relevance of neuroscience to our understanding of the self, as Stent and others have suggested, be the path to follow?

Holism and Dualism

Holism is a philosophy that espouses the whole as the basic unit of analysis because wholes are viewed as independent of their components (Blitz 1992). Therefore, according to holism, knowledge of the components is neither necessary nor sufficient to understand the whole (Blitz 1992). As with reductionism, advocates of this approach can be found in biological sciences as well as social sciences. In cognitive science, some argue that the mind can be studied independently of the brain, whereas in sociology, some defend that social facts can always be understood without studying individual psychology (Bunge 1996, 1998).

In philosophy of mind, holism translates into dualism given that the mind—considered as a whole—can be considered independent of the brain. Apart from Descartes's thesis, many contemporary philosophers have argued for a form of dualism. For example, in a classic essay, Nagel has sustained that qualitative properties are not amenable to objective scientific inquiry (Nagel 1974). Similarly, Ricoeur argued in his dialogue with neurobiologist Changeux for semantic dualism, because language used to describe oneself phenomenologically is betrayed by scientific investigation of the same language or concept (Nagel 1974; Changeux and Ricoeur 2000). Though it is not within the scope of this chapter to review differences between the various forms of dualism, when we examine more closely how holism and its dualism counterpart would approach the neuroscience of ethics, we find that some of the ethical consequences of neuroscience could be ill captured. This point was stressed by Cole-Turner in the context of pharmacology-based enhancement: "Some, of course, will argue that psychopharmacology or genetic alteration may affect the body or the brain but not the person as person, not the soul or the mind, not the self as a psychological dimension of being. . . . This view is based on some form of dualism of brain and mind or body and soul and is probably very widespread, even if its religious or philosophical antecedents have disappeared" (Cole-Turner 1998).

The opposing positions of reductionism and holism converge in their inability to fully attend to the challenges of neuroscience research because they are ill suited to realistically reflect the impact of neuroscience on ethics. Either they emphasize technical issues and threaten the value of personhood with eliminativism, or they highlight ethical issues while rejecting the possibility of a relationship between the mind and the brain.

Reductionism is conducive to the belief that folk psychology is false and will eventually be eliminated; dualism (holism) does not sufficiently consider the specific contribution of neuroscience in understanding the components of the mind-brain. Both are too restrictive in scope and perspective to frame the ethical and social challenges posed by neuroscience. This now leads to the exploration of emergentism, which can be viewed as a middle-ground position between reductionism and holism (dualism).

Emergentism

Emergentism states that some properties of wholes are not the properties of any of their components and therefore knowledge of the parts is necessary but not sufficient to understand the whole (Blitz 1992). Qualitative novel properties are possible with increasing complexity of biological organization, but these novel emergent properties of the whole are not independent of their components, as holism would suggest.

This form of scientific emergentism has been defended in philosophy of biology (Mayr 1985, 1988; Blitz 1992; Mahner and Bunge 1997), philosophy of mind (Bunge 1977a, 1977b, 1980), and more implicitly by some neuroscientists (Changeux and Dehaene 1989). For example, biological life is an emergent property of cell activity, but none of the cell's organelles are living things as such (Mahner and Bunge 1997). In the same manner, mind properties emerge from the interaction of nervous system components, but these properties do not all reduce to their components. This is in accordance with the neuroscientific hypothesis that consciousness is an integrative process stemming from synchronized activity of various brain regions. It is also consistent with the discovery of neural networking principles that indicate emergent properties of brain activity.

Accordingly, emergentism contrasts with the radical stance of holism, for which mind properties are not amenable to scientific investigation. Emergentism is more in line with the commitment of reductionism to current neuroscience research, that studying the brain is a fruitful strategy for understanding the mind and its dysfunctions. However, it also provides for an understanding that certain higher-level mind properties are part of our ontology and will not necessarily be simply eliminated by lower-order explanations. Some content of ordinary ethics language may be lost if we follow strong reductionist commitments. This potential negative consequence is brought to the foreground by emergentism, which

Table 9.2
Mind–body approaches and the neuroscience of ethics

Philosophy	Blitz (1992)		Adapted from Racine (2002)	
	Part–whole: ontology	Part–whole: epistemology	Mind–body thesis	Ethical consequences of neuroscience of ethics
Reductionism	Properties of the whole are always found among the properties of their parts—all properties are resultants.	Knowledge of the part is both necessary and sufficient to understand the whole.	Reductive monism and eliminativism: The mind does not exist because it does not reduce to its components, the activity of the nervous system. Mind concepts must be eliminated.	Neuroscience of ethics does not raise particular issues because mind-related issues are based on false folk psychology concepts. Traditional ethics language is or will be reshaped by scientific ontology. Ethics could be evacuated.
Holism	The basic unit is that of the whole—wholes are independent of parts.	Knowledge of the parts is neither necessary nor sufficient to understand the whole.	Dualism: Mind is a whole and cannot be explained or understood from its components, the activity of the nervous system.	Neuroscience of ethics does not raise particular issues because the mind is independent of the body. Respect for traditional ethical norms is maintained.
Emergentism	Some properties of wholes are not the properties of any of their parts.	Knowledge of the parts is necessary but not sufficient to understand the whole.	Emergentist monism: Understanding the activity of the components of brain systems is necessary but insufficient to understand higher-level properties of the brain.	Neuroscience of ethics could reveal the working of the mind-brain. New perspectives could be generated by the neuroscience of ethics given that the components of the brain give rise to mind-level phenomenon.

recognizes the relationship between mind and brain and views the potential impact of the neuroscience of ethics as dealing with higher-order brain properties that have some ontological standing. (By rejecting the value of neuroscience in this regard, holism neglects this issue.) Consequently, in emergentism, ethical discussion should be anchored in the interactions between mind-level descriptions and brain processes. Neither dualism nor reductionism provides the grounds to capture this feature of neuroscience. In this respect, emergentism promises to be a constructive and an insightful theoretical and interpretive framework to grasp social issues and the consequences of neuroscience.

Emergentism and the Relationship between Mind Properties and Biological Properties

Levels of Analysis (Function and Relation)
The emergentist approach recognizes the existence of multiple levels of physical, biological, and social organization that can generate emergent properties of physical, biological, or social systems. As such, this basic idea can appear simple, but it is still imprecise on how it can guide and constrain potential interpretations stemming from neuroscience, especially the neuroscience of moral behavior and personality. The framework in which the nervous system is thought to be organized—multiple levels (e.g., molecular, cellular, networks, and networks of networks)—is generally well accepted in neuroscience and has been proposed by others as a guiding principle for the modeling of cognitive function (Changeux and Dehaene 1989).

Building on the work of Bunge (1980) and Mahner and Bunge (1997), I would like to better define the notion of emergence that is at the core of emergentism as a philosophical approach. An emergent property is a property that is possessed by a system but by none of its components. An emergent property appears when interactions between components create a new feature of the system. Mahner and Bunge (1997) distinguish two forms of emergent properties: intrinsic and relational. In a biological system, an intrinsic emergent property is the property of the global system *(b)* that none of its components possesses, while a relational emergent property is a property that *(b)* acquires because *(b)* is itself part of a larger system. For example, being a living thing is an emergent intrinsic property of a cell because it is not a property of its components, like the mitochondria and the endoplasmic ribosome. However, being a predator, for instance, is a relational property that a system possesses not intrinsically but only in relationship to another biological system (Mahner and Bunge 1997). Recognizing the existence of emergent properties does not lead to the conclusion that they are mysterious, unexplainable properties like some have wrongly suggested (Kim 1996, 1998). On the contrary, it makes sense of global properties in ways that are consistent with the rest of biological inquiry. Emergent properties also exist in the social world and in social systems.

Again based on Bunge and Mahner's work, I would like to distinguish two different types of analysis: functional and relational. Analysis of function is equivalent to the understanding of the activities of a biological organ. For example, let's take an organism that I will call system B with a subsystem b (e.g., the digestive system). A functional analysis of the subsystem b would be the analysis of what b does, that is, understanding the processes that happen within this subsystem (Mahner and Bunge 1997). Relational analysis (or analysis of relational properties) involves understanding the role that a subsystem like b plays in the system B. These two types of analysis can be in fact two aspects of the same scientific goal and inquiry, but they point to different foci. Therefore, examining the process of digestion, the analysis of function (the biochemical reactions involved in the digestion of nutrients) in the stomach is not necessarily equivalent to relational analysis, trying to examine the role that the digestive system plays in the organism.

Types of Analysis (Causal and Descriptive)

In the literature, different forms of distinctions have been proposed to delineate the task of cognitive science and cognitive neuroscience. For example, inspired by computer sciences, some have proposed a distinction between the software (the mind) and the hardware (the brain) to identify two distinct levels of analysis (Pylyshyn 1985; Johnson-Laird 1988), a strategy inspired by Turing (Turing 1950). Others have distinguished computations (the computation task to be performed) from algorithms (the instructions contained in a "program") and the implementation (the physical realization of the program; Marr 1982). However, there are in fact multiple levels at which one can distinguish the analysis of system function and the understanding of the system's role. Further, based on Andy Clark's (1989) distinction between descriptive and causal cognitive sciences, I would like to propose two others types of analysis that can be performed with the function-relation distinction. Descriptive analysis attempts to describe abstractly cognitive function while a causal analysis attempts to understand the causal mechanisms underlying cognition. Causal analysis relies on the identification of mechanisms, characterizing the activities of components in a neuronal or cognitive system. Descriptive analysis models the system by generally sketching its function (the activities of a system) in a more abstract way (e.g., functional algorithms). Consequently, the ontological soundness of descriptive analysis is less well established than that of causal analysis. Both types of analysis can be relevant to understanding multiple levels of organization. One can try to understand the causal mechanisms involved in retina cell development (cellular level) or the causal mechanisms involved in visual perception (network level). Descriptive and causal analyses can be considered two different aspects, or dimensions, of a more comprehensive explanation of a system or subsystem.

Typology of Epistemological Strategies

I now propose to combine the two distinctions presented above (functional/relational and causal/descriptive) to yield a more complete overview of different epistemological strategies (see table 9.3). Based on these distinctions, four different possibilities exist. Neuroscience research can try to explain (functional-causal; FC) the processes within a subsystem like an organ or try to describe or model the processes and activities of this subsystem (functional-descriptive; FD). Research could also be interested in understanding the causal mechanisms supporting the role of a subsystem (relational-causal; RC) or describing through modeling or with the help of algorithms the role of a subsystem (relational-descriptive; RD). An example from vision research will help clarify how these distinctions can be applied. Let's take a cone cell as a subsystem of a system, the photopic system, the role of which is to produce color vision among other things. (The photopic system is itself part of a super system, the visual system, which is a network of networks.) In this case, an FC strategy could be used to understand the neurochemical activities of the action potential of the cell; an FD strategy could be used to produce an algorithm capturing

Table 9.3
Typology of epistemological strategies to understand neuronal and cognitive function

	Nature of property to understand	
Nature of research goal	Functional	Relational
Explain	Functional-causal (FC)	Relational-causal (RC)
Describe	Functional-descriptive (FD)	Relational-descriptive (RD)

an activation rule guiding the action potential of the cell; an RC strategy could be used to try to explain causally how the action potential contributes to the perception of a color; and finally, an RD strategy can generate an algorithm describing or modeling how different action potentials contribute to the perception of a color.

Emergentism and Eliminativism

I have distinguished between different emergent properties and the different strategies that can be combined to understand them. However, this does not mean that all research strategies are equally useful at different levels of biological organization. An RD strategy targeting some basic molecular processes may be too early to make any sense; while some attempts to use an FC strategy of causal mechanisms involved in higher-order cognitive processes may seem premature without an overall RC understanding of the role of a subsystem.

I want to observe that the ontological status of general descriptions is fuzzier than causal explanations because of the approximations and generalizations implied in modeling functional and relational properties. This is especially relevant regarding cognitive functions such as thought processes and psychological properties because an FC understanding of them is often limited, and an FD understanding is limited by lay descriptions based on phenomenology, self-reports, and folk psychology. This does not mean that it is impossible to understand those processes, but an FD understanding of them is contrived by the approximate folk psychological language we generally use to describe cognitive function. This has been highlighted in Dennett's pragmatism in philosophy of mind, which views commonsensical folk psychology as a useful tool in the interim of more scientific explanations of psychological processes and mind-level properties. Dennett calls this the intentional stance. In this sense, understanding ourselves and other individuals through common folk psychology is a useful, perhaps unavoidable tool, which can be refined based on neuroscience research. In other words, the uncertain nature of the ontological status of folk psychological explanations should not disqualify it as a useful first step in describing cognitive systems. Descriptions, especially descriptions of relational properties like models and algorithms, don't necessarily have the goal of describing mechanisms, but they can serve as general and sometimes approximate sketches of a system's activities and roles. Consequently, folk psychology as a strategy to describe cognitive function should not be viewed, at least in its entirety, as a nonrevisable form of understanding cognitive processes.

These clarifications should make it clear that emergentism's attitude to the mind–body problem and the relationship between psychological and biological properties is starkly different from eliminativism. Eliminativism argues that FD and RD understandings of the mind cannot rely at all on folk psychology. These understandings are so false that they will be eliminated by advances in neuroscience. The problem is that reductionism does not recognize the temporary usefulness of FD and RD explanations at any level of organization, and eliminativism is actually incoherent without the descriptive activities that researchers engage in to explain lower-level properties and relationships. Holism (dualism) is another pitfall, however, since it argues that FD and RD understandings of the mind-brain can be detached from the biology of the mind-brain, and therefore holism separates FD and RD explanations from FC and RC explanations. This point of view was argued by Fodor, who saw cognitive sciences as primarily concerned with the algorithms and computations of the mind, that is, with descriptions of its functional and relational properties, because of the multiple realizations of cognitive functions (Fodor 1974, 1975). Again, this is inconsistent with the overall intents of neuroscience research and the tenets of scientific research more generally speaking since a broader and fuller understanding of biological systems—their functional and their relational properties—is sought in this research. However, a descriptive understanding does not replace and is not necessarily eliminated by a causal explanation. Both undertakings can be useful to explain properties of biological systems, including the mind-brain. Rigid realism regarding folk psychology does not make room for further revisions based on advances in neuroscience research. Holism would be as equally narrow as eliminativism.

Implications and Limits of the Pragmatic Approach

Pragmatism has definite advantages over eliminativist materialism and holism, which translates into dualism in philosophy of mind and neuroscience. Emergentism captures the complex multilevel organization of the nervous system and argues for the role of different forms of understanding and therefore diverse epistemological strategies. Accordingly, the neuroscience of moral decision making can aim to describe more abstract relationships between biological and social systems while also investigating the causal mechanisms underlying these. Emergentism recognizes the value of neuroscience research as eliminativist materialism does but also recognizes the limits of neuroscience as it ventures into higher-order properties like moral decision making. Apart from acknowledging scientific value, the emergentist framework also emphasizes that important limitations in current neuroscience research should prevent sweeping statements about a comprehensive understanding of moral decision making. This position recognizes the complexity created by the interaction of biological and social systems involved in such cognition and behaviors as well as our limited understanding of them. In a nutshell, pragmatism promotes in general the idea that a neuroscientific understanding of moral reasoning and of most cognitive processes is possible (in principle) and should therefore bring added understanding of the mechanisms involved in moral cognition and behavior but that other forms of research and other disciplinary approaches can also shed light (perhaps even more so than neuroscience) on the nature of decision making because of the multiplicity of levels involved.

The proposed typology is also imperfect and should be viewed as a heuristic framework that makes progress possible and sets cautionary boundaries to the claims that can be made early on in the neuroscience of ethics. In particular, it highlights biological complexity and the need to understand the big picture before making statements based on a limited understanding of the biological or relational properties of a neuronal system that would erroneously suggest a comprehensive understanding of complex emergent properties. The last section of this chapter addresses some more specific challenges that have shaped the discussion on the neuroscience of ethics. Many of these arguments rely on underlying eliminativist or holistic assumptions, and I argue that emergentism brings some clarifications that help take into account challenges while allowing neuroscience to move forward in a prudential fashion.

Pragmatic Neuroethics and Arguments against the Neuroscience of Ethics

Pragmatic neuroethics as reviewed in chapter 3 is inspired by a commitment to interdisciplinary and multidimensional approaches to ethics. This was unambiguously stated by John Dewey in *Human Nature and Conduct* (1922). Such pragmatic and interdisciplinary thinking was also captured in early bioethics writings. Potter viewed bioethics as a bridge between the biological sciences and the humanities (Potter 1970), while Callahan expressed dissatisfaction with monodisciplinary and overly theoretical views on ethics (Callahan 1976). The neuroscience of ethics and social neuroscience have reinvigorated the interest (see chapter 3 on the fourth wave of naturalism in bioethics) in the biological underpinnings of moral decision making and moral behavior. Authors like Greene (2003), Cacioppo (Cacioppo et al. 2000), and Haidt (2007) have brought forward new frameworks to examine these biological underpinnings, as presented in table 9.1. Not surprisingly, the neuroscience of ethics is an increasingly active field of inquiry. However, there is still much resistance to this research, particularly to the neuroscience of ethics' potential contribution to inform practical ethics and real-world decision making. Several arguments and challenges are commonly put forward to argue against this area of neuroscience (e.g., neurological determinism, naturalistic fallacy, semantic dualism, biological reductionism, and threats to ethics). I counter-argue that based on the emergentist framework, none of these arguments are definitive and should better be viewed as both cautionary warnings and practical guideposts.

Neurological Determinism
At first glance, the contribution of neuroscience research to bioethics appears to jeopardize beliefs in free will and support forms of determinism.

Using neuroscience evidence and explanations could jeopardize our belief in free will viewed as a form of "uncaused causation" or as somehow separated from causal processes. Further, neuroscience research showing how different reactions and behaviors are based on automatic responses and neuronal processing may undermine more broadly held beliefs in human agency and responsibility (Gazzaniga 2005). Neuroscience could therefore lead us to consider notions such as free will and responsibility obsolete and worthy of elimination from a scientific point of view.

Discussions on free will and responsibility involve complex philosophical and scientific debates. Leaving aside the philosophical discussions on the metaphysics of free will, I will simply highlight here that the form of strong determinism that critics have in mind relies on a flawed understanding of the complexity of biological systems and of the different epistemological strategies of neuroscience. First, physicochemical systems could perhaps follow strong forms of determinism, but such determinism does not square with common understandings of the biological sciences (Walsh 1995). This point has been well presented by the biologist and philosopher of biology Ernst Mayr. Mayr argued that the biological sciences do not entirely comply with deterministic philosophies of science given the interaction of biological systems with their internal (physiological) and external environments (Mayr 1988). Indeed, neuronal plasticity and constant interactions between the central nervous system (CNS) and other systems contribute to the CNS's evolutionary relevance as a complex input–output information-processing system. Biological sciences, while not committing to strong forms of determinism—where general laws would explain everything, and every event could be explained and predicted from antecedent causes—can be committed to softer and more realistic models of explanation (Mahner and Bunge 1997). This view is a better fit with the existence of emergent and relational properties of the brain's systems and implies fewer metaphysical commitments to general determinism.

Second, biological systems are open and dynamic and are generally more complex than inorganic systems because of the emergent properties created by their molecular and cellular composition and organization. This is why Mayr stated that biological sciences do not yield predictive models as some of the basic physical sciences do (Mayr 1988). Most biological explanations therefore are not general laws but probabilities with several exceptions (Mayr 1985). This does not mean there is no continuity between organic and inorganic systems, since the basic principles guiding chemical reactions are the same, but the organization of biological systems is different, and distinct emergent properties are generated by their organization.

Third, the complexity of the nervous system, which surpasses all other biological systems, makes simple-minded determinism even more unlikely. The brain comprises 10^{11} neurons and 10^{14} synapses as part of a highly complex organization with emergent properties. Some neuronal processes do appear fairly mechanical even though quite complex (e.g., synaptic neurotransmitter-receptor interactions). However, higher-order properties of the brain reflect even more complexity, openness, and plasticity. Even for fairly simple signals like pain, complex nondeterministic processes in the brain are guided by reactions to internal and external stimuli. For example, downward pain modulation (pain suppression) occurs in the periaqueductal gray matter (a mesenphecalic structure in the medullar reticular formation of the brain stem). This area projects to the raphe nuclei, which contains essentially serotoninergic neurons that project to the dorsal root of the spinal cord. Serotonine acts to (1) inhibit neurons that transmit pain in ascending pathways and (2) excite enkephalinergic inhibitory interneurons (Martin 1998). This pain modulation is guided by afferent input from telencephalic and diencephalic structures of the brain and allows us to continue to function despite feeling pain. This in a nutshell means that we should not fear the implications of strong forms of reductionism (beyond the hasty reductionist claims that can be damaging as such). Most forms of strong determinism are likely based on metaphysical arguments seeking some provocative partial piece of neuroscience evidence supporting an almost ideological or religious belief in deterministic causation. For example, eliminativists are simply swayed by thinking of the brain as simple, dismissing the emergent properties conferring adaptability and openness to the brain as an adaptive biosocial organ. Neuroscience can therefore inform our thinking on moral behavior and cognition without implying strong forms of neurological determinism.

Naturalistic Fallacy

The naturalistic fallacy was first highlighted by the philosopher David Hume in 1739 in his *Treatise of Human Nature* (Hume 1975 [1739]; see also chapter 3 in this volume). Hume noticed a fallacy or at least a logical problem in deriving a statement about what ought to be from statements on what is, between the "is" and the "ought," between *descriptive* discourse and *normative* discourse. The philosopher G. E. Moore's *Principia Ethica* (1903) radicalized this distinction and sustained that "the good," the definitive ethical property, was a non-natural property, that is, a property that could not be reduced to a factual property (Moore 1971). This meant that when something was judged good in an ethical sense, the judgment could not be converted to a statement about the pleasant nature of the property because that judgment itself was susceptible to being evaluated as good or bad. The translation of the property of being good into a natural property involved a naturalistic fallacy.

Hume's historical identification of the naturalistic fallacy, and subsequent philosophical discussions highlighting the slide from an "is" to an "ought," remains a common reference in bioethics scholarship. Much of the interest in the distinction lies in preventing hasty reasoning that slides from matters of fact to value judgments, to what we should pursue as individuals and societies. Generally speaking, the identification and critique of naturalistic fallacies remains a rampart against crude forms of biology-based moral-political ideologies. Any meaningful discussion of the neuroscience of ethics, however, must start by acknowledging that radical forms of is-ought distinctions also have serious problems, such as precluding the existence of any concrete sources of the "ought." As Callahan has highlighted, "is" represents all we have, and it is clear that real-world ethical reasoning and behavior is based on real-world experiences and perspectives (Callahan 1996). If one precludes a priori sources of ethical authority such as religious revelations or revelations of reason in the form of metaphysical transcendental conditions (e.g., synthetic a priori judgments), then ethical judgments must be partly based on experience and induction. The contrary is incompatible with emergentism, and pragmatic naturalism, as a scientifically informed approach that strives to capture different disciplinary insights into the multiple levels of biological and social organization. And in this sense, Dewey was right that scholarly research can inform our views on ethical reasoning and behavior and nourish intuitions about what is ethical or not (Dewey 1922). As I highlight in chapter 3, bioethics itself has generally rejected a strong is-ought divide by acknowledging the context-sensitive nature of biomedical ethics reasoning. In this respect, moral reasoning is very similar to other forms of solution-seeking endeavors. Both an informed perspective on the circumstances of a case or ethical problem and reflection are necessary components for sound bioethics problem solving and recommendations in a pluralistic society. This is one of the reasons, in contrast to any radical is-ought divide, empirical research in bioethics is now a lively and respectable area of scholarship (Sugarman, Faden, and Weinstein 2001) and contributes to the evolution of bioethics as a form of practice distinct from normative disciplines such as theology and philosophy, which nevertheless still nourish bioethics (Andre 2002). For example, if the neuroscience of ethics (or other forms of empirical research) shows how moral reasoning is constrained and influenced by context and culture, then we need to take into account this knowledge to shape good and practical recommendations. In this sense, just like qualitative research has informed us tremendously on dying and end-of-life decision-making processes, neuroscience and moral psychology could help us further understand what moral reasoning and behavior are and how they are engaged in bioethics situations. To maximize its relevance and impact, however, the contribution of neuroscience to our empirical understanding of moral psychology will also need to interact with relevant nonbiology-based research to fully describe and explain higher-level emergent properties that involve social interactions. In sum, far from corroborating any conservative reasoning that self-advantageously deduces a preferred view on the "ought" from a specific take on the "is," the pragmatic and emergentist interpretation of neuroscience's contribution is that neuroscience can alter our implicit and explicit beliefs about how moral cognition and behavior work. The contribution of neuroscience is in this respect a welcome addition to the evolving pool of empirical bioethics research and is not inherently committed to strong forms of theoretical eliminativism. Rather, a form of revisionism based on the enrichment provided by multiple disciplinary perspectives on the mind-brain involved in moral reasoning and action is more likely. More bridging of naturally occurring real-world bioethics problems with neuroscience research (which is typically conducted in a controlled environment) could be an interesting way to test emerging neuroscience-informed insights and models of moral reasoning and behavior.

Semantic Dualism

Substance dualism, that there is, as Descartes historically described, a material substance (or *res extensa*) and a thinking substance, the mind (*res cogitans*; Descartes 1992), is an incoherent philosophical perspective that generates all kinds of philosophical puzzles (e.g., how does the mind interact with the body? how does the mind cause physical processes?). In addition, it is a doctrine that does not square with modern science and evidence from various neuroscience subdisciplines (neuropsychology, neurophysiology, neurochemistry). Old-fashioned dualism has no scientific credibility, and it is always hard to believe that a scientific mind like Descartes ever believed in it beyond its usefulness to sidetrack religious authorities from his own provocative mechanistic views of the human body. In response to the evolution of neuroscience, a version of a dualistic argument has been presented by Gunther Stent, who, like Kant, sustained that there are "two worlds." One is constructed by the laws of theoretical reason and is governed by the laws of causality; the other is constructed by the practical reason of ethics and is governed by the laws of freedom (Stent 1990). It is easy to figure out that a disguised substance dualism is at work here.

Another strange form of dualism remains vibrant in some academic headquarters, *semantic* dualism. For someone sympathetic to pragmatic naturalism and emergentism, semantic dualism is one of the most puzzling and perplexing arguments put forward against the neuroscience of ethics. There are different versions of semantic dualism, but the basic and common underlying take on this position is that the language used to describe the mind is incommensurable with the language used to describe the brain. For example, the French philosopher Ricoeur systematically argued, in his dialogue with neuroscientist Jean-Pierre Changeux, that brain properties are different from mind properties (Changeux and Ricoeur 2000). According to this phenomenology-inspired argument, use of neuroscience to explore the biological bases of the self or to further define the nature of morality confuses brain properties with mind properties (Changeux and Ricoeur 2000). Ricoeur states that we commit a semantic amalgam (*amalgame sémantique*), a kind of fallacy created by the use of semantic properties grounded in two different levels of discourse (Changeux and Ricoeur 2000). An example of this is when following colloquial neuroessentialism, we say that "the *brain* thinks" (Changeux and Ricoeur 2000). For Ricoeur, thought refers to what the body experiences phenomenologically (*corps-sujet*, or *corps propre*), while the brain is an organ of the body, the designation of which comes from objective discourse (*corps-objet*). Even the neuroscientist Michael Gazzaniga relies on a form of semantic dualism when, in *The Ethical Brain*, he maintains in the discussion of neuroscience's impact on free will that "neuroscience will never find the brain correlate of responsibility, because this is something we ascribe to humans—to people—not to brains. It is a moral value we demand of our fellow, rule-following human beings. . . . Psychiatrists and brain scientists might be able to tell us what someone's mental state is but cannot tell us (without being arbitrary) when someone has too little control to be held responsible" (Gazzaniga 2005).

Based on these examples, it is easy to imagine how semantic dualists could argue, for example, that the emotional neural networks and brain activation patterns investigated by fMRI do not have the same semantic content as when we speak of moral emotions; in one case, we are examining brain activity, while in the other, we are self-reporting phenomenological experience and using language with different semantic properties.

The basic problem with semantic dualism is that it grossly conflates epistemology with ontology. Just because we have two different bits of language about a biological (or another type of) property of a thing, it neither follows that there are two different things nor that the content describing the property does not overlap. The world is one, and beings and things exist in a physical sense, but of course our description of them can be extensively pluralistic and even include room for the narratives of beings that possess sentience and the ability to express a perspective on the world. This being said, there is no legitimate reason to transform differences in language into any doctrine of semantic dualism. Just speaking in different ways about a phenomenon does not create de facto two different things or two different properties of a single thing. Historically, philosopher Thomas Nagel presented such a form of radical dualism in his paper "What Is It Like to Be a Bat?" His argument brought out the challenge of explaining the nature of subjective experience, called "qualia" by philosophers. But there is no reason to apprehend that in principle, an understanding of subjective experience is impossible. Of course one can counter-argue that neuroscience will not reveal what it is like to be in a certain state. But this is perfectly fine if one acknowledges that neuroscience is not an ontology; it is an epistemology, an understanding of the world (not the world itself) and does not need to be committed to explaining away subjective experience but to simply trying to explain it fully and carefully in its complexity. Common sense (e.g., we communicate on the basis that there is enough experience shared in different subjective experiences to make sense of language and communication) and scholarly research (e.g., qualitative research on the experience of patients) show, for example, how strong forms of semantic dualism that stress differences between subjective and objective perspectives are wrong.

Emergentism takes a very different approach to this issue. It acknowledges, contrary to semantic dualism, that our understanding of certain mind properties can be revised based on neuroscientific evidence (Bickle 1992). Folk psychology, or so called propositional attitude psychology, can be seen as a tool, a simple and convenient practical stance, that as humans we conveniently adopt (Dennett 1981) and that can be refined to reflect the evolving scientific understanding of morality. For example, in their paper on the concept of person, Farah and Heberlein (2007) reviewed how cognitive neuroscience research could inform how the concept of person actually works and the challenges introduced by using this concept to designate human beings. Current neuroscience explanations of the concept of person may not capture the essence of such a complex ethical concept on which there are multiple perspectives, such as the concept of person. However, Farah and Heberlein's contribution has the merit of identifying some interesting challenges in clarifying the boundaries of ambiguous but frequently used concepts such as person and personhood. And if we better understand how our concept of person works, perhaps we can be more attentive to how we apply it and increase our insight into the genesis of ethical problems created by its use. In addition, current neuroscience evidence can bring bioethicists to consider aspects of moral concepts and moral reasoning that may be left unattended (e.g., the existence of separate person- and nonperson-recognition systems), even though this may have important practical implications (e.g., defining the status of persons in beginning-of-life contexts).

This being said, it is also important to realize that current neuroscience research does not capture the full description and complexity of higher-order properties that describe cognitive functions like moral reasoning and moral emotions. Most ethical constructs are defined in several ways, and it is naïve to think that one can straightforwardly examine the neuronal underpinnings of such ill-defined and socially constructed objects. But the biology of a socially constructed object is still the biology of something—something that is shaped by the environment.

Semantic dualism does have the merit of tempering reductionist interpretations in neuroscience. It also highlights the challenges in accounting for subjective experience from third-party and intersubjective perspectives. This is why I insist on the need for interdisciplinary definitions of these objects of research like moral emotions and moral reasoning. For higher-order properties, constructs are fuzzy and there is an obvious need for increased clarity. However, to clarify the nature of these properties, qualitative research and other forms of nonbiological inquiry are required to prepare the description and characterization of the neuronal aspect of such properties. Limits in capturing the phenomenological complexity of moral reasoning will temper claims to our understanding of the biology of moral reasoning.

Biological Reductionism and Eliminativism

Several years ago, some authors voiced the fear that neuroscience will reduce ethical concepts to the point of examining only their trivial components, which are theoretically and practically irrelevant (MacIntyre 1998). Others, including some philosophers and neuroscientists, have argued that typical folk psychological explanations of ethics (and many other areas of human lives) will not be reducible to lower-level explanations and will therefore be eliminated because of their inherent inaccuracy (P. S. Churchland 1986).

From a pragmatic and moderate naturalistic perspective immersed in emergentism, it is hard to imagine that nothing could be gained from neuroscience's investigation into the realm of ethics. It is true that in comparison to qualitative research, neuroscience is perhaps less equipped to approach the meaning of moral concepts and behaviors. However, this is different from saying that, in principle, nothing can be learned because neuroscience targets lower-level properties. There is a gap, a big gap, but to make this gap impossible to bridge is to bet on ignorance instead of knowledge. The emergentist approach sketched above suggests that neuroscience may have a role in bringing fresh perspectives on the description of cognitive and neuronal processes in moral decision making and behavior. If highly emotional ethical decisions were handled by different neuronal subsystems than less emotionally charged decisions, then practical ethics could benefit from including further consideration of this aspect of moral decision making (Greene et al. 2001). For example, the handling of case discussions by clinical ethicists could take explicitly into account the emotional state of patients, family members, and providers when initiating discussions (Racine 2008b). Such research could thus change our views, that is, our description of moral properties, while providing ways to concretely address and intervene in processes involved in moral decision making and behavior. Once multiple levels of biological organization are acknowledged and the potential contribution of different disciplinary perspectives are actively sought based on this premise, the antineuroscience argument cannot hold beyond sheer dogmatism.

From the same emergentist perspective, it is also clear that sweeping eliminativism cannot be held a priori. Each research endeavor will have to examine closely how different disciplinary explanations approaching multiple levels of organization will or will not fit together. The pragmatic perspective suggests that how an explanation will interact with previous explanations should be determined a posteriori. If a previous theoretical framework will be eliminated, or an alleged property explained away, this possibility should be considered openly, not become an ideology to advocate. Further, emergentism makes sense of both intrinsic and relational emergent properties that, combined, argue for the role of research endeavors that fully take into account the complexity of biological (and social) systems and avoid blunt reductionism of higher-order properties.

In sum, the progressive integration of neuroscience in bioethics will not necessarily do injustice to the nature of moral concepts if we do this well. Further, we should also not expect complete explanations of moral concepts by reductionist neuroscience in the immediate future. As long as we acknowledge a form of multilevel scientific approach, we can benefit from the progressive study of interacting biological and social systems (Bunge 1977a). In fact, more broadly speaking, any empirical examination of moral concepts and moral behavior faces the challenge of relying on a reduced predefined domain of normative behavior. In other words, what the empirical bioethics researcher considers to be relevant to study (e.g., respect of patient preferences in end-of-life care) is in part informed by a combination of implicit and explicit commitments to what is considered by the researcher to be constitutive of the moral domain (e.g., normative justification for the importance of respect for autonomy in the given example). As the neuroscience of ethics moves forward, the issue of intertheoretic reduction must be further addressed to respect the normative dimensions of bioethics and to ensure that neuroscience fits in multilevel interdisciplinary research approaches.

Threats to Ethics (Neuroscience Is Dangerous for Ethics)

Perhaps at the root of some of the arguments against the neuroscience of ethics is fear, a fear that the input of neuroscience in ethics will be dangerous. Part of the task of ethics is to create and protect academic and public spaces for dialogue to address the role of values in decisions. In the era of technologically driven biomedicine and decades of increasingly bureaucratic models of organization of care, ethics has been considered a rampart against impersonal medicine and disrespect for persons. The perspective provided by neuroscience could be viewed as reinforcing the trend of seductive overly objective and technologically driven evidence-based medicine. Would the discourse of neuroscience, embedded to some extent in the values of modern science, technology, and medicine, provide the critical resources to make room for ethics (Held 1996)? Would it narrow down ethics and make ethics a science-based process? Would the scientific methods and concepts of neuroscience risk trumping other forms of bioethics discourses and scholarship and therefore impoverish ethics (Stent 1990)? How will the neuroethics community prevent early neurorealist conclusions, as displayed in chapter 4, that neuroscience evidence is inherently more informative and powerful than research yielded by, say, social science approaches?

The risks of overly objective medicine are great and should not be minimized. Indeed, part of the role of bioethics is to help voice the concerns of persons and ensure that they are respected as persons and not simply as biological systems (Andre 2002). To do this, we need the humanities and perspectives that encapsulate the broadest sets of views on what ethics is and its impact on healthcare experiences and medical decisions.

Nonetheless, neuroscience does promise to bring new insights to ethics, and rejecting this knowledge about how ethics work cannot be done without undermining ethics in general. Ignoring how ethics work cannot be in itself an ally of moral excellence and moral praiseworthiness. Clearly, strong, sweeping reductionist interpretations of neuroscience research are not compatible with such broad perspectives. But they are not only ethically problematic; they are also scientifically mistaken because they depict ethics simplistically and attribute to higher-order properties a rigid and unrevisable description.

Even if some agreement on the interpretation of neuroscience of ethics research within academia were possible, the dangerousness of the neuroscience of ethics would likely remain beyond academia, in the public domain. As seen in chapter 5 and in previous research, neuroscience research and neurotechnological innovation are often reported in the media without attention to the limitations inherent in study designs, such as the limited number of participants and other factors influencing the external validity of results and therefore their real-world meaning and use (Racine, Bar-Ilan, and Illes 2005, 2006). In addition, emerging popular interpretations of neuroscience take the form of neuroessentialist and neurorealist beliefs that prepare the public psyche for hasty social use of results, that is, neuropolicy. There appears to be evidence from a psychological and cognitive science perspective that neuroscience explanations lead to neurorealism, that they can give an added and illegitimate sense of objectivity to poor scientific explanations (McCabe and Castel 2008; Weisberg et al. 2008). Another psychological study has shown that when deterministic neuroscience explanations of behavior are presented to volunteers, these volunteers tend to increase their unethical cheating behaviors presumably because their own sense of their capacity to act freely is undermined (Vohs and Schooler 2008). The philosopher and writer Sartre has well characterized this kind of threat to ethics based on determinism, which undermines the capacity of individuals to act differently and be responsible for their actions (Sartre 1996). It is therefore necessary that forms of nonreductionist materialism like emergentism as well as interdisciplinary perspectives permeate public discussions about the impact of the neuroscience of ethics and social behaviors. To counter reductionist and nonbenign messages, neuroethics will need to avoid disseminating forms of scientism and a technological fix that reduce our take on ethics, individuals, and society as a whole while keeping in mind the interest of neuroscience research. These are in fact some of the very ills that bioethics currently tackles in the delivery of healthcare. The neuroscience of ethics should preserve (not explain away) the moral ideals that make our individual and collective existences better. Fostering interdisciplinary perspectives upstream in research design and downstream in discussion of research are important avenues to explore. Those involved in generating research must play an active role in ensuring careful interpretation and use of their research. Those who summon neuroscience evidence to support their claims about ethics must be held accountable to the highest scientific standards.

Conclusion

This chapter reviewed some promises of social neuroscience and of the neuroscience of ethics. Insights into social behavior, emotions, altruism, and pro-social behavior could have wide-ranging implications for science and society. Some authors have suggested that neuroscience will alter fundamentally how we view ethics. Others have countered that neuroscience will not change anything in our understanding of ethics or that the neuroscience of ethics is inherently problematic because of logical fallacies or dangers posed to ethics. I argue from a pragmatist and emergentist perspective that such arguments are not definitive and that, rather, they bring qualifications to the neuroscience of ethics and the interpretation of such research. The thinking laid out in this chapter highlights the need to integrate the neuroscience of ethics in an interdisciplinary understanding of ethics based on an open-minded view about the complexity of ethics and behavior.

10

Conclusion: Neuroethics and Future Challenges for Neuroscience, Ethics, and Society

Neuroscience is fast advancing, and even though we still have much work ahead of us to improve treatment and understanding of neurological and psychiatric disorders, the time to work collaboratively toward these aims is now. Throughout this book I underscore several challenges that we face with advances in neuroscience, for example, with the evolution of social neuroscience, neuroimaging in disorders of consciousness (DOC), public understanding of neuroscience innovation, and the use of neuropharmaceuticals to enhance cognitive performance. I have tried to delineate possible approaches to deal with challenges in these areas, but much more work is undoubtedly needed to better characterize the issues at stake, recommend more specific guidance, and, importantly, assess the outcomes of any implementation of recommendations and policies to tackle these issues. It is also clear that the number of important questions to address is daunting, and it is hard to do justice to even a minority of them.

Based on the view of pragmatic neuroethics and the content of preceding chapters, I comment in this concluding chapter on a few recurring themes that are of particular relevance as neuroethics moves forward. I have chosen to make concluding remarks on three major challenges for neuroscience, ethics, and society: (1) public engagement and the divergences between lay and expert perspectives; (2) the development of nonbiological perspectives in face of emerging neuroessentialism and neuropolicy; and (3) the development of a pluralistic neuroethics within a bioethics of broader scope.

Bridging the Gap between Expert and Nonexpert Perspectives: Multidirectional Approaches

Much of what I present in chapters 5 and 8 on the public understanding of neuroscience and on the misunderstandings created by media coverage of DOC (e.g., the Terri Schiavo case) suggests that neuroscience literacy should be improved to foster a balanced understanding of neuroscience innovation. At the same time, it is inappropriate to view public communication as a collection of unidirectional processes where experts channel messages to lay publics. First, the creation of news and public information is an interactive process as such and, even in its simplest forms, involves multiple stakeholders. Second, from an ethical and pragmatic standpoint, there are broad implications of some neurotechnologies, such as neuro-stimulation, neuropharmacology, and neuroimaging. Given such broad implications, it is clear that communication and public discourse must also broaden to include the perspectives and experiences of all those concerned by the implications and consequences of neuroscience advances. This is essential because citizens and patients are experts with respect to their own experiences and lives (Racine, Bar-Ilan, and Illes 2005). Third, beyond gaps in knowledge between experts and nonexperts, there are actually more elemental questions regarding the meanings and definitions of the issues at stake. What many bioethicists call "cognitive enhancers" is viewed as a form of prescription drug misuse in public health discourses. This suggests that there could be fundamentally different takes on this issue even within academia. In the context of chronic DOC, the language and interpretations of experts (e.g., regarding the behaviors of persistent vegetative state patients) differ substantially from those of nonexperts. The same is true of views on social neuroscience and its potential to disrupt commonsensical folk psychological explanations of, for example, free will and moral decision making. Accordingly, not only are there knowledge gaps to fill between expert and nonexpert perspectives, but the nature of many areas of neuroscience research generate fundamental questions on the relationship between mind and body, culture and nature, in ways that clearly show the need to broaden current debates. Figure 10.1 captures the pragmatic idea that multiple stakeholders need to be engaged in the description of ethics questions to enrich debates and research in neuroethics. Multidirectional communication encourages genuine open dialogue and the mutual enrichment of all parties. While the accuracy of scientific information is not a trivial goal, according to this model, differences in interpretation should promote self-reflection and further discussion. Ensuring this form of pragmatic inquiry and debate is integral to science in a pluralistic democratic society (Racine, Bar-Ilan, and Illes 2005) and reflects the shared responsibility of stakeholders to participate based on their capacities. The engagement of stakeholders and the improvement of multidirectional communication processes is a colossal task. Nonetheless, everyone can participate in their capacity to such processes to foster broader and meaningful ethics dialogue. For the researcher, this can mean making efforts to respond to requests by journalists and to participate in public information and debate. For journalists, this can mean attempting to remediate some of the shortcomings of

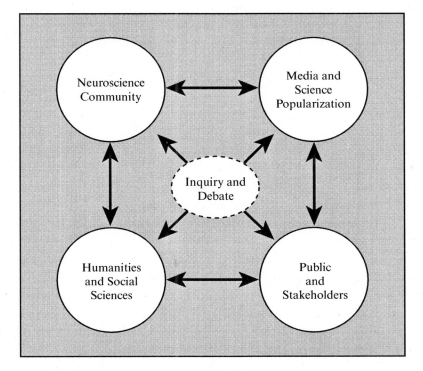

Figure 10.1
Multidirectional model of science communication in neuroscience and neuroethics.
First published in *Nature Reviews Neuroscience* (Racine, Bar-Ilan, and Illes 2005).

conventional journalism by participating in other forms of public information. For policy makers, this can signify that public consultation procedures must genuinely take into account multiple ethical perspectives. For patients and citizens, this could mean participating in public debates and refraining from uncritically accepting ethical and scientific opinions.

Advancing Nonbiomedical Research and Perspectives in Neurology and Psychiatry

In this book, I highlight many challenges related to fears that neuroscience will introduce a deterministic, mechanistic, and reductionist take on human "nature," the human individual, and human experience. A corollary to this perception is the threat that neuroscience could represent to human values by diminishing beliefs in free will and jeopardizing the integrity of fundamental views and concepts (e.g., personhood, moral reasoning, consciousness, subjective experience) used to describe and explicate what it is to be a human being. Moving beyond various conceptual issues, interventions in the brain, such as neuropharmacology-based performance enhancement, raise similar questions about the role of biological and neuroscience-based approaches to mind and behavior. Will neuroscience replace traditional means of dealing with challenges, that is, through the help of cultural traditions? For example, will the pursuit of self-discipline to improve productivity, focus, and concentration be replaced by prescription stimulants to enhance the healthy? Will self-reflection and responses of social networks sparked by the sorrow of losing a close relative be replaced by mood dampeners? The "replacement" of traditional means by biological ones would of course be a big shift and does not necessarily constitute the only way in which tradition and biological innovation can interact. (Please note that my use of the terms "tradition" and "innovation" corresponds to their Latin meaning— see chapter 4 for explanations—and neither imply that traditions are obsolete behaviors and modes of thinking nor that innovation is *creatio de novo*). Biological means based on science and technology can become part of culture as they evolve and can be integrated in ways that do not drastically disrupt or jeopardize the essence of cultures (this is the case with many forms of technological innovation). However, one of the questions sparked by the "neuroscience revolution" is whether neuroscience

will actually bring about changes that are so drastic and funda
their nature that they will jeopardize essential beliefs and thus c
shake humanistic traditions both in their content (e.g., humanism, belief
in free will and personal responsibility) and in their practice (e.g., moral
education approaches, value of work and discipline to self-achieve).

The concerns created by deterministic interpretations of neuroscience
have important historical roots intertwined with the history of neuroscience. It is important to look historically to understand attitudes and
resources that could help us today. The study of mind and behavior has
been a longstanding theater of discussion of scientific reductionism and its
implications, such as phrenology in the nineteenth century and behaviorism in the early twentieth century. But resistance to deterministic and
essentialist interpretations has also found voices historically. For example,
the British neurophysiologist and Nobel prize-winner Charles Sherrington
refused to promote the neuroessentialism that permeated academic thinking in the 1930s and 1940s. A cautious and reflective man, Sherrington
believed that, considering the knowledge of his era, essentialist interpretations of neuroscience would threaten "high culture" and human values.
Sherrington was also a writer, poet, and devoted practitioner of what is
now called the medical humanities. He articulated a vision where the mind
was the locus of human culture and morality. According to his views, the
mind–body problem was more an issue about the relationship between
culture and science (Smith 2001). Consequently, Sherrington perceived
monism and materialism as threats to the cultural legacy of the humanities. Other historical examples (e.g., Jean Pierre Flourens' battle against
phrenology; Wilder Penfield's attempts to foster interdisciplinary neuroscience approaches) should be considered to help nourish thinking about the
reductionist implications of neuroscience as well as to keep in mind the
values and resources that have promoted broader thinking. These historical examples show how neuroscientists have positively interacted with
social expectations and beliefs in the interpretation of the broader significance of their writings. (Of course "bad examples" could be found, and
there is much to learn from these too.)

The pragmatic thinking that permeates this book (and its emergentist
philosophy of neuroscience) and the corollary requirements to adopt interdisciplinary approaches and foster broad and inclusive dialogue suggest
that we need to be ambitious in attempting to understand the mind-brain

yet cautious in interpretations of what neuroscience findings mean in a broader scholarly and social context. What this means concretely is that neuroscience, because of the questions that it tackles and the complex nature of these questions, has to be an essentially interdisciplinary task. This is beginning to be reflected in neuroethics education, research, and policy activities now present in some leading professional neuroscience societies and neuroscience programs. In addition, ethical and social issues are increasingly discussed openly in basic and clinical sciences. Nonetheless, fostering broader interdisciplinary approaches that bridge basic science, clinical care, and ethics is a colossal task in need of support and resources. Some of the things we need to be doing increasingly is exposing neuroscience students to the medical humanities and social sciences; prompting discussions of neuroscience's implications in humanities and social science programs; supporting within healthcare and health services communities the role of nontraditional approaches and therapies in neurological and psychiatric care (e.g., nutrition, lifestyle); actively seeking the participation of all those involved in promoting broad and inclusive approaches; increasing support for neuroscience research and nonbiological perspectives; and listening in particular to patient narratives and the voices of caregivers through research that gathers their important voices in the understanding and treatment of the mind-brain. As such, what I suggest from a pragmatic perspective is that scholarly and social contexts matter and that consequently, we need to actively create and seek out exemplary conditions in which broad interdisciplinary approaches can take root and grow. Once exemplar practices are rooted, these can inspire others to move ahead.

Developing a Practical and Pluralistic Approach for Neuroethics in a Wider-Ranging International Bioethics

The first chapters of this book review the first years of scholarship in neuroethics and explain how this young field is already pluralistic in its objectives, methods, and approaches. At this stage of early development in particular, pluralism should be welcomed and encouraged to maintain, and even extend, the scope of perspectives on ethical, social, and legal issues generated by the evolution of neuroscience and clinical care. Pluralism also carries multiple intellectual and practical resources that are crucial to generating creative solutions by and for individuals and collectivities to handle challenges locally and collaboratively. The pragmatic view of neuroethics, which should coexist alongside other views and approaches, stresses the need for multiple theoretical and practical perspectives, the importance of empirical (especially qualitative) research to ensure that the approaches we adopt are well grounded, and taking into consideration the perspectives and experiences of stakeholders. These goals need to be pursued within an intercultural and community dialogue beyond the detrimental legacy of the "culture wars" on academia, society, and international collaboration. In conclusion, let's hope that we can envision the future where the best of ourselves can serve to improve treatment and understanding for those who suffer from illnesses of the mind-brain, and that neuroethics, along other forms of social and cultural innovation, will capture and help propel these goals forward.

References

3TU Centre for Ethics and Technology. 2007. [cited June 22, 2007]. Available from http://www.ethicsandtechnology.eu/index.php/projects/detail/neuroethics_ethical_legal_and_conceptual_aspects_of_neuroscience/

Abelson, J., P. G. Forest, J. Eyles, P. Smith, E. Martin, and J.-P. Gauvin. 2003. Deliberations about deliberative methods: Issues in the design and evaluation of public participation processes. Social Science & Medicine 57:239–251.

Ad Hoc Committee of the Harvard Medical School to Examine the Definition of Brain Death. 1968. A definition of irreversible coma. Journal of the American Medical Association 205:337–340.

Aleman, A., and M. Swart. 2008. Sex differences in neural activation to facial expressions denoting contempt and disgust. PLoS ONE 3:e3622 1-7.

Alexander, L. 1949. Medical science under dictatorship. New England Journal of Medicine 241:39–47.

American Academy of Neurology. 1989. Position of the American Academy of Neurology on certain aspects of the care and management of the persistent vegetative state patient. Neurology 39:125–126.

American Academy of Neurology. 1993. Position of the American Academy of Neurology on certain aspects of the care and management of profoundly irreversibly paralyzed patients with retained consciousness and cognition. Neurology 43:222–223.

American Congress of Rehabilitation Medicine. 1995. Recommendations for use of uniform nomenclature pertinent to patients with severe alterations in consciousness. Archives of Physical Medicine and Rehabilitation 76:205–209.

Andre, J. 2002. *Bioethics as a Practice*. Chapel Hill: University of North Carolina Press.

Andrews, K., L. Murphy, R. Munday, and C. Littlewood. 1996. Misdiagnosis of the vegetative state: Retrospective study in a rehabilitation unit. British Medical Journal 313:13–16.

Andrews, P., E. Azoulay, M. Antonelli, L. Brochard, C. Brun-Buisson, G. Dobb, J. Y. Fagon, H. Gerlach, J. Groeneveld, J. Mancebo, P. Metnitz, S. Nava, J. Pugin, M. Pinsky, P. Radermacher, C. Richard, R. Tasker, and B. Vallet. 2005. Year in review in intensive care medicine, 2004. III. Outcome, ICU organisation, scoring, quality of life, ethics, psychological problems and communication in the ICU, immunity and hemodynamics during sepsis, pediatric and neonatal critical care, experimental studies. Intensive Care Medicine 31:356–372.

Annas, G. J. 2005. "Culture of life politics" at the bedside—The case of Terri Schiavo. New England Journal of Medicine 352:1710–1715.

Anonymous. 2002. Rats turned into remote-controlled "robots." *Seattle Times*, May 2.

Anonymous. 2004. Dispatch: The mind's place of untruth. *Guardian*, December 2.

Appel, J. M. 2008. When the boss turns pusher: A proposal for employee protections in the age of cosmetic neurology. Journal of Medical Ethics 34:616–618.

Asch, D. A., K. Faber-Langendoen, J. A. Shea, and N. A. Christakis. 1999. The sequence of withdrawing life-sustaining treatment from patients. American Journal of Medicine 107:153–156.

Atkinson, T. 2002. Lifestyle drug market booming. Nature Medicine 8:909.

Austin, M. 2000. The enemy within: As science makes bold advances in researching and identifying the genes that cause disease, workplace discrimination fears grow ever more real. *Denver Post*, July 2.

Bacon, D., M. A. Williams, and J. Gordon. 2007. Position statement on laws and regulations concerning life-sustaining treatment, including artificial nutrition and hydration, for patients lacking decision-making capacity. Neurology 68: 1097–1100.

Bacon, J. 2004. Group to prove pornography is addictive. *Daily Universe*, May 12.

Baird, R. 1997. Medical ethics: Warned or harmed? Will genetic understanding of mental disorders add to their social stigma? *Guardian*, April 2.

Barch, D. M., and C. S. Carter. 2005. Amphetamine improves cognitive function in medicated individuals with schizophrenia and in healthy volunteers. Schizophrenia Research 77:43–58.

Baron, L., S. D. Shemie, J. Teitelbaum, and C. J. Doig. 2006. History, concept and controversies in the neurological determination of death. Canadian Journal of Anaesthesia 53:602–608.

Bauby, J.-D. 1997. *Le scaphandre et le papillon*. Paris: Robert Laffont.

Beauchamp, T., and J. Childress. 2001. *Principles of Biomedical Ethics*. 5th ed. Oxford: Oxford University Press.

Beaulieu, A. 2001. Voxels in the brain. Social Studies of Science 31:635-680.

Beaulieu, A. 2002. Images are not the (only) truth: Brain mapping, visual knowledge and iconoclasm. Science, Technology & Human Values 27:53–86.

Becker, K. J., A. B. Baxter, W. A. Cohen, H. M. Bybee, D. L. Tirschwell, D. W. Newell, H. R. Winn, and W. T. Longstreth. 2001. Withdrawal of support in intracerebral hemorrhage may lead to self-fulfilling prophecies. Neurology 56:766–772.

Beddington, J., C. L. Cooper, J. Field, U. Goswami, F. A. Huppert, R. Jenkins, H. S. Jones, T. B. Kirkwood, B. J. Sahakian, and S. M. Thomas. 2008. The mental wealth of nations. Nature 455:1057–1060.

Bekinschtein, T., R. Leiguarda, J. Armony, A. Owen, S. Carpintiero, J. Niklison, L. Olmos, L. Sigman, and F. Manes. 2004. Emotion processing in the minimally conscious state. Journal of Neurology, Neurosurgery, and Psychiatry 75:788.

Bell, E., and E. Racine. 2009. Enthusiasm for fMRI often overlooks its dependence on task selection and performance. American Journal of Bioethics 9:23-25.

Bell, M. D., E. Moss, and P. G. Murphy. 2004. Brainstem death testing in the UK—Time for reappraisal? British Journal of Anaesthesia 92:633–640.

Bellantoni, L. 2003. What good is a pragmatic bioethics? Journal of Medicine and Philosophy 28:615–633.

Benabid, A. L. 2007. What the future holds for deep brain stimulation. Expert Review of Medical Devices 4:895–903.

Berlin, I. 2002. *Liberty: Incorporating Four Essays on Liberty*. vol. 9. Ed. H. Hardy. Oxford, New York: Oxford University Press.

Bernat, J. 2008. *Ethical Issues in Neurology*. 3rd ed. Philadelphia, PA: Lippincott, Williams and Wilkins.

Bernat, J. L. 2004. Ethical aspects of determining and communicating prognosis in critical care. Neurocritical Care 1:107–117.

Bernat, J. L. 2006a. Chronic disorders of consciousness. Lancet 367:1181–1192.

Bernat, J. L. 2006b. The whole-brain concept of death remains optimum public policy. Journal of Law, Medicine & Ethics 34:35–43.

Bernat, J. L., and D. A. Rottenberg. 2007. Conscious awareness in PVS and MCS: The borderlands of neurology. Neurology 68:885–886.

Berthoz, S., J. Grezes, J. L. Armony, R. E. Passingham, and R. J. Dolan. 2006. Affective response to one's own moral violations. NeuroImage 31:945–950.

Bickle, J. 1992. Revisionary physicalism. Biology and Philosophy 7:411–430.

Blake, J. 2001. Magnetic appeal. New therapy that fights depression sparks a current of optimism. *Seattle Times*, March 27.

Blakeslee, S. 1996. Pulsing magnets offer new method of mapping brain. *New York Times*, May 21.

Blakeslee, S. 2004. If you have a "buy button" in your brain, what pushes it? *New York Times*, October 19.

Blitz, D. 1992. *Emergent Evolution: Qualitative Novelty and the Levels of Reality*. Boston: Kluwer Academic Press.

Bodenheimer, T. 2000. Uneasy alliance—Clinical investigators and the pharmaceutical industry. New England Journal of Medicine 342:1539–1544.

Boly, M., M. E. Faymonville, P. Peigneux, B. Lambermont, P. Damas, G. Del Fiore, C. Degueldre, G. Franck, A. Luxen, M. Lamy, G. Moonen, P. Maquet, and S. Laureys.

2004. Auditory processing in severely brain injured patients: Differences between the minimally conscious state and the persistent vegetative state. Archives of Neurology 61:233–238.

Boly, M., M. E. Faymonville, C. Schnakers, P. Peigneux, B. Lambermont, C. Phillips, P. Lancellotti, A. Luxen, M. Lamy, G. Moonen, P. Maquet, and S. Laureys. 2008. Perception of pain in the minimally conscious state with PET activation: An observational study. Lancet Neurology 7:1013–1020.

Borg, J. S., D. Lieberman, and K. A. Kiehl. 2008. Infection, incest, and iniquity: Investigating the neural correlates of disgust and morality. Journal of Cognitive Neuroscience 20:1529–1546.

Borry, P., P. Schotsmans, and K. Dierickx. 2005. The birth of the empirical turn in bioethics. Bioethics 19:49–71.

Bowman, K. W. 2000. Communication, negotiation, and mediation: Dealing with conflict in end-of-life decisions. Journal of Palliative Care 16 (Suppl): S17–S23.

Bray, C. L., K. S. Cahill, J. T. Oshier, C. S. Peden, D. W. Theriaque, T. R. Flotte, and P. W. Stacpoole. 2004. Methylphenidate does not improve cognitive function in healthy sleep-deprived young adults. Journal of Investigative Medicine 52: 192–201.

Brendel, D. H. 2006. *Healing Psychiatry: Bridging the Science/Humanism Divide.* Cambridge, MA: MIT Press.

British Medical Association. 2007. *Boosting your brainpower: Ethical aspects of cognitive enhancement.* London, UK: British Medical Association.

Bruer, J. T. 1998. The brain and child development: Time for some critical thinking. Public Health Reports 113:388–397.

Buechler, C. M., P. A. Blostein, A. Koestner, K. Hurt, M. Schaars, and J. McKernan. 1998. Variation among trauma centers' calculation of Glasgow Coma Scale score: Results of a national survey. Journal of Trauma 45:429–432.

Buford, C., and F. Allhoff. 2005. Neuroscience and metaphysics. American Journal of Bioethics 5:34–36.

Bunge, M. 1977a. Emergence and the mind. Neuroscience 2:501–509.

Bunge, M. 1977b. Levels and reduction. American Journal of Physiology 233: R75–R82.

Bunge, M. 1980. *The Mind-Body Problem: A Psychobiological Approach.* Oxford: Pergamon Press.

Bunge, M. 1996. *Finding Philosophy in Social Science.* New Haven, CT: Yale University Press.

Bunge, M. 1998. *Social Science under Debate: A Philosophical Perspective.* Toronto, Buffalo: University of Toronto Press.

Bush, S. S. 2006. Neurocognitive enhancement: Ethical considerations for an emerging subspecialty. Applied Neuropsychology 13:125–136.

Cacioppo, J. T., and G. G. Berntson. 1992. Social psychological contributions to the decade of the brain. Doctrine of multilevel analysis. American Psychologist 47:1019–1028.

Cacioppo, J. T., G. G. Berntson, J. F. Sheridan, and M. K. McClintock. 2000. Multi-level integrative analyses of human behavior: Social neuroscience and the complementing nature of social and biological approaches. Psychological Bulletin 126:829–843.

Callahan, D. 1976. Bioethics as a discipline. In *Biomedical Ethics and the Law*, ed. J. Humber and R. F. Almeder, 1–11. New York: Plenum Press.

Callahan, D. 1994. Bioethics: Private choice and common good. Hastings Center Report 24:28–31.

Callahan, D. 1996. Can nature serve as a moral guide? Hastings Center Report 26:21–22.

Callahan, D. 2005. Bioethics and the culture wars. Cambridge Quarterly of Healthcare Ethics 14:424–431.

Canadian Council for Donation and Transplantation. 2005. *Donation after cardiocirculatory death: A Canadian forum.* Edmonton, Alberta: The Canadian Council for Donation and Transplantation.

Caplan, A. L. 2003. Is better best? Scientific American (September):104–105.

Carey, B. 2005. Signs of awareness seen in brain-injured patients. *New York Times*, February 8.

Cartlidge, N. 2001. States related to or confused with coma. Journal of Neurology, Neurosurgery, and Psychiatry 71 (Suppl 1):i18–i19.

Caulfield, T. 2004. The commercialisation of medical and scientific reporting. PLoS Med 1:e38.

Center for Cognitive Neuroscience at the University of Pennsylvania. [cited June 22, 2007]. Available from http://www.neuroethics.upenn.edu/

Centre for Ethics. 2007. [cited June 22, 2007]. Available from http://www.ethics.emory.edu/content/view/396/98/

Changeux, J.-P. 1981. Les progrès des sciences du système nerveux concernent-ils les philosophes? Bulletin de la Société française de Philosophie 75:73–105.

Changeux, J.-P. 1983. *L'homme neuronal.* Paris: Hachette.

Changeux, J. P., and S. Dehaene. 1989. Neuronal models of cognitive functions. Cognition 33:63–109.

Changeux, J.-P., and P. Ricoeur. 2000. *Ce qui nous fait penser: La nature et la règle.* Paris: Odile Jacob.

Chatterjee, A. 2004. Cosmetic neurology: The controversy over enhancing movement, mentation, and mood. Neurology 63:968–974.

Childs, N. L., W. N. Mercer, and H. W. Childs. 1993. Accuracy of diagnosis of persistent vegetative state. Neurology 43:1465–1467.

Christakis, N. A. 1997. The ellipsis of prognosis in modern medical thought. Social Science & Medicine 44:301–315.

Christakis, N. A. 1999. Prognostication and bioethics. Daedalus 128:197–214.

Christakis, N. A., and T. J. Iwashyna. 1998. Attitude and self-reported practice regarding prognostication in a national sample of internists. Archives of Internal Medicine 158:2389–2395.

Christakis, N. A., and E. B. Lamont. 2000. Extent and determinants of error in doctors' prognoses in terminally ill patients: Prospective cohort study. British Medical Journal 320:469–472.

Churchland, P. M. 1981. Eliminative materialism and the propositional attitudes. Journal of Philosophy 77:67–90.

Churchland, P. M. 1989. *A Neurocomputational Perspective: The Nature of Mind and the Structure of Science*. Cambridge, MA: Bradford Books/MIT Press.

Churchland, P. M. 1995. *The Engine of Reason, the Seat of the Soul: A Philosophical Journey into the Brain*. Cambridge, MA: Bradford Books/MIT Press.

Churchland, P. S. 1986. *Neurophilosophy: Toward a Unified Science of the Mind-Brain*. Cambridge, MA: Bradford Book/MIT Press.

Churchland, P. S. 2002. *Brain-Wise: Studies in Neurophilosophy*. Cambridge, MA: MIT Press.

Ciaramelli, E., M. Muccioli, E. Ladavas, and G. di Pellegrino. 2007. Selective deficit in personal moral judgment following damage to ventromedial prefrontal cortex. Social Cognitive and Affective Neuroscience 2:84–92.

Clark, A. 1989. *Microcognition: Philosophy, Cognitive Sciences, Concepts, and Representational Changes*. Cambridge, MA: MIT Press.

Clarke, E., and L. S. Jacyna. 1987. *Nineteenth-Century Origins of Neuroscience Concepts*. Berkeley: University of California Press.

Cohen, E. 2006. Conservative bioethics and the search for wisdom. Hastings Center Report 36:44–56.

Colburn, D. 1999. The infinite brain: People used to think the brain was static and inevitably declined with age. Actually, the brain never stops changing—and we never stop learning. *Washington Post*, September 28.

Cole-Turner, R. 1998. Do Means Matter? In *Enhancing Human Traits: Ethical and Social Implications*, ed. E. Parens, 151–161. Washington, D.C.: Georgetown University Press.

Coleman, M. R., J. M. Rodd, M. H. Davis, I. S. Johnsrude, D. K. Menon, J. D. Pickard, and A. M. Owen. 2007. Do vegetative patients retain aspects of language comprehension? Evidence from fMRI. Brain 130:2494–2507.

Connor, S. 1995. The last great frontier: The brain is the ultimate enigma. *Independent*, May 21.

Connor, S. 2002. Genetic test may identify boys who will grow up to be violent. *Independent*, August 2.

Conrad, P. 2001. Genetic optimism: Framing genes and mental illness in the news. Culture, Medicine, and Psychiatry 25:225-247.

Cook, D., G. Rocker, J. Marshall, P. Sjokvist, P. Dodek, L. Griffith, A. Freitag, J. Varon, C. Bradley, M. Levy, S. Finfer, C. Hamielec, J. McMullin, B. Weaver, S. Walter, G. Guyatt; Level of Care Study Investigators, and the Canadian Critical Care Trials Group. 2003. Withdrawal of mechanical ventilation in anticipation of death in the intensive care unit. New England Journal of Medicine 349: 1123–1132.

Cook, D. J., M. Giacomini, N. Johnson, and D. Willms. 1999. Life support in the intensive care unit: A qualitative investigation of technological purposes. Canadian Critical Care Trials Group. Canadian Medical Association Journal 161:1109–1113.

Cook, D. J., G. H. Guyatt, R. Jaeschke, J. Reeve, A. Spanier, D. King, D. W. Molloy, A. Willan, and D. L. Streiner. 1995. Determinants in Canadian health care workers of the decision to withdraw life support from the critically ill. Canadian Critical Care Trials Group. Journal of the American Medical Association 273:703–708.

Coveney, C. M., B. Nerlich, and P. Martin. 2009. Modafinil in the media: Metaphors, medicalisation and the body. Social Science & Medicine 68:487–495.

Craig, D. A. 2000. Ethical language and themes in news coverage of genetic testing. Journalism and Mass Communication Quarterly 77:160-174.

Cranford, R. E. 1989. The neurologist as ethics consultant and as a member of the institutional ethics committee. Neurologic Clinics 7:697–713.

Crick, F. 1995. *The Astonishing Hypothesis: The Scientific Search for the Soul.* London: Simon & Schuster.

Crossman, J., M. Bankes, A. Bhan, and H. A. Crockard. 1998. The Glasgow Coma Score: Reliable evidence? Injury 29:435–437.

Cummins, H. J. 1997. What's on Baby's mind? Researchers studying how an infant's brain develops are intrigued by what's going on in the heads of their tiny subjects. *Star Tribune*, August 27.

Curtis, J. R. 2004. Communicating about end-of-life care with patients and families in the intensive care unit. Critical Care Clinics 20:363–380.

Dalgleish, T. 2004. The emotional brain. Nature Reviews Neuroscience 5:583–589.

Damasio, A. R. 1994. *Descartes' Error*. New Jersey: Penguin Putnam Pubs.

De Vries, R. 2005. Framing neuroethics: A sociological assessment of the neuroethical imagination. American Journal of Bioethics 5:25–27.

De Vries, R. 2007. Who will guard the guardians of neuroscience? Firing the neuroethical imagination. EMBO Reports 8:S65–S69.

December, A. 2004. Is it aging? Is it Alzheimer's? Tests will predict who is developing Alzheimer's and who will benefit most from treatment. *Boston Globe*, July 6.

Dennett, D. 1981. *Brainstorms: Philosophical Essays on Mind and Psychology*. Cambridge, MA: MIT Press.

Department of Energy. *Ethical, Legal, and Social Issues* [cited June 29, 2009]. Available from http://www.ornl.gov/sci/techresources/Human_Genome/elsi/elsi.shtml

Descartes, R. 1992 [1641]. *Méditations métaphysiques, objections et réponses, suivies de quatre lettres*. Manchecourt: GF-Flammarion.

Devictor, D. J., and D. T. Nguyen. 2001. Forgoing life-sustaining treatments: How the decision is made in French pediatric intensive care units. Critical Care Medicine 29:1356–1359.

Dewey, J. 1922. *Human Nature and Conduct: An Introduction to Social Psychology*. New York: Holt.

Di, H. B., S. M. Yu, X. C. Weng, S. Laureys, D. Yu, J. Q. Li, P. M. Qin, Y. H. Zhu, S. Z. Zhang, and Y. Z. Chen. 2007. Cerebral response to patient's own name in the vegetative and minimally conscious states. Neurology 68:895–899.

Diefenbach, G. J., D. Diefenbach, A. Baumeister, and M. West. 1999. Portrayal of lobotomy in the popular press: 1935–1960. Journal of the History of the Neurosciences 8:60–69.

DiPietro, J. A. 2000. Baby and the brain: Advances in child development. Annual Review of Public Health 21:455–471.

Dobson, R. 1997. Navigating the maps of the mind: The latest advancements in mind mapping will bring us closer to solving the age-old mysteries of the brain. *Independent*, March 9.

Doig, C. J., K. Young, J. Teitelbaum, and S. D. Shemie. 2006. Determining brain death in Canadian intensive care units. Canadian Journal of Anaesthesia 53:609–612.

Donnelley, S. 1996. Nature as reality check. Hastings Center Report 26:26–27.

Donnelley, S. 2002. Natural responsibilities. Philosophy, biology, and ethics in Ernst Mayr and Hans Jonas. Hastings Center Report 32:36–43.

Doucet, H. 2005. Imagining a neuroethics which would go further than genethics. American Journal of Bioethics 5:29–31.

Doucet, H. 2007. Anthropological challenges raised by neuroscience: Some ethical reflections. Cambridge Quarterly of Healthcare Ethics 16:219–226.

Doucet, H., J.-M. Larouche, and K. R. Melchin, eds. 2001. *Ethical Deliberation in Multiprofessional Health Care Teams*. Ottawa: University of Ottawa Press.

Downie, J., and M. Hadskis. 2005. Finding the right compass for issue-mapping in neuroimaging. American Journal of Bioethics 5:27–29.

Downie, J., and J. Marshall. 2007. Pediatric neuroimaging ethics. Cambridge Quarterly of Healthcare Ethics 16:147–160.

Dudai, Y. 2004. The neurosciences: The danger that we think that we have understood it all. In *The New Brain Sciences: Perils and Prospects*, eds. D. Rees and S. Rose, 167–180. Cambridge: Cambridge University Press.

Dumit, J. 2004. *Picturing Personhood: Brain Scans and Biomedical Identity*. Princeton: Princeton University Press.

Eaton, M. L., and J. Illes. 2007. Commercializing cognitive neurotechnology—the ethical terrain. Nature Biotechnology 25:393–397.

Economist. 2002. Open your mind. Editorial, May 25.

Eisenberg, A. 2002. What's next. Don't point, just think: The brain wave as joystick. *New York Times*, March 28.

Elias, M. 2000. Brain scans search for Alzheimer's before it strikes. *USA Today*, May 16.

Elliott, R., B. J. Sahakian, K. Matthews, A. Bannerjea, J. Rimmer, and T. W. Robbins. 1997. Effects of methylphenidate on spatial working memory and planning in healthy young adults. Psychopharmacology 131:196–206.

Emory university asked to halt neuromarketing experiments. 2003. *ActionScript* 1–5.

Engelhardt, H. T. 1996. *The Foundations of Bioethics*. 2nd ed. New York: Oxford University Press.

Eslinger, P. J., and A. R. Damasio. 1985. Severe disturbance of higher cognition after bilateral frontal lobe ablation: Patient EVR. Neurology 35:1731–1741.

Evans, J. H. 2002. *Playing God? Human Genetic Engineering and the Rationalization of Public Bioethical Debate*. Chicago: Chicago University Press.

Evenson, B. 2003. The guilty mind: What if a brain scan could catch a murderer? *National Post*, February 8.

Evers, K. 2005. Neuroethics: A philosophical challenge. American Journal of Bioethics 5:31–33.

Evers, K. 2007a. Perspectives on memory manipulation: Using beta-blockers to cure post-traumatic stress disorder. Cambridge Quarterly of Healthcare Ethics 16:138–146.

Evers, K. 2007b. Towards a philosophy for neuroethics. An informed materialist view of the brain might help to develop theoretical frameworks for applied neuroethics. EMBO Reports 8:S48–S51.

Fackelmann, K. 2001. $3 million brain scanner is new weapon in drug fight. *USA Today*, February 1.

Fagot-Largeault, A. 1987. Vers un nouveau naturalisme: Bioéthique et normalité. Prospective et Santé 40:33–38.

Fagot-Largeault, A. 1993. Normativité biologique et normativité sociale. In *Fondements naturels de l'éthique*, ed. J.-P. Changeux, 191–225. Paris: Odile Jacob.

Farah, M. J. 2002. Emerging ethical issues in neuroscience. Nature Neuroscience 5:1123–1129.

Farah, M. J. 2007. Social, legal, and ethical implications of cognitive neuroscience: "Neuroethics" for short. Journal of Cognitive Neuroscience 19:363–364.

Farah, M. J., and A. S. Heberlein. 2007. Personhood and neuroscience: Naturalizing or nihilating? American Journal of Bioethics 7:37–48.

Farah, M. J., J. Illes, R. Cook-Deegan, H. Gardner, E. Kandel, P. King, E. Parens, B. Sahakian, and P. R. Wolpe. 2004. Neurocognitive enhancement: What can we do and what should we do? Nature Reviews Neuroscience 5:421–425.

Farah, M. J., and P. R. Wolpe. 2004. Monitoring and manipulating brain function: New neuroscience technologies and their ethical implications. Hastings Center Report 34:35–45.

Farah, M. J., and P. Wolpe. 2004. Neuroethics: Toward broader discussion (author reply). Hastings Center Report 34:4–5.

Finger, E. C., A. A. Marsh, N. Kamel, D. G. Mitchell, and J. R. Blair. 2006. Caught in the act: The impact of audience on the neural response to morally and socially inappropriate behavior. NeuroImage 33:414–421.

Fins, J. J. 2000. A proposed ethical framework for international cognitive neuroscience: A consideration of deep brain stimulation in impaired consciousness. Neurological Research 22:273–278.

Fins, J. J. 2003. Constructing an ethical stereotaxy for severe brain injury: Balancing risks, benefits and access. Nature Reviews Neuroscience 4:323–327.

Fins, J. J. 2005a. Clinical pragmatism and the care of brain damaged patients: Toward a palliative neuroethics for disorders of consciousness. Progress in Brain Research 150:565–582.

Fins, J. J. 2005b. Rethinking disorders of consciousness: New research and its implications. Hastings Center Report 35:22–24.

Fins, J. J. 2008a. A leg to stand on: Sir William Osler and Wilder Penfield's "Neuroethics." American Journal of Bioethics 8:37–46.

Fins, J. J. 2008b. Neuroethics and neuroimaging: Moving toward transparency. American Journal of Bioethics 8:46–52.

Fins, J. J., M. D. Bacchetta, and F. G. Miller. 1997. Clinical pragmatism: A method of moral problem solving. Kennedy Institute of Ethics Journal 7:129–145.

Fins, J. J., and J. Illes. 2008. Lights, camera, inaction? Neuroimaging and disorders of consciousness. American Journal of Bioethics 8:W1–W3.

Fins, J. J., J. Illes, J. L. Bernat, J. Hirsch, S. Laureys, and E. Murphy. 2008. Neuroimaging and disorders of consciousness: Envisioning an ethical research agenda. American Journal of Bioethics 8:3–12.

Fins, J. J., A. R. Rezai, and B. D. Greenberg. 2006. Psychosurgery: Avoiding an ethical redux while advancing a therapeutic future. Neurosurgery 59:713–716.

Fins, J. J., and N. D. Schiff. 2006. Shades of gray: New insights into the vegetative state. Hastings Center Report 36:8.

Firn, D. 2003. University wins go-ahead for animal test lab. *Financial Times* (North American Edition), November 22.

Fishkin, J. S. 1991. *Democracy and Deliberation: New Directions for Democratic Reform*. New Haven, CT: Yale University Press.

Fixmer, R. 1999. The soul of the next new machine: Humans; how the wedding of brain and computer could change the universe. *New York Times*, November 6.

Flower, R. 2004. Lifestyle drugs: Pharmacology and the social agenda. Trends in Pharmacological Sciences 25:182–185.

Fodor, J. 1974. Special sciences. Synthese 28:97–115.

Fodor, J. 1975. *The Language of Thought*. Cambridge, MA: Harvard University Press.

Foreman, J. 2004. Answers to alcoholism become clearer: Both environment and genetics to play significant roles in the risk of developing the disease. *Star Tribune*, October 24.

Fowler, L. F. 1855. *Familiar Lessons on Astronomy: Designed for the Use of Children and Youth in Schools and Families*. New York: Fowler & Wells.

Fraix, V., J. L. Houeto, C. Lagrange, C. Le Pen, P. Krystkowiak, D. Guehl, C. Ardouin, M. L. Welter, F. Maurel, L. Defebvre, A. Rougier, A. L. Benabid, V. Mesnage, M. Ligier, S. Blond, P. Burbaud, B. Bioulac, A. Destée, P. Cornu, P. Pollak; SPARK Study Group. 2006. Clinical and economic results of bilateral subthalamic nucleus stimulation in Parkinson's disease. Journal of Neurology, Neurosurgery, and Psychiatry 77:443–449.

Francis, D., J. Diorio, D. Liu, and M. J. Meaney. 1999. Nongenomic transmission across generations of maternal behavior and stress responses in the rat. Science 286:1155–1158.

Freundlich, N. 2004. Genetic predictions: Just swab away. *New York Times*, March 21.

Friedman, L. S., and E. D. Richter. 2004. Relationship between conflicts of interest and research results. Journal of General Internal Medicine 19:51–56.

Fuchs, T. 2006. Ethical issues in neuroscience. Current Opinion in Psychiatry 19:600–607.

Fukushi, T., O. Sakura, and H. Koizumi. 2007. Ethical considerations of neuroscience research: The perspectives on neuroethics in Japan. Neuroscience Research 57:10–16.

Ganz, F. D., J. Benbenishty, M. Hersch, A. Fischer, G. Gurman, and C. L. Sprung. 2006. The impact of regional culture on intensive care end of life decision making: An Israeli perspective from the ETHICUS study. Journal of Medical Ethics 32:196–199.

Garreau, J. 2006. "Smart pills" are on the rise. But is taking them wise? *Washington Post*, June 11.

Garros, D., R. J. Rosychuk, and P. N. Cox. 2003. Circumstances surrounding end of life in a pediatric intensive care unit. Pediatrics 112:e371.

Gazzaniga, M. S. 2005. *The Ethical Brain*. New York: Dana Press.

Giacino, J. T., S. Ashwal, N. Childs, R. Cranford, B. Jennett, D. I. Katz, J. P. Kelly, J. H. Rosenberg, J. Whyte, R. D. Zafonte, and N. D. Zasler. 2002. The minimally conscious state: Definition and diagnostic criteria. Neurology 58:349–353.

Gill-Thwaites, H. 2006. Lotteries, loopholes and luck: Misdiagnosis in the vegetative state patient. Brain Injury 20:1321–1328.

Giridharadas, A. 2008. India's novel use of brain scans in courts is debated. *New York Times*, September 14.

Glannon, W. 2006a. Neuroethics. Bioethics 20:37–52.

Glannon, W. 2006b. Psychopharmacology and memory. Journal of Medical Ethics 32:74–78.

Glannon, W. 2007. *Bioethics and the Brain*. New York: Oxford University Press.

Goggin, M. L., and W. A. Blanpied, eds. 1986. *Governing Science and Technology in a Democracy*. Knoxville: University of Tennessee Press.

Goldberg, C. 2003. Brain imaging poses questions of privacy. *Milwaukee Journal Sentinel*, May 18.

Gostin, L. O. 1980. Ethical considerations of psychosurgery: The unhappy legacy of the prefrontal lobotomy. Journal of Medical Ethics 6:149–154.

Government Office for Science. 2008. Foresight Mental Capital and Wellbeing Project (2008). Final Project report—Executive Summary. London: Government Office for Science.

Graff Low, K., and A. E. Gendaszek. 2002. Illicit use of psychostimulants among college students: A preliminary study. Psychology Health and Medicine 7:283–287.

Gray, J. R., and P. M. Thompson. 2004. Neurobiology of intelligence: Science and ethics. Nature Reviews Neuroscience 5:471–482.

Greely, H. 2007. On neuroethics. Science 318:533.

Greely, H., B. Sahakian, J. Harris, R. C. Kessler, M. Gazzaniga, P. Campbell, and M. J. Farah. 2008. Towards responsible use of cognitive-enhancing drugs by the healthy. Nature 456:702–705.

Greely, H. T., and J. Illes. 2007. Neuroscience-based lie detection: The urgent need for regulation. American Journal of Law & Medicine 33:377–431.

Greenberg, B. D. 2002. Update on deep brain stimulation. Journal of Electroconvulsive Therapy 18:193–196.

Greenberg, D. L. 2007. Comment on "Detecting awareness in the vegetative state." Science 315:1221.

Greene, J. D. 2003. From neural "is" to moral "ought": What are the moral implications of neuroscientific moral psychology? Nature Reviews Neuroscience 4:847–850.

Greene, J. D., L. E. Nystrom, A. D. Engell, J. M. Darley, and J. D. Cohen. 2004. The neural bases of cognitive conflict and control in moral judgment. Neuron 44:389–400.

Greene, J. D., R. B. Sommerville, L. E. Nystrom, J. M. Darley, and J. D. Cohen. 2001. An fMRI investigation of emotional engagement in moral judgment. Science 293:2105–2108.

Griffiths, K. 2001. About-turn on genetic testing: Insurers agree on five-year ban on demands for DNA profiles. *Independent*, October 27.

Gura, T. 2005. Educational Research: Big plans for little brains. Nature 435:1156–1158.

Gutmann, A., and D. Thompson. 1997. Deliberating about Bioethics. Hastings Center Report 27:38–41.

Habermas, J. 1968. *Technik und Wissenschaft als "Ideologie."* Frankfurt am Main: Suhrkamp.

Habermas, J. 1991. *Moral Consciousness and Communicative Action.* Cambridge, MA: MIT Press.

Habermas, J. 1997. *Between Facts and Norms: Contributions to a Discourse Theory of Law and Democracy.* Translated by W. Rehg. Cambridge: MIT Press.

Habermas, J. 1999. *De l'éthique de la discussion.* Paris: Flammarion.

Haidt, J. 2007. The new synthesis in moral psychology. Science 316:998–1002.

Hall, K. M., M. M. Irwin, K. A. Bowman, W. Frankenberger, and D. C. Jewett. 2005. Illicit use of prescribed stimulant medication among college students. Journal of American College Health 53:167–174.

Hall, S. S. 1998. The scientific method: Test-tube moms. *New York Times,* April 5.

Hall, S. S. 1999. Journey to the center of my mind. *New York Times,* June 6.

Hamani, C., M. P. McAndrews, M. Cohn, M. Oh, D. Zumsteg, C. M. Shapiro, R. A. Wennberg, and A. M. Lozano. 2008. Memory enhancement induced by hypothalamic/fornix deep brain stimulation. Annals of Neurology 63:119–123.

Hammes, B. J., J. Klevan, M. Kempf, and M. S. Williams. 2005. Pediatric advance care planning. Journal of Palliative Medicine 8:766–773.

Harada, T., S. Itakura, F. Xu, K. Lee, S. Nakashita, D. N. Saito, and N. Sadato. 2009. Neural correlates of the judgment of lying: A functional magnetic resonance imaging study. Neuroscience Research 63:24–34.

Harenski, C. L., O. Antonenko, M. S. Shane, and K. A. Kiehl. 2008. Gender differences in neural mechanisms underlying moral sensitivity. Social Cognitive and Affective Neuroscience 3:313–321.

Harenski, C. L., and S. Hamann. 2006. Neural correlates of regulating negative emotions related to moral violations. NeuroImage 30:313–324.

Harris, J. 1992. *Wonderwoman and Superman: Ethics and Human Biotechnology.* Oxford: Oxford University Press.

Harris, J. 2007. *Enhancing Evolution: The Ethical Case for Making Better People.* Princeton: Princeton University Press.

Hawkes, N. 2002. Only 1 in 20 has "pacemaker" to still Parkinson's tremors. Times (London), March 26.

Heekeren, H. R., I. Wartenburger, H. Schmidt, K. Prehn, H. P. Schwintowski, and A. Villringer. 2005. Influence of bodily harm on neural correlates of semantic and moral decision-making. NeuroImage 24:887–897.

Heekeren, H. R., I. Wartenburger, H. Schmidt, H. P. Schwintowski, and A. Villringer. 2003. An fMRI study of simple ethical decision-making. Neuroreport 14:1215–1219.

Held, V. 1996. Whose agenda? Ethics versus cognitive science. In *Mind and Morals: Essays on Ethics and Cognitive Science*, ed. M. F. Larry May, 69–87. Cambridge, MA: MIT Press.

Hellmore, E. 1998. She thinks she believes in God. In fact, it's just chemical reactions taking place in the neurons of her temporal lobes: Science has gone in search of the soul. *Observer*, May 3.

Hewitt, J. 2002. Psycho-affective disorder in intensive care units: A review. Journal of Clinical Nursing 11:575–584.

Hickie, I. 2004. Can we reduce the burden of depression? The Australian experience with beyondblue: The national depression initiative. Australasian Psychiatry 12 (Suppl):S38–S46.

Hirsch, J. 2005. Raising consciousness. Journal of Clinical Investigation 115:1102.

Hollon, M. F. 2004. Direct-to-consumer marketing of prescription drugs: A current perspective for neurologists and psychiatrists. CNS Drugs 18:69–77.

Hopkin, M. 2006. "Vegetative" patient shows signs of conscious thought. Nature 443:132–133.

Hornby, K., S. D. Shemie, J. Teitelbaum, and C. Doig. 2006. Variability in hospital-based brain death guidelines in Canada. Canadian Journal of Anaesthesia 53: 613–619.

Hsu, M., C. Anen, and S. R. Quartz. 2008. The right and the good: Distributive justice and neural encoding of equity and efficiency. Science 320:1092–1095.

Huber, G., ed. 1996. *Cerveau et psychisme humains: quelle éthique? Collection Éthique et Sciences*. Paris: John Libbey Eurotext.

Hulette, C. 2003. Brain banking in the United States. Journal of Neuropathology and Experimental Neurology 62:715–722.

Hume, D. 1975 [1739]. *A Treatise of Human Nature*. Oxford: Clarendon Press.

Hunter, J. D. 1992. *Culture Wars: The Struggle to Define America*. New York: Basic Books.

Illes, J. 2004a. A fish story: Brain maps, lie detection and personhood. Cerebrum 6:73–80.

Illes, J. 2004b. Medical Imaging: A hub for the new field of neuroethics. Academic Radiology 11:721–723.

Illes, J. 2007a. Empirical neuroethics. Can brain imaging visualize human thought? Why is neuroethics interested in such a possibility? EMBO Reports 8:S57–S60.

Illes, J. 2007b. Ipsa scientia potestas est (knowledge is power). American Journal of Bioethics 7:1–2.

Illes, J. 2008. Brain screening and incidental findings: Flocking to folly? Lancet Neurology 7:23–24.

Illes, J., ed. 2006. *Neuroethics: Defining the Issues in Theory, Practice, and Policy.* Oxford: Oxford University Press.

Illes, J., and S. J. Bird. 2006. Neuroethics: A modern context for ethics in neuroscience. Trends in Neurosciences 29:511–517.

Illes, J., J. E. Desmond, L. F. Huang, T. A. Raffin, and S. W. Atlas. 2002. Ethical and practical considerations in managing incidental findings in functional magnetic resonance imaging. Brain and Cognition 50:358–365.

Illes, J., E. Fan, B. Koenig, T. A. Raffin, D. Kann, and S. W. Atlas. 2003. Self-referred whole-body CT imaging: Current implications for health care consumers. Radiology 228:346–351.

Illes, J., and M. Kirschen. 2003. New prospects and ethical challenges for neuroimaging within and outside the health care system. AJNR. American Journal of Neuroradiology 24:1932–1934.

Illes, J., M. P. Kirschen, and J. D. Gabrieli. 2003. From neuroimaging to neuroethics. Nature Neuroscience 6:205.

Illes, J., and E. Racine. 2005a. Imaging or imagining? A neuroethics challenge informed by genetics. American Journal of Bioethics 5:5–18.

Illes, J., and E. Racine. 2005b. Neuroethics: A dialogue on a continuum from tradition to innovation. American Journal of Bioethics 5:W3-4.

Illes, J., and E. Racine. 2007. Neuroethics: From neurotechnology to healthcare. Cambridge Quarterly of Healthcare Ethics 16:125–128.

Illes, J., E. Racine, and M. Kirschen. 2006. A picture is worth a thousand words, but which one thousand? In *Neuroethics: Defining the Issues in Research, Practice and Policy*, ed. J. Illes, 149–168. Oxford: Oxford University Press.

Illes, J., and T. A. Raffin. 2002. Neuroethics: An emerging new discipline in the study of brain and cognition. Brain and Cognition 50:341–344.

Illes, J., A. Rosen, M. Greicius, and E. Racine. 2007. Prospects for prediction: Ethics analysis of neuroimaging in Alzheimer's disease. Annals of the New York Academy of Sciences 1097:278–295.

Jansen, L. A. 1998. Assessing clinical pragmatism. Kennedy Institute of Ethics Journal 8:23–36.

Jeffrey, D. 2005. *Patient-Centred Ethics and Communication at the End of Life.* Oxford: Radcliffe Publishing.

Jennett, B., and F. Plum. 1972. Persistent vegetative state after brain damage. A syndrome in search of a name. Lancet 299:734–737.

Jennings, B. 1990. Bioethics and Democracy. Centennial Review 34:207–225.

Joffe, A. R., and N. Anton. 2006. Brain death: Understanding of the conceptual basis by pediatric intensivists in Canada. Archives of Pediatrics & Adolescent Medicine 160:747–752.

Johannes Gutenberg-University of Mainz. 2007. [cited June 22, 2007]. Available from http://www.neuroethik.ifzn.uni-mainz.de/index.php?L=1

Johnson, D. 2008. How do you know unless you look?: Brain imaging, biopower and practical neuroscience. Journal of Medical Humanities 29:147–161.

Johnson, N., D. Cook, M. Giacomini, and D. Willms. 2000. Towards a "good" death: End-of-life narratives constructed in an intensive care unit. Culture, Medicine and Psychiatry 24:275–295.

Johnson-Laird, P. N. 1988. *The Computer and the Brain: An Introduction to Cognitive Science*. Cambridge, MA: Harvard University Press.

Johnston, S. C. 2000. Prognostication matters. Muscle & Nerve 23:839–842.

Jones, D. G. 2008. Neuroethics: Adrift from a clinical base. American Journal of Bioethics 8:49–50.

Jonsen, A. R. 2008. Encephaloethics: A history of the ethics of the brain. American Journal of Bioethics 8:37–42.

Jonsen, A. R., M. Siegler, and W. T. Winslade. 1998. *Clinical Ethics: A Practical Approach to Ethical Decision in Clinical Medicine*. 4th ed. New York: McGraw Hill.

Joss, S., and J. Durant, eds. 1995. *Public Participation in Science: The Role of Consensus Conference in Europe*. London: Science Museum with the support of the European Commission Directorate General XII.

Kandel, E. R. 1998. A new intellectual framework for psychiatry. American Journal of Psychiatry 155:457–469.

Kant, I. 2002 [1785]. *Groundwork for the Metaphysics of Morals*, Translated by A. Zweig, Edited by T. E. Hill, Jr. and A. Zweig. Oxford, New York: Oxford University Press.

Katzman, G. L., A. P. Dagher, and N. J. Patronas. 1999. Incidental findings on brain magnetic resonance imaging from 1000 asymptomatic volunteers. Journal of the American Medical Association 282:36–39.

Kédia, G., S. Berthoz, M. Wessa, D. Hilton, and J. L. Martinot. 2008. An agent harms a victim: A functional magnetic resonance imaging study on specific moral emotions. Journal of Cognitive Neuroscience 20:1788–1798.

Keenan, S. P., K. D. Busche, L. M. Chen, R. Esmail, K. J. Inman, and W. J. Sibbald. 1998. Withdrawal and withholding of life support in the intensive care unit: A comparison of teaching and community hospitals. The Southwestern Ontario Critical Care Research Network. Critical Care Medicine 26:245–251.

Kennedy, D. 2005. Neuroimaging: Revolutionary research tool or a post-modern phrenology? American Journal of Bioethics 5:19.

Khan, M. 2003. Study drugs draw concern. *Miami Herald*, July 6.

Kim, B. S., J. Illes, R. T. Kaplan, A. Reiss, and S. W. Atlas. 2002. Incidental findings on pediatric MR images of the brain. AJNR. American Journal of Neuroradiology 23:1674–1677.

Kim, J. 1996. *Philosophy of Mind*. Boulder, CO: Westview Press.

Kim, J. 1998. *Mind in a Physical World: An Essay on the Mind-Body Problem*. Cambridge, MA: MIT Press.

Kliemann, D., L. Young, J. Scholz, and R. Saxe. 2008. The influence of prior record on moral judgment. Neuropsychologia 46:2949–2957.

Koehler, P. J., and E. F. Wijdicks. 2008. Historical study of coma: Looking back through medical and neurological texts. Brain 131:877–889.

Kopell, B. H., B. Greenberg, and A. R. Rezai. 2004. Deep brain stimulation for psychiatric disorders. Journal of Clinical Neurophysiology 21:51–67.

Kramer, P. D. 2000. The valorization of sadness. Hastings Center Report 30:13–18.

Krämer, U. M., H. Jansma, C. Tempelmann, and T. F. Munte. 2007. Tit-for-tat: The neural basis of reactive aggression. NeuroImage 38:203–211.

Krimsky, S., L. S. Rothenberg, P. Stott, and G. Kyle. 1996. Financial interests of authors in scientific journals: A pilot study of 14 publications. Science and Engineering Ethics 2:395–410.

Kua, E., M. Reder, and M. J. Grossel. 2004. Science in the news: A study of reporting genomics. Public Understanding of Science (Bristol, England) 13:309–322.

Kubu, C. S., and P. J. Ford. 2007. Ethics in the clinical application of neural implants. Cambridge Quarterly of Healthcare Ethics 16:317–321.

Kuehn, B. M. 2007. Scientists probe deep brain stimulation: Some promise for brain injury, psychiatric illness. Journal of the American Medical Association 298:2249–2251.

Kulynych, J. 2002. Legal and ethical issues in neuroimaging research: Human subjects protection, medical privacy, and the public communication of research results. Brain and Cognition 50:345–357.

Lamb, G. M. 2004. Strange food for thought: The brain-gain revolution is already under way. But will these "neural enhancement" drugs turn us into Einsteins or Frankensteins? *Christian Science Monitor*, 17 June.

Lancet. 2006. Memory enhancement—neuroethical dilemma. Editorial, 368:620.

Langleben, D. D., L. Schroeder, J. A. Maldjian, R. C. Gur, S. McDonald, J. D. Ragland, C. P. O'Brien, and A. R. Childress. 2002. Brain activity during simulated deception: An event-related functional magnetic resonance study. NeuroImage 15:727–732.

Larson, P. S. 2008. Deep brain stimulation for psychiatric disorders. Neurotherapeutics 5:50–58.

Laureys, S., M. E. Faymonville, P. Peigneux, P. Damas, B. Lambermont, F. Del Fiore, C. Degueldre, J. Aerts, A. Luxen, G. Franck, M. Lamy, G. Moonen, and P. Maquet. 2002. Cortical processing of noxious somatosensory stimuli in the persistent vegetative state. NeuroImage 17:732–741.

Laureys, S., F. Perrin, M. E. Faymonville, C. Schnakers, M. Boly, V. Bartsch, S. Majerus, G. Moonen, and P. Maquet. 2004. Cerebral processing in the minimally conscious state. Neurology 63:916–918.

Leighton, N. 2004. They're reading our minds. Sunday Times (London) January 25.

Leshner, A. I. 2005. It's time to go public with neuroethics. American Journal of Bioethics 5:1–2.

Levy, N. 2007. *Neuroethics: Challenges for the 21st Century.* Cambridge: Cambridge University Press.

Lexchin, J. 2001. Lifestyle drugs: Issues for debate. Canadian Medical Association Journal 164:1449–1451.

Lieberman, M. D., A. Hariri, J. M. Jarcho, N. I. Eisenberger, and S. Y. Bookheimer. 2005. An fMRI investigation of race-related amygdala activity in African-American and Caucasian-American individuals. Nature Neuroscience 8:720–722.

Lippman, A. 1991. Prenatal genetic testing and screening: Constructing needs and reinforcing inequalities. American Journal of Law and Medicine 17:15–50.

Lippman, A. 1992. Led (astray) by genetic maps: The cartography of the human genome and health care. Social Science & Medicine 35:1469–1476.

Logothetis, N. K. 2007. The ins and outs of fMRI signals. Nature Neuroscience 10:1230–1232.

Long, K. R. 2002. The ethics of rewiring the brain: Technique combines psychiatry, neurology in quest to improve lives. *Plain Dealer*, March 3.

Lozano, A. M., and C. Hamani. 2004. The future of deep brain stimulation. Journal of Clinical Physiology 21:68–69.

Lycan, W. 1987. *Consciousness.* Cambridge, MA: MIT Press.

Lynch, G. 2002. Memory enhancement: The search for mechanism-based drugs. Nature Neuroscience 5 (Suppl):1035–1038.

Macciocchi, S. N., and W. A. Alves. 1997. Ethical considerations in neuroclinical trials. Neurosurgical Review 20:161–170.

Macdermid, A. 1997. Hi-tech hairnet that reads minds. *Glasgow Herald*, January 23.

MacIntyre, A. 1998. What can moral philosophers learn from the study of the brain? Philosophy and Phenomenological Research 58:865–869.

Macklin, R. 2006. The new conservatives in bioethics: Who are they and what do they seek? Hastings Center Report 36:34–43.

MacLean, P. D. 1967. The brain in relation to empathy and medical education. Journal of Nervous and Mental Disease 144:374–382.

Maher, B. 2008. Poll results: Look who's doping. Nature 452:674–675.

Mahner, M., and M. Bunge. 1997. *Foundations of Biophilosophy.* New York: Springer.

Mahowald, M. B. 1994. So many ways to think. An overview of approaches to ethical issues in geriatrics. Clinics in Geriatric Medicine 10:403–418.

Marcin, J. P., M. M. Pollack, K. M. Patel, B. M. Sprague, and U. E. Ruttimann. 1999. Prognostication and certainty in the pediatric intensive care unit. Pediatrics 104:868–873.

Marcin, J. P., R. K. Pretzlaff, M. M. Pollack, K. M. Patel, and U. E. Ruttimann. 2004. Certainty and mortality prediction in critically ill children. Journal of Medical Ethics 30:304–307.

Marcus, S. J., ed. 2002. *Neuroethics: Mapping the Field, Conference Proceedings.* Washington, DC: Dana Press.

Mariani, S. M. 2003. Neuroethics: How to leave the cave without going astray. Medscape 5:1–5.

Marr, D. 1982. *Vision: A Computational Investigation into the Human Representation and Processing of Visual Information.* San Francisco: W.H. Freeman and Company.

Martin, J. H. 1998. *Neuroanatomy.* New York: McGraw-Hill.

Martinson, B. C., M. S. Anderson, and R. De Vries. 2005. Scientists behaving badly. Nature 435:737–738.

Masri, C., C. A. Farrell, J. Lacroix, G. Rocker, and S. D. Shemie. 2000. Decision making and end-of-life care in critically ill children. Journal of Palliative Care 16 (Suppl):S45–S52.

Mathews, D. J., J. Sugarman, H. Bok, D. M. Blass, J. T. Coyle, P. Duggan, J. Finkel, H. T. Greely, A. Hillis, A. Hoke, R. Johnson, M. Johnston, J. Kahn, D. Kerr, J. Kurtzberg, S. M. Liao, J.W. McDonald, G. McKhann, K. B. Nelson, M. Rao, A. Regenberg, A. W. Siegel, K. Smith, D. Solter, H. Song, A. Vescovi, W. Young, J.D. Gearhart, and R. Faden. 2008. Cell-based interventions for neurologic conditions: Ethical challenges for early human trials. Neurology 71:288–293.

Mauron, A. 2003. Renovating the house of being. Annals of the New York Academy of Sciences 1001:240–252.

Mayr, E. 1985. How Biology Differs from the Physical Sciences? In *Evolution at the Crossroads: The New Biology and the New Philosophy of Science*, ed. D. J. Depew and B. H. Weber, 43–63. Cambridge, MA: MIT Press.

Mayr, E. 1988. Is biology an autonomous science? *Toward a New Philosophy of Biology*, 6–23. Cambridge, MA: Harvard University Press.

McCabe, D. P., and A. D. Castel. 2008. Seeing is believing: The effect of brain images on judgments of scientific reasoning. Cognition 107:343–352.

McCarthy, M. 2007. Prescription drug abuse up sharply in the USA. Lancet 369:1505–1506.

McClure, S. M., J. Li, D. Tomlin, K. S. Cypert, L. M. Montague, and P. R. Montague. 2004. Neural correlates of behavioral preference for culturally familiar drinks. Neuron 44:379–387.

McGinn, C. 2002. Machine dreams. *New York Times*, May 5.

McIntyre, M., and J. Mazzolini. 1997. Their every move is electric: With pacemaker-sized stimulators and tiny computers, researchers are bypassing spines and nerves and giving paralysis and stroke victims some function. *Plain Dealer*, August 10.

Mcnaught, A. 1996. Brain waves. *Scotsman*, May 6.

Mehta, M. A., A. M. Owen, B. J. Sahakian, N. Mavaddat, J. D. Pickard, and T. W. Robbins. 2000. Methylphenidate enhances working memory by modulating discrete frontal and parietal lobe regions in the human brain. Journal of Neuroscience 20:RC65.

Mejia, R. E., and M. M. Pollack. 1995. Variability in brain death determination practices in children. Journal of the American Medical Association 274:550–553.

Mink, R. B., and M. M. Pollack. 1992. Resuscitation and withdrawal of therapy in pediatric intensive care. Pediatrics 89:961–963.

Moll, J., R. de Oliveira-Souza, I. E. Bramati, and J. Grafman. 2002. Functional networks in emotional moral and nonmoral social judgments. NeuroImage 16: 696–703.

Moll, J., R. de Oliveira-Souza, P. J. Eslinger, I. E. Bramati, J. Mourão-Miranda, P. A. Andreiuolo, and L. Pessoa. 2002. The neural correlates of moral sensitivity: A functional magnetic resonance imaging investigation of basic and moral emotions. Journal of Neuroscience 22:2730–2736.

Moll, J., R. de Oliveira-Souza, F. T. Moll, F. A. Ignácio, I. E. Bramati, E. M. Caparelli-Dáquer, and P. J. Eslinger. 2005. The moral affiliations of disgust: A functional MRI study. Cognitive and Behavioral Neurology 18:68–78.

Moll, J., P. J. Eslinger, and R. de Oliveira-Souza. 2001. Frontopolar and anterior temporal cortex activation in a moral judgment task: Preliminary functional MRI results in normal subjects. Arquivos de Neuro-Psiquiatria 59:657–664.

Moore, G. E. 1971. *Principia Ethica*. Cambridge: Cambridge University Press.

Moreno, J. 1999. Bioethics is a naturalism. In *Pragmatic Bioethics*, ed. G. McGee, 5–17. Nashville: Vanderbilt University Press.

Moruzzi, G., and H. W. Magoun. 1949. Brain stem reticular formation and activation of the EEG. Electroencephalography and Clinical Neurophysiology 1:455–473.

Multi-Society Task Force on PVS. 1994. Medical aspects of the persistent vegetative state (1). New England Journal of Medicine 330:1499–1508.

Multi-Society Task Force on PVS. 1994. Medical aspects of the persistent vegetative state (2). New England Journal of Medicine 330:1572–1579.

Naccache, L. 2006. Is she conscious? Science 313:1395–1396.

Nachev, P., and M. Husain. 2007. Comment on "Detecting awareness in the vegetative state." Science 315:1221.

Nagel, T. 1974. What is it like to be a bat? Philosophical Review 83:435–450.

Nagourney, E. 2001. Vital signs: Patterns; surprise! Brain likes thrill of unknown. *New York Times*, April 17.

National Conference of Commissioners on Uniform State Laws. 1980. *Uniform Determination of Death Act*. Kauai, HI.

National Health and Medical Research Council. 2008. *Post-coma Unresponsiveness and Minimally Responsive State: A Guide for Families and Careers of People with Profound Brain Damage.* Canberra: Government of Australia.

National Institute on Drug Abuse. 2005. *Prescription Drugs: Abuse and Addiction. Research Report Series.* National Institute on Drug Abuse, National Institutes of Health, Bethesda, MD.

Nature Neuroscience. 1998. Does neuroscience threaten human values? Editorial, 1:535–536.

Nature Neuroscience. 2004. Brain Scam? Editorial, 7:683.

Nelkin, D. 2001. Beyond risk: Reporting about genetics in the post-Asilomar press. Perspectives in Biology and Medicine 44:199–207.

Neuroethics New Emerging Team. 2008. [cited June 22 2008]. Available from http://www.neuroethics.ca

Neuroethics Research Unit. 2007. [cited June 22, 2007]. Available from http://www.ircm.qc.ca/en/recherche/statique/unite46.html

New York Times. 1995. Testing for cancer risks. Editorial, March 28.

Noble, H. B. 1999. Pain at work: Startling images and new hope. *New York Times*, August 10.

Norton, B. G. 1996. Moral naturalism and adaptive management. Hastings Center Report 26:24-26.

Novel Tech Ethics. 2007. [cited June 22 2007]. Available from http://www.novel techethics.ca/site_neuro_project_detail.php?page=136&project=15

Nut, A. E. 2005. The science of the brain leads to new doubts, fears. *Star-Ledger*, December 18.

Olshansky, S. J., and T. T. Perls. 2008. New developments in the illegal provision of growth hormone for "anti-aging" and bodybuilding. Journal of the American Medical Association 299:2792–2794.

Olson, S. 2005. Brain scans raise privacy concerns. Science 307:1548–1550.

Owen, A. M., and M. R. Coleman. 2008. Functional neuroimaging of the vegetative state. Nature Reviews Neuroscience 9:235–243.

Owen, A. M., M. R. Coleman, M. Boly, M. H. Davis, S. Laureys, and J. D. Pickard. 2006. Detecting awareness in the vegetative state. Science 313:1402.

Owen, A. M., M. R. Coleman, D. K. Menon, I. S. Johnsrude, J. M. Rodd, M. H. Davis, K. Taylor, and J. D. Pickard. 2005. Residual auditory function in persistent vegetative state: A combined PET and fMRI study. Neuropsychological Rehabilitation 15:290–306.

Parens, E. 2005. Authenticity and ambivalence: Toward understanding the enhancement debate. Hastings Center Report 35:34–41.

Parens, E. 2006. Creativity, gratitude, and the enhancement debate. In *Neuroethics: Defining the Issues in Theory, Practice, and Policy.* ed. J. Illes, 75–86. Oxford: Oxford University Press.

Parens, E., ed. 1998. *Enhancing Human Traits: Ethical and Social Implications*. Washington, D.C.: Georgetown University Press.

Parens, E., and J. Johnston. 2006. Against hyphenated ethics. *Bioethics Forum* (Friday, September 8, 2006), http://www.bioethicsforum.org/genethics-neuroethics-nanoethics.asp

Parens, E., and J. Johnston. 2007. Does it make sense to speak of neuroethics? Three problems with keying ethics to hot new science and technology. EMBO Reports 8:S61–S64.

Parker, M., and S. D. Shemie. 2002. Pro/con ethics debate: Should mechanical ventilation be continued to allow for progression to brain death so that organs can be donated? Critical Care (London, England) 6:399–402.

Payne, K., R. M. Taylor, C. Stocking, and G. A. Sachs. 1996. Physicians' attitudes about the care of patients in the persistent vegetative state: A national survey. Annals of Internal Medicine 125:104–110.

Pellegrino, E. 2006. Balint Lecture. *ASBH Summer Conference: Bioethics and Politics*. Albany, New York.

Pence, G. E. 2004. Comas: Karen Quinlan and Nancy Kruzan. In *Classic Cases on Medical Ethics*, 29–57. Boston: McGraw-Hill.

Perry, J. E., L. R. Churchill, and H. S. Kirshner. 2005. The Terri Schiavo case: Legal, ethical, and medical perspectives. Annals of Internal Medicine 143:744–748.

Peterson, L. 2001. Be careful in presuming elder dementia. *Tampa Tribune*, July 24.

Phillips, S. 2006. An espresso in the morning is just so last year. Times Higher Education (March Suppl):10.

Pitman, R., K. Sanders, R. Zusman, A. R. Healy, F. Cheema, N. B. Lasko, L. Cahill, and S. P. Orr. 2002. Pilot study of secondary prevention of posttraumatic stress disorder with propranolol. Biological Psychiatry 51:189–192.

Plassmann, H., J. O'Doherty, and A. Rangel. 2007. Orbitofrontal cortex encodes willingness to pay in everyday economic transactions. Journal of Neuroscience 27:9984–9988.

Pollack, A. 2004. With tiny brain implants, just thinking may make it so. *New York Times*, April 13.

Pontius, A. A. 1973. Neuro-ethics of "walking" in the newborn. Perceptual and Motor Skills 37:235–245.

Pontius, A. A. 1993. Neuroethics vs. neurophysiologically and neuropsychologically uninformed influences in child-rearing, education, emerging hunter-gatherers, and artificial intelligence models of the brain. Psychological Reports 72:451–458.

Posner, J. B., C. B. Saper, N. D. Schiff, and F. Plum. 2007. *Plum and Posner's Diagnosis of Stupor and Coma*. Edited by W. J. Herdmen. Contemporary Neurology Series. Fourth Edition. New York: Oxford University Press.

Potter, V. R. 1970. Bioethics: The science of survival. Perspectives in Biology and Medicine 14:127–153.

Potter, V. R. 1971. *Bioethics: Bridge to the Future.* Englewood Cliffs, NJ: Prentice-Hall.

Potter, V. R. 1972. Bioethics for whom? Annals of the New York Academy of Sciences 196:200–205.

Prehn, K., I. Wartenburger, K. Meriau, C. Scheibe, O. R. Goodenough, A. Villringer, E. van der Meer, and H. R. Heekeren. 2008. Individual differences in moral judgment competence influence neural correlates of socio-normative judgments. Social Cognitive and Affective Neuroscience 3:33–46.

Prendergast, T. J., M. T. Claessens, and J. M. Luce. 1998. A national survey of end-of-life care for critically ill patients. American Journal of Respiratory and Critical Care Medicine 158:1163–1167.

President's Council on Bioethics. 2003. *Beyond Therapy.* Washington, DC: President's Council on Bioethics/Harper Collins.

President's Council on Bioethics. 2004. Staff working paper: An overview of the impact of neuroscience evidence in criminal law. Available at http://www.bioethics.gov/background/neuroscience_evidence.html.

Prudhomme B. P., K. A. Becker-Blease, and K. Grace-Bishop. 2006. Stimulant medication use, misuse, and abuse in an undergraduate and graduate student sample. Journal of American College Health 54:261–268.

Pylyshyn, Z. W. 1985. *Computation and Cognition: Toward a Foundation for Cognitive Science.* Cambridge, MA: MIT Press.

Racine, E. 2002. Therapy or enhancement, philosophy of neuroscience and the ethics of neurotechnology. Ethica 14: 70–100

Racine, E. 2003. Discourse ethics as an ethics of responsibility: Comparison and evaluation of citizen involvement in population genomics. Journal of Law, Medicine & Ethics 31:390–397.

Racine, E. 2007. Identifying challenges and conditions for the use of neuroscience in bioethics. American Journal of Bioethics 7:74–76.

Racine, E. 2008a. Comment on "Does it make sense to speak of neuroethics?". EMBO Reports 9:2–3.

Racine, E. 2008b. Enriching our views on clinical ethics: Results of a qualitative study of the moral psychology of healthcare ethics committee members. Journal of Bioethical Inquiry 5:57–67.

Racine, E. 2008c. Interdisciplinary approaches for a pragmatic neuroethics. American Journal of Bioethics 8:52–53.

Racine, E. 2008d. Which naturalism for bioethics? A defense of moderate (pragmatic) naturalism. Bioethics 22:92–100.

Racine, E., R. Amaram, M. Seidler, M. Karczewska, and J. Illes. 2008. Media coverage of the persistent vegetative state and end-of-life decision-making. Neurology 71:1027–1032.

Racine, E., O. Bar-Ilan, and J. Illes. 2005. fMRI in the public eye. Nature Reviews Neuroscience 6:159–164.

Racine, E., O. Bar-Ilan, and J. Illes. 2006. Brain imaging: A decade of coverage in the print media. Science Communication 28:122–142.

Racine, E., and E. Bell, 2008. Clinical and public translation of neuroimaging research in disorders of consciousness challenges current diagnostic and public understanding paradigms. American Journal of Bioethics 8:13–5; discussion W1–W3.

Racine, E., D. DuRousseau, and J. Illes. 2007. From the bench to headlines: Ethical issues in performance-enhancing technologies. Technology 11:37–54.

Racine, E., and C. Forlini. 2008. Cognitive enhancement, lifestyle choice or misuse of prescription drugs? Ethics blind spots in current debates. *Neuroethics* (Published online September 4).

Racine, E., I. Gareau, H. Doucet, D. Laudy, G. Jobin, and P. Schraedley-Desmond. 2006. Hyped biomedical science or uncritical reporting? Press coverage of genomics (1992–2001) in Québec. Social Science & Medicine 62:1278–1290.

Racine, E., and J. Illes. 2006. Neuroethical responsibilities. Canadian Journal of Neurological Sciences 33:269–277.

Racine, E., and J. Illes. 2007. Emerging ethical challenges in advanced neuroimaging research: Review, recommendations and research agenda. Journal of Empirical Research on Human Research Ethics (JERHRE) 2:1–10.

Racine, E., and J. Illes. 2008. Neuroethics. In *Cambridge Textbook of Bioethics*, eds. P. Singer and A. Viens, 495–503. Cambridge: Cambridge University Press.

Racine, E., and J. Illes. 2009. "Emergentism" at the crossroads of philosophy, neurotechnology, and the enhancement debate. In *Handbook of Philosophy and Neuroscience*, ed. J. Bickle, 431–453. New York: Oxford University Press.

Racine, E., M. Lansberg, M.-J. Dion, C. Wijman, and J. Illes. 2007. A qualitative study of prognostication and end-of-life decision-making in critically-ill neurological patients. Paper read at International Conference in Clinical Ethics, June 2, 2007, Toronto.

Racine, E., H. Z. A. Van der Loos, and J. Illes. 2007. Internet marketing of neuroproducts: New practices and healthcare policy challenges. Cambridge Quarterly of Healthcare Ethics 16:181–194.

Racine, E., S. Waldman, and J. Illes. 2005. Ethics and scientific accuracy in print media coverage of modern neurotechnology. Society for Neuroscience Annual Meeting, Washington, D.C., November 11–16.

Racine, E., S. Waldman, N. Palmour, D. Risse, and J. Illes. 2007. Currents of hope: Neurostimulation techniques in US and UK print media. Cambridge Quarterly of Healthcare Ethics 16:312–316.

Randolph, A. G., M. B. Zollo, R. S. Wigton, and T. S. Yeh. 1997. Factors explaining variability among caregivers in the intent to restrict life-support interventions in a pediatric intensive care unit. Critical Care Medicine 25:435–439.

Rebagliato, M., M. Cuttini, L. Broggin, I. Berbik, U. de Vonderweid, G. Hansen, M. Kaminski, L. A. Kollée, A. Kucinskas, S. Lenoir, A. Levin, J. Persson, M. Reid, R. Saracci; EURONIC Study Group (European Project on Parents' Information and Ethical Decision Making in Neonatal Intensive Care Units). 2000. Neonatal end-of-life decision making: Physicians' attitudes and relationship with self-reported practices in 10 European countries. Journal of the American Medical Association 284:2451–2459.

Reid, L., and F. Baylis. 2005. Brains, genes, and the making of the self. American Journal of Bioethics 5:21–23.

Reiser, S. J. 1991. The public and the expert in biomedical policy controversies. In *Biomedical Politics*, ed. K. E. Hanna, 325–331. Washington, D.C.: National Academy Press.

Robertson, D., J. Snarey, O. Ousley, K. Harenski, F. DuBois Bowman, R. Gilkey, and C. Kilts. 2007. The neural processing of moral sensitivity to issues of justice and care. Neuropsychologia 45:755–766.

Rocker, G., D. Cook, P. Sjokvist, B. Weaver, S. Finfer, E. McDonald, J. Marshall, A. Kirby, M. Levy, P. Dodek, D. Heyland, G. Guyatt; Level of Care Study Investigators; Canadian Critical Care Trials Group. 2004. Clinician predictions of intensive care unit mortality. Critical Care Medicine 32:1149–1154.

Rocker, G., and D. Heyland. 2003. New research initiatives in Canada for end-of-life and palliative care. Canadian Medical Association Journal 169:300–301.

Rocker, G. M., D. J. Cook, and S. D. Shemie. 2006. Practice variation in end of life care in the ICU: Implications for patients with severe brain injury. Canadian Journal of Anaesthesia 53:814–819.

Rodriguez, P. 2006. Talking brains: A cognitive semantic analysis of an emerging folk neuropsychology. Public Understanding of Neuroscience 15:301–330.

Rorty, R. 1965. Mind-body identity, privacy, and categories. Review of Metaphysics 19:24–54.

Rose, S. P. 2002. "Smart drugs": Do they work? Are they ethical? Will they be legal? Nature Reviews Neuroscience 3:975–979.

Rose, S. P. R. 2003. How to (or not to) communicate science. Biochemical Society Transactions 31:307–312.

Roskies, A. 2002. Neuroethics for the new millenium. Neuron 35:21–23.

Rousseau, J.-J. 1819. *Oeuvres complètes de J.J. Rousseau*. Edited by V. H. Perroneau. Édition ornée de gravures. vol. 12. Paris: Dupont.

Rousseau, J.-J. 1992 [1762]. *Du contrat social*. Paris: GF-Flammarion.

Rowe, G., and L. J. Frewer, 2000. Public participation methods: A framework for evaluation. Science, Technology & Human Values 25:3–29.

Royal College of Physicians. 2003. *The Vegetative State: Guidance on Diagnosis and Management*. London: Royal College of Physicians.

Ruskin, G. 2004. Commercial alert asks Senate Commerce Committee to investigate neuromarketing. *Commercial Alert*, 1–4.

Safire, W. 2002a. Neuroethics belongs in public eye. *Dayton Daily News*, May 17.

Safire, W. 2002b. Visions for a new field of neuroethics. In *Neuroethics: Mapping the Field*. ed. S. J. Marus, 3–9. Washington, DC: Dana Press.

Safire, W. 2003. A fatal operation raises troubling questions: Neuroethics. *International Herald Tribune*, July 11.

Sahakian, B., and S. Morein-Zamir. 2007. Professor's little helper. Nature 450:1157–1159.

Sample, I., and D. Adam. 2003. The brain can't lie: Brain scans reveal how you think and feel and even how you might behave. No wonder CIA and big businesses are interested. *Guardian*, November 20.

Sandel, M. J. 2004. The case against perfection: What's wrong with designer children, bionic athletes, and genetic engineering. Atlantic Monthly 292:50–54, 56–60, 62.

Sartre, J.-P. 1996. *L'existentialisme est un humanisme*. Folio/Essais. Saint-Amand: Gallimard.

Savulescu, J., and A. Sandberg. 2008. Neuroenhancement of love and marriage: The chemicals between us. Neuroethics 1:31–44.

Schaich Borg, J., C. Hynes, J. Van Horn, S. Grafton, and W. Sinnott-Armstrong. 2006. Consequences, action, and intention as factors in moral judgments: An fMRI investigation. Journal of Cognitive Neuroscience 18:803–817.

Schick, A. 2005. Neuro exceptionalism? American Journal of Bioethics 5:36–38.

Schiff, N. D., J. T. Giacino, K. Kalmar, J. D. Victor, K. Baker, M. Gerber, B. Fritz, B. Eisenberg, T. Biondi, J. O'Connor, E. J. Kobylarz, S. Farris, A. Machado, C. McCagg, F. Plum, J. J. Fins, and A. R. Rezai. 2007. Behavioural improvements with thalamic stimulation after severe traumatic brain injury. Nature 448:600–603 with corrigendum in Nature 452:120.

Schiff, N. D., D. Rodriguez-Moreno, A. Kamal, K. H. Kim, J. T. Giacino, F. Plum, and J. Hirsch. 2005. fMRI reveals large-scale network activation in minimally conscious patients. Neurology 64:514–523.

Schmickle, S. 2000. Not knowing can be as hard as knowing: As Kristin LaVine considers whether to be tested for Huntington's, uncertainty is never far away. *Star Tribune*, November 5.

Schmidt-Felzmann, H. 2003. Pragmatic principles—methodological pragmatism in the principle-based approach to bioethics. Journal of Medicine and Philosophy 28:581–596.

Sellars, W. 1963. *Science, Perception, and Reality*. New York: Humanities Press.

Sententia, W. 2004. Neuroethical considerations: Cognitive liberty and converging technologies for improving human cognition. Annals of the New York Academy of Sciences 1013:221–228.

Shanteau, J., and K. Linin. 1990. Subjective meaning of terms used in organ donation: Analysis of word associations. In *Organ Donation and Transplantation: Psychological and Behavioral Factors*, eds. J. Shanteau and R. Harris, 37–49. Washington, DC: American Psychological Association.

Shaver, K. 1998. "Subtle" brain damage found in Aron, Doctor says. *Washington Post*, March 11.

Shevell, M. I. 1999. Neurosciences in the Third Reich: From ivory tower to death camps. Canadian Journal of Neurological Sciences 26:132–138.

Shevell, M. I. 2004. Ethical issues in pediatric critical care neurology. Seminars in Pediatric Neurology 11:179–184.

Shevell, M. I., A. Majnemer, and S. P. Miller. 1999. Neonatal neurologic prognostication: The asphyxiated term newborn. Pediatric Neurology 21:776–784.

Shewmon, D. A. 2001. The brain and somatic integration: Insights into the standard biological rationale for equating "brain death" with death. Journal of Medicine and Philosophy 26:457–478.

Shewmon, D. A. 2004. A critical analysis of conceptual domains of the vegetative state: Sorting fact from fancy. NeuroRehabilitation 19:343–347.

Siminoff, L. A., C. Burant, and S. J. Youngner. 2004. Death and organ procurement: Public beliefs and attitudes. Kennedy Institute of Ethics Journal 14:217–234.

Siminoff, L. A., M. B. Mercer, and R. Arnold. 2003. Families' understanding of brain death. Progress in Transplantation 13:218–224.

Singer, T., S. J. Kiebel, J. S. Winston, R. J. Dolan, and C. D. Frith. 2004. Brain responses to the acquired moral status of faces. Neuron 41:653–662.

Singh, I. 2008. Beyond polemics: Science and ethics of ADHD. Nature Reviews Neuroscience 9:957–964.

Singh, L. 2005. Will the "real boy" please behave: Dosing dilemmas for parents of boys with ADHD. American Journal of Bioethics 5:34–47.

Smart, A. 2003. Reporting the dawn of the post-genomic era: Who wants to live forever? Sociology of Health & Illness 25:24–49.

Smith, R. 2001. Representations of mind: C.S. Sherrington and scientific opinion, c. 1930–1950. Science in Context 14:511–539.

Solomon, M. Z. 2005. Realizing bioethics' goals in practice: Ten ways "is" can help "ought." Hastings Center Report 35:40–47.

Sprung, C. L., S. L. Cohen, P. Sjokvist, M. Baras, H. H. Bulow, S. Hovilehto, D. Ledoux, A. Lippert, P. Maia, D. Phelan, W. Schobersberger, E. Wennberg, T. Woodcock; Ethicus Study Group. 2003. End-of-life practices in European intensive care units: The Ethicus Study. Journal of the American Medical Association 290:790–797.

Stent, G. S. 1990. The poverty of neurophilosophy. Journal of Medicine and Philosophy 15:539–557.

Stevens, R. D., and A. Bhardwaj. 2006. Approach to the comatose patient. Critical Care Medicine 34:31–41.

Sugarman, J., R. Faden, and J. Weinstein. 2001. A decade of empirical research in medical ethics. In Methods in Medical Ethics, eds. J. Sugarman and D. P. Sulmasy, 19–28. Washington, D.C.: Georgetown University Press.

Takahashi, H., M. Kato, M. Matsuura, M. Koeda, N. Yahata, T. Suhara, and Y. Okubo. 2008. Neural correlates of human virtue judgment. Cerebral Cortex 18:1886–1891.

Takahashi, H., N. Yahata, M. Koeda, T. Matsuda, K. Asai, and Y. Okubo. 2004. Brain activation associated with evaluative processes of guilt and embarrassment: An fMRI study. NeuroImage 23:967–974.

Talwar, S. K., S. Xu, E. S. Hawley, S. A. Weiss, K. A. Moxon, and J. K. Chapin. 2002. Rat navigation guided by remote control. Nature 417:37–38.

Tamber, C. 2005. Brave neuro world. *Daily Record*, December 30.

Tambor, E. S., B. A. Bernhardt, J. Rodgers, N. A. Holtzman, and G. Geller. 2002. Mapping the human genome: An assessment of media coverage and public reaction. Genetics in Medicine 4:31–36.

Taylor, C. 1989. *Sources of the Self: The Making of Modern Identity*. Cambridge, MA: Harvard University Press.

Teasdale, G., and B. Jennett. 1974. Assessment of coma and impaired consciousness. A practical scale. Lancet 2:81–84.

Teter, C. J., S. E. McCabe, J. A. Cranford, C. J. Boyd, and S. K. Guthrie. 2005. Prevalence and motives for illicit use of prescription stimulants in an undergraduate student sample. Journal of American College Health 53:253–262.

Teter, C. J., S. E. McCabe, K. LaGrange, J. A. Cranford, and C. J. Boyd. 2006. Illicit use of specific prescription stimulants among college students: Prevalence, motives, and routes of administration. Pharmacotherapy 26:1501–1510.

Thomas, D. 1997. Keeping pace with Parkinson's: Doctors can't prevent or cure the disease, but they're working to alleviate the worst symptoms. *Omaha World Herald*, November 10.

Thompson, R. A., and C. A. Nelson. 2001. Developmental science and the media. American Psychologist 56:5–15.

Thompson, T., R. Barbour, and L. Schwartz. 2003. Adherence to advance directives in critical care decision making: A vignette study. British Medical Journal 327:1011-1014.

Toga, A. W. 2002. Imaging databases and neuroscience. Neuroscientist 8:423–436.

Tomlinson, T. 1990. Misunderstanding death on a respirator. Bioethics 4:253–264.

Tomlinson, T., and H. Brody. 1988. Ethics and communication in do-not-resuscitate orders. New England Journal of Medicine 318:43–46.

Torassa, U. 2002. Alzheimer's Disease on the medical front. Fade to black: Research into detecting Alzheimer's disease earlier will help ease anxiety. *San Francisco Chronicle*, June 2.

Toulmin, S. 1982. How medicine saved the life of ethics. Perspectives in Biology and Medicine 25:736–750.

Tovino, S. A. 2007. Functional neuroimaging and the law: Trends and directions for future scholarship. American Journal of Bioethics 7:44–56.

Trueland, J. 1999. Magnetic fields used to treat depression. *Scotsman*, May 18.

Truog, R. D. 2007. Brain death—too flawed to endure, too ingrained to abandon. Journal of Law, Medicine & Ethics 35:273–281.

Turing, A. L. 1950. Computing machinery and intelligence. Mind 59:433–460.

Turner, D. C., and B. J. Sahakian. 2006. Neuroethics of cognitive enhancement. BioSocieties 1:113–123.

Turner, E. H., A. M. Matthews, E. Linardatos, R. A. Tell, and R. Rosenthal. 2008. Selective publication of antidepressant trials and its influence on apparent efficacy. New England Journal of Medicine 358:252–260.

Turner, L. 2003. The tyranny of "genethics." Nature Biotechnology 21:1282.

U.S. Food and Drug Administration. *FDA approves humanitarian device exemption for deep brain stimulator for severe obsessive-compulsive disorder* [cited June 29, 2009]. Available from http://www.fda.gov/bbs/topics/NEWS/2009/NEW01959.html

van Djick, J. 2003. After the "Two cultures": Toward a "(multi)cultural practice of science communication. Science Communication 25:177–190.

Vastag, B. 2004. Poised to challenge need for sleep, "wakefulness enhancer" rouses concerns. Journal of the American Medical Association 291:167–170.

Vohs, K. D., and J. W. Schooler. 2008. The value of believing in free will: Encouraging a belief in determinism increases cheating. Psychological Science 19:49–54.

Walsh-Kelly, C. M., K. R. Lang, J. Chevako, E. L. Blank, N. Korom, K. Kirk, and A. Gray. 1999. Advance directives in a pediatric emergency department. Pediatrics 103:826–830.

Walsh, A. 1995. *Biosociology: An Emerging Paradigm*. Westport, CT: Praeger Publishers.

Warren, O. J., D. R. Leff, T. Athanasiou, C. Kennard, and A. Darzi. 2008. The neurocognitive enhancement of surgeons: An ethical perspective. Journal of Surgical Research 152:167–172.

Weber, F., and H. Knopf. 2006. Incidental findings in Magnetic Resonance Imaging of the brains of healthy young men. Journal of the Neurological Sciences 210:81–84.

Weijer, C. 2005. A death in the family: Reflections on the Terri Schiavo case. Canadian Medical Association Journal 172:1197–1198.

Weisberg, D. S., F. C. Keil, J. Goodstein, E. Rawson, and J. R. Gray. 2008. The seductive allure of neuroscience explanations. Journal of Cognitive Neuroscience 20:470–477.

Wijdicks, E. F. 2001. The diagnosis of brain death. New England Journal of Medicine 344:1215–1221.

Wijdicks, E. F., and C. A. Wijdicks. 2006. The portrayal of coma in contemporary motion pictures. Neurology 66:1300–1303.

Wijdicks, E. F., and M. F. Wijdicks. 2006. Coverage of coma in headlines of US newspapers from 2001 through 2005. Mayo Clinic Proceedings 81:1332–1336.

Wikipedia. *Neuroethics* [cited June 22, 2007]. Available from http://en.wikipedia.org/wiki/Neuroethics

Wilens, T. E., L. A. Adler, J. Adams, S. Sgambati, J. Rotrosen, R. Sawtelle, L. Utzinger, and S. Fusillo. 2008. Misuse and diversion of stimulants prescribed for ADHD: A systematic review of the literature. Journal of the American Academy of Child and Adolescent Psychiatry 47:21–31.

Wilfond, B. S., and W. G. Magnuson. 2005. On the proliferation of bioethics sub-disciplines: Do we really need "genethics" and "neuroethics"? American Journal of Bioethics 5:20–21.

Wilkie, T. 1996. When ignorance is bliss: Most people at risk of genetic illness are refusing to have DNA tests. Tom Wilkie examines the facts that are confounding scientists. *Independent*, March 25.

Wilson, F. C., J. Harpur, T. Watson, and J. I. Morrow. 2002. Vegetative state and minimally responsive patients—regional survey, long-term case outcomes and service recommendations. NeuroRehabilitation 17:231–236.

Wise, J. 1997. The long wait: Jacqui Wise hears how genetic testing can bring heartache as well as hope. *Guardian*, March 4.

Wise, R. 1997. Clinton to back bill against genetic bias in insurance. *Atlanta Journal-Constitution*, July 14.

Wolf, S. M. 1994. Shifting paradigms in bioethics and health law: The rise of a new pragmatism. American Journal of Law & Medicine 20:395–415.

Wolpe, P. R. 2002. The neuroscience revolution. Hastings Center Report 32:8.

Wolpe, P. R. 2004. Neuroethics. In *The Encyclopedia of Bioethics*, ed. S. G. Post, 1894–1898. New York: MacMillan Reference.

Wolpe, P. R., K. R. Foster, and D. D. Langleben. 2005. Emerging neurotechnologies for lie-detection: Promises and perils. American Journal of Bioethics 5:39–49.

World Health Organization. 2001. *The World Health Report 2001. Mental Health: New Understanding, New Hope.* Geneva: World Health Organization.

World Health Organization. 2006. *Neurological Disorders: Public Health Challenges.* Geneva: World Health Organization.

Yesavage, J., M. Mumenthaler, J. L. Taylor, L. Friedman, R. O'Hara, J. Sheikh, J. Tinklenberg, and P. J. Whitehouse. 2003. Donepezil and flight simulator performance: Effects on retention of complex skills. Neurology 59:123–125.

Young, L., and R. Saxe. 2008. The neural basis of belief encoding and integration in moral judgment. NeuroImage 40:1912–1920.

Young, S. N. 2003. Lifestyle drugs, mood, behaviour and cognition. Journal of Psychiatry & Neuroscience 28 (9):87–89.

Youngner, S. J., C. S. Landefeld, C. J. Coulton, B. W. Juknialis, and M. Leary. 1989. Brain death and organ retrieval. A cross-sectional survey of knowledge and concepts among health professionals. Journal of the American Medical Association 261:2205–2210.

Zardetto-Smith, A. M., K. Mu, C. Phelps, L. Houtz, and C. Royeen. 2002. Brains rule! fun = learning = neuroscience literacy. Neuroscientist 8:396–404.

Zernike, K. 2005. The difference between steroids and Ritalin is . . . *New York Times*, March 20.

Zimmer, C. 2003. What if there is something going on in there? New research suggests that many vegetative patients are more conscious than previously supposed—and might eventually be curable. A whole new way of thinking about pulling the plug. *New York Times Magazine* 9:52–56.

Zuckerman, D. 2003. Hype in health reporting: "Checkbook science" buys distortion of medical news. International Journal of Health Services 33:383–389.

Index

AD, x, 1, 2, 7, 17, 100, 102, 114, 122
Addiction, xvi, 45
ADHD, 87, 114
Advanced directives, 162
Akinetic mutism, 149
Alexander, Leo, 139
Alzheimer's disease. *See* AD
American Academy of Neurology
  and the minimally conscious state (MCS), 148
  and patients lacking decision-making capacity, 175 (*see also* Capacity in decision making, impaired
  and the persistent vegetative state (PVS), 18, 140, 168
  and physician involvement in direct-to-consumer advertising (DTCA), 111
Amygdala
  in emotions, 157, 185, 188
  in decision making, 187
  in moral emotions, 188
  in moral transgressions, 186
Aneurysm, 6
Animal rights, 40–42, 49, 105
Anterior cingulate cortex, 155, 185, 188. *See also* Cingulate (cortex)
Antidepressant, 10, 84, 122
Antinaturalism. *See also* Naturalism; Pragmatic naturalism
  in bioethics, 55, 56, 62–64
  critique of, 62–63, 69
  definition of, 60

discussion of, 60–61, 69
  in philosophy, 54, 56, 59
ARAS, 139, 141–142
Aristotle
  and the golden mean, 138
  and moral excellence, ix, 138
  and naturalism, 54
  and phronesis, 57
Ascending reticular activation system. *See* ARAS
Attention deficit/hyperactivity disorder. *See* ADHD
Authenticity, 43, 135
Autonomy (of ethics as a discipline), 62
Autonomy, respect for
  in cognitive enhancement, 121, 124, 127–128, 130, 132
  in decision making, xiii, 37, 40, 40–42, 47, 66, 68, 83, 89, 100, 104
  in ethical dilemmas, 136
  individual autonomy, 131, 132, 134, 135
  in liberalism, 128, 131, 135
  in patient decision making, 162
  public autonomy, 44, 131, 133, 134
  in social neuroscience and the neuroscience of ethics, 183, 190, 211

Basal ganglia, 185
Baylis, Françoise, xvi, 71, 81, 88–89
Beauchamp, Tom
  and metaethics, 64
  and naturalism, 63, 67–68

Beauchamp, Tom (cont.)
  and reflective equilibrium, 68
  and respect for autonomy, 6
Behaviorism, 219
Belmont Report, 78, 83
Berlin, Isaiah, 124, 128
Bernat, James
  and brain death, 144, 145
  and coma, 145
  and disorders of consciousness
    (DOC), 139, 141, 142, 147
  and ethical challenges of poor neuro-
    logical prognosis, 7, 161, 163, 166,
    170, 175
  and the definition of neuroethics, 28,
    29, 76
  and neuroimaging research on dis-
    orders of consciousness (DOC), 20,
    150, 155, 177
  and the persistent vegetative state
    (PVS), 18, 146, 147, 168, 174
Brain-based education, 2, 3, 114, 180.
  See also Education
Brain-computer interface, 38, 116.
  See also Brain-machine interface
Brain death (irreversible coma, "coma
  dépassé"). *See also* Neurological
  determination of death
  acceptance of by the medical com-
    munity, 18, 139
  and the Ad Hoc Committee of the
    Harvard Medical School, 143
  and "coma dépassé," 142
  confusion about, 142, 172
  critiques of, 145
  determination of, 18, 19, 139, 144,
    173
  and disorders of consciousness
    (DOC), 140, 141, 142, 158
  ethical issues associated with, 29,
    143–144, 162
  history of, 25
  and irreversible coma, 142
  media coverage of, 168
  and National Conference of Commis-
    sioners on Uniform State Law, 144

  and Pope Pius XII, 142
  and the Uniform Death Determina-
    tion Act (UDDA) 144–145
Brain imaging. *See also* fMRI; Neuroimaging; PET; SPECT
  in disorders of consciousness (DOC),
    144
  in marketing, 102
  in the media, 23, 158
Brain-machine interface, 32. *See also*
  Brain-computer interface
Brain injury. *See* EOL decision
  making; Stroke; Traumatic brain
  injury
Brainome, 48
Brain privacy, 25, 43. *See also* Thought
  privacy
Brandel, David, 24
Brocher Foundation, xvi
Bunge, Mario, 192–193, 195–196,
  202, 210
Burden (public health burden of
  neurological and psychiatric disorders), ix–x, 7

Callahan, Daniel
  and the culture wars, 135
  and the is-ought distinction, 57, 62,
    66, 204
  and naturalism, 57, 62–64, 66, 201,
    204
  and the nature of bioethics, 75, 85,
    96, 136–137, 201
  and the public good, 136–137
Capacity (decision-making capacity).
  See also Competency in decision
  making
  discussion of in the neuroethics
    literature, 37, 40–42, 83, 212
  impaired, 6, 21, 175–176, 183
  media discussions of, 104
Caplan, Arthur, xix, 11, 122, 125
Categorical imperative, 131, 133–134
Central nervous system. *See* CNS
Changeux, Jean-Pierre, 181, 192–193,
  195, 206–207

Chatterjee, Anjan, 87
Childress, James
and metaethics, 64
and naturalism, 63, 67–68
and reflective equilibrium, 68
and respect for autonomy, 6
Churchland, Patricia
and ethics, 191
and folk psychology, 108, 190, 209
and neurophilosophy, 109, 181, 190
Churchland, Paul, 108, 181, 190–191
Cingulate cortex, 155, 184, 185, 187, 188
Citizens' juries, 137
Clinical ethics, 58, 90, 167
Clinical neuroethics, 4–7, 27
CNS, 12, 80, 113, 202
Coercion, 43, 127
Cognition. *See also* Cognitive enhancement
in cognitive neuroscience, 2, 5, 22, 187, 197, 200, 208
and neuroethics, 32, 36, 59, 88, 184, 200, 204–205
in the persistent vegetative state (PVS), 147, 154, 174
Cognitive enhancement (neurocognitive enhancement). *See also* Commercialization; Culture wars; Discrimination; Justice; Pragmatism; Prescription abuse; Prescription misuse; Privacy
and conservatism, 122, 129
definition of, 10, 129
discussion of in the neuroethics literature, 10–12, 14 43–44, 45, 49, 84–85, 87
and moderate liberalism, 130
and moral acceptability, 125–126
and moral praiseworthiness, 125–126
social and economic pressures in, 136
Cognitive system, 197, 199
Coma. *See also* Glasgow Coma Scale; Irreversible coma
causes of, 139, 145

diagnosis of, 18, 139–141, 144–145
and ethical issues, 161, 163–165
history of, 141
in the media, 168, 174
prognosis of, 18, 139, 145
"Coma dépassé." *See* Brain death
Commercialization
in cognitive enhancement, 127
discussion of in the neuroethics literature, 40–42, 45
discussion of in media coverage of neuroscience, 103, 107, 109–110, 113
Communication. *See also* Unidirectional communication; Multidirectional communication
of poor neurological prognosis, 7, 146, 149, 159, 161–1634, 165, 166, 170–172, 175, 177
science communication, 8, 115–119, 208, 216
Competency (decision-making competency), 16, 21. *See also* Capacity in decision making
Confidentiality, 43, 103
Conflict of interest, 45, 103
Consciousness. *See* DOC
Consent. *See* Informed consent
Conservatism, 128–131, 137
Cranford, Ronald, 28–30, 34, 40, 76, 80, 86
Culture wars
and bioethics, 136–138, 221
in cognitive enhancement, 121–124
context of, 121, 135

Damasio, Antonio, 9
DBS. *See also* Informed consent
costs of, 15–16
in essential tremor (ET), 14–15
in major depressive disorder (MDD), 15, 17
mechanisms of action, 15
media coverage of, 16, 99

DBS (cont.)
number of completed DBS surgeries,
15
in obsessive compulsive disorder
(OCD), 15, 17
in Parkinson's disease (PD), 14–15
in the persistent vegetative state
(PVS), 148–149
in Tourette syndrome (TS), 15, 17
Decision making. See Amygdala;
Autonomy, respect for; Capacity
in decision making; Competency in
decision making; Emotion (in decision making); Justice; Shared
decision making
Deep brain stimulation. See DBS
Deliberation, 131, 134, 137–138
Dennett, Daniel, 198–199, 208
Depression. See also MDD
in deep brain stimulation (DBS), 27,
100
public health aspects of, x, 6–8, 14,
23, 91
Descarries, Laurent, 180
Descartes, René, 192, 206
Determinism (neurological determinism), 103, 201–203, 212, 218.
See also Free will
Dewey, John
in bioethics, 58–59
in ethics, 63, 67, 201
and naturalism, 57, 67, 201,
204–205
and pragmatism, 57, 138, 182
and reductionism, 87
Dignity, 40–41, 48, 50, 104, 129,
131
Direct-to-consumer advertising. See
DTCA
Discourse ethics, 131, 134
Discrimination
in cognitive enhancement, 127
discussion of in media coverage of
neuroscience, 103
discussion of in the neuroethics
literature, 40–42, 47

of neurological and psychiatric
patients, ix, 8, 91, 99
Disorders of consciousness. See DOC
DLPFC, 184, 185, 188
DOC, 18, 20, 139–159, 161–178,
215, 216. See also Coma; fMRI;
MCS; Permanent vegetative state;
PET; PVS; VS
Dorsolateral prefrontal cortex. See
DLPFC
Dorsomedial frontal cortex, 186
Doucet, Hubert, xv, 71, 80, 123, 172
Downie, Jocelyn, xvi, 21, 45, 82
DTCA, 10, 24, 110–111
Dualism. See also Holism
semantic, 183, 192, 210, 206–209
substance, 192–195, 199–200,
206

Education. See also Brain-based
education
and democracy, 113
and disorders of consciousness
(DOC), 147, 173
and neuroethics, 219–220
and neuroscience, 2–3, 30, 107, 114,
180
and phrenology, 113, 181
EEG, 99, 144
Electroencephalography. See EEG
ELSI program (in genetics and
genomics), 78–79, 95
Emergentism. See also Properties
and eliminativism, 198–201, 210,
212
and ethics, 204, 209
philosophy of, xiii, 179, 190,
193–195
and semantic dualism, 206, 208
Emotion in decision making, xiii, 5, 8,
9, 22, 157, 175, 179, 182, 207, 210,
213
Empathy, xiii, 2, 98, 125, 176, 179,
181
End-of-life decision making. See EOL
decision making

Engelhardt, H. Tristram, 191
EOL decision making
  and bereavement, 172
  and communication, 20, 154, 170
  in the context of the persistent
    vegetative state (PVS), 174–175,
    177
  in the intensive care unit (ICU), 170,
    171
  in the pediatric context, 162
  in severe brain injury, 162, 171–173,
    176
  and withdrawal of life support, 7,
    121, 167, 171
Epilepsy, 7, 32
Epistemology
  antinaturalistic, 56
  in the mind-body problem, 194,
    207–208
  naturalistic, 55, 59, 66
  in neuroethics, 97, 117
  and functional-causal (FC) explana-
    tion, 197–199
  and functional-descriptive (FD) exp-
    lanation, 197–199
  and relational-causal (RC) explana-
    tion, 197–198
  and relational-descriptive (RD) exp-
    lanation, 197–199
Eslinger, Paul, 9, 188, 189
Essential tremor (ET), 14–15
Ethical principles, 58, 60, 63, 91, 125,
  136
Eugenics, 40–42, 49, 102. *See also*
  Nazi experiments
Evers, Kathinka, 38, 54, 72, 79,
  85–86

Fagot-Largeault, Anne, 54, 57, 58, 64
Farah, Martha
  and cognitive enhancement, 10, 122
  and the definition of neuroethics, 32,
    36–37, 39–40, 83, 94
  and personhood, 9, 59, 94, 208
  and safety, 46
FC explanation. *See* Epistemology

FD explanation. *See* Epistemology
Fins, Joe
  and cognitive enhancement, 87
  on deep brain stimulation (DBS), 16
  and the definition of neuroethics, 28,
    51, 72, 75, 76, 85, 86
  on disorders of consciousness (DOC),
    19, 21, 140, 142, 152–153, 174,
    177
  and pragmatism, 54, 58–59
fMRI
  and lie detection, 3, 102
  media coverage of, 24, 99–100, 107,
    110, 154
  and the minimally conscious state
    (MCS), 151, 156–157
  and moral decision-making, 182,
    184–189, 207
  and neuroessentialism, 101,
    105–106
  and neuropolicy, 107
  and neurorealism, 106
  and personality, 22
  technical aspects of, 22–23
  and the vegetative state (VS), 40, 151,
    152, 153, 154
Fodor, Jerry, 199
Folk psychology (propositional attitude psychology), 108, 190, 191,
  193, 194, 190, 199, 200, 208
FPC, 189
Free will. *See also* Determinism
  discussion of in the neuroethics
    literature, 31, 33, 42, 45, 83
  and neuroscience, 9, 108, 109, 190,
    216
  and responsibility, 207, 219
Frontopolar cortex. *See* FPC
Functional-causal explanation. *See*
  Epistemology
Functional-descriptive explanation.
  See Epistemology
Functional magnetic resonance imag-
  ing. *See* fMRI
Functional neuroimaging. *See* Neuro-
  imaging

Galen, 141
GCS, 145, 165, 172
Genethics, 72, 76, 78, 79
Genetics
  and ethics, 32, 39, 40, 43, 71, 77, 78,
    89, 81, 82, 83, 84, 88, 90, 95, 132
  genetic alteration, 192
  genetic analysis, 2
  genetic discrimination, 103
  genetic engineering, 126
  genetic essentialism, 92
  genetic information, 104, 105
  geneticization, 109
  genetic research, 16, 100
  genetic selection, 105
  media coverage of, 16, 110
  neurogenetic testing, 99, 100, 101, 110
Genomics
  and ethics, 32, 78, 79
  media coverage of, 110
  research in, 16, 32, 78
Glannon, Walter, xv, 4, 46, 76, 122
Glasgow Coma Scale. See GCS
Goulon, Maurice, 142, 143
Greely, Henry, 3, 11, 79
Greene, Joshua, 8, 9, 22, 181–182,
  188, 189, 201, 210

Habermas, Jürgen, 68, 115, 131–134.
  See also Discourse ethics
Hadskis, Michael, 45, 82
Hippocrates, 141
Holism, 190, 192–195, 199–200. See
  also Dualism
Human Genome Project, 78
Huntington's disease, 100, 105
Huxley, Thomas, 61

ICU, 162, 166, 170, 171, 173
Identity. See Personal identity
Illes, Judy
  acknowledgment, xv, xvi
  and cognitive enhancement, 127
  and the definition of neuroethics, 4,
    33, 34, 37, 38, 39, 71–72, 75, 76,
    79, 80, 82, 86, 88, 138

and direct-to-consumer advertising
  (DTCA), 10, 110, 111, 114
and disorders of consciousness
  (DOC), 150, 153, 177
and lie detection, 3, 183
and the ethics of neuroimaging,
  21–22, 23, 24, 43, 48, 97, 98, 175,
and the history of neuroethics, 49,
  83
and incidental findings, 5
Neuroethics: defining the issues in
  theory, practice, and policy, 4
and public understanding of neuroscience, 24, 42, 47, 82, 92, 93, 95,
  98, 99, 101, 108, 110, 115, 116,
  117, 118, 212, 216, 217
Incidental findings, 5, 6, 21, 43, 50
Informed consent. See also Autonomy,
  respect for; Capacity; Competency;
  Persons, respect for
in deep brain stimulation (DBS), 14,
  16
discussion of in media coverage of
  neuroscience, 104
discussion of in the neuroethics
  literature, 37, 40–43, 50, 83
in severe brain injury, 5
Insula, 157, 184
Intelligence, 23, 105
Intensive care unit. See ICU
Irreversible coma. See Brain death
Is-ought distinction, 57, 60–68,
  204–205

Jennett, Bryan, 18, 145–146, 170
Jonsen, Albert R., 67, 142, 143
Justice
  in cognitive enhancement, 128
  discussion of in the neuroethics
    literature, 41, 42, 48, 90
  discussion of in media coverage of
    neuroscience, 109
  in moral decision making, 185

Kandel, Erik, 109
Kant, Immanuel, 131–134, 206

Kennedy, Donald, 48, 71, 97, 113
Knowledge transfer, 170

Laureys, Steven, 155, 156
Liberalism, 125, 128–131, 134, 137
Lippman, Abby, 109
Lobotomy, 16, 114, 191. *See also*
  Psychosurgery
Locked-in syndrome, 144, 149

MacLean, Paul, 181
Magnetic resonance imaging. *See* MRI
Magnetoencephalography. *See* MEG
Mahner, Martin, 193, 195–196, 202
Major depressive disorder. *See* MDD
Manifest image, 108–109, 114, 159,
  191. *See also* Scientific image
Marr, David, 196
Materialism, 190, 200, 212, 219
Mathews, Debra J. H., 6
Mayr, Ernst, 193, 202–203
MCS
  acceptance of the diagnosis for, 18,
    148
  behaviors in, 148, 150, 155
  diagnosis of, 18, 139, 148, 150, 155,
    156, 157, 172
  and ethics, 19, 20
  history of, 18, 148
  media coverage of, 158, 159, 168, 170
  prognosis of, 148, 149
  recovery from, 149, 150, 172
  neuroimaging research on, 20, 151,
    153, 155, 156–157, 170, 172
MDD, 15, 17
Meaney, Michael, 180
Medial prefrontal cortex. *See* MPFC
MEG, 21
Memory enhancement 12, 15, 55, 122.
  See also Cognitive enhancement
Metaethics, 60, 62, 64, 65, 67
Methylphenidate, 11, 12, 84, 122.
  See also Ritalin; Stimulants
Mind-body problem, 86, 92, 183, 189,
  190, 199, 219
Mind control, 21, 22, 49, 50, 103

Mind reading, 21, 22, 25, 50, 51, 99,
  106, 107, 113, 175
Minimally conscious state. *See* MCS
Minimally responsive state, 148
Modafinil, 43
Moderate liberalism, 128, 131, 135,
  137. *See also* Cognitive enhance-
  ment; Moral acceptability
Moderate pragmatic naturalism. *See*
  Pragmatic naturalism
Moll, Jorge R., 187, 188, 189
Mollaret, Pierre, 142–143
Moore, George E., 61, 204
Moral acceptability. *See also* Moral
  acceptability test; Moral praiseworthiness; Moral praiseworthiness test
  definition of, 124–126
  and Habermas, 131
  and Kant, 132
  and moderate liberalism, 130, 131,
    132
  policy implications of, 128
Moral acceptability test, 125–127,
  130. *See also* Moral acceptability;
  Moral praiseworthiness; Moral
  praiseworthiness test
Moral emotions, 98, 182, 184–189,
  207, 209. *See also* Moral judgment
Moral excellence, ix, 124, 126, 134,
  138, 212. *See also* Virtues
Moral judgment
  in bioethics, 63
  emotions in, 9, 182, 184, 186, 187,
    188, 189 (*see also* Moral emotions)
  and neuroscience, 184–189
Moral praiseworthiness. *See also*
  Moral acceptability; Moral acceptability test; Moral praiseworthiness
  test
  and conservatism, 125, 129, 130
  definition of, 124–126
  and democracy, 135
  and Dewey, 139
  and Habermas, 131, 134
  and moral excellence, 126, 212
  policy implications of, 128

Moral praiseworthiness (cont.)
  and pragmatism, 138
  and public good, 131
Moral praiseworthiness test, 125–126,
  127–128. See also Moral accept-
  ability; Moral acceptability test;
  Moral praiseworthiness
Moral reasoning
  and dialogue between tradition and
    innovation, 138
  and moral praiseworthiness, 138
  and neuroscience, xiii, 8, 9, 39, 59,
    108, 179, 182, 189, 200, 205, 206,
    208–209
  and solution seeking, 205
Moreno, Jonathan, 54, 58, 63, 64
MPFC, 184, 186, 187, 188
MRI, 3, 45, 47
Multidirectional communication,
    116–117, 216–217. See also Com-
    munication; Unidirectional
    communication
Multiple sclerosis, 15
Multi-Society Task Force on PVS, 18,
    20, 140, 145, 147, 168

Nagel, Thomas, 207
National Conference of Commis-
    sioners on Uniform State Law, 142,
    144
Naturalism. See also Pragmatic natu-
    ralism; Pragmatic neuroethics
  in bioethics, 53–45, 57–69
  epistemological, 58
  moderate (see Pragmatic naturalism)
  philosophic, 58
  strong naturalism, 54, 55, 64–69
Naturalistic fallacy, 55, 57, 60, 61, 66,
    183, 201, 204. See also Is-ought
    distinction
Nazi experiments, 25, 42, 83. See also
    Eugenics
Nervous system, 1, 2, 12, 25, 42, 49,
    74, 190, 193, 194, 195, 200, 203.
    See also CNS
Neural implant, 105

Neural network, 191, 193, 207
Neurocognitive enhancement. See
    Cognitive enhancement
Neuroeconomics, 24
Neuroessentialism. See also fMRI;
    Neuroimaging
  consequences of, 24, 82, 107, 219
  definition of, 24, 91–93, 101,
    105–106
  examples of, 105–106, 207
Neuroethics
  areas of, 4–9 (see also Clinical
    neuroethics, Pragmatic neuroethics;
    Research neuroethics; Theoretical
    neuroethics)
  attributes of, 35–42
  as a branch of bioethics, 36, 38
  common view of, 35, 81
  context-based issues in, 42
  and critique of narrow focus, 77–81
  and critique of reinventing the
    bioethics wheel, 81–85
  definitions of, 28–40
  and detrimental specialization in
    bioethics, 74–77
  and disciplinary primacy, 85, 87
  as a new discipline, 36, 39, 73–74,
    88–89
  healthcare driven, 33, 34
  history of, 28–30
  knowledge-driven, 30–32, 33,
  as a new field, 33, 38, 88–91
  as a new movement, 36, 39
  origins of the term, 29
  pluralism in, 4, 28, 71, 73, 79, 87
  and reductionism, 91–95
  salient challenges in, 1–4, 10–25
  technology-driven, 32, 33, 75
  and uniqueness of brain, 30, 36, 37,
    42, 50, 51, 71–72, 75, 80, 88, 100
Neuroethics: Mapping the Field
    Conference, 30, 34, 50
Neurogenetics
  media coverage of, 99, 100, 101,
    110
  neurogenetic testing, x, 2

Neuroimaging (functional neuroimaging). *See also* Brain imaging; EEG; fMRI; PET
and behavior, 38
commercial aspects of, 24, 109–113
and databases, 43
and disorders of consciousness (DOC), 18–21, 139–140, 148, 150, 153–155, 157–159, 170, 172, 173, 174, 176, 177, 178, 215
and ethics, 4, 6, 34, 43
functional and structural, 3
and genetics, 82
and incidental findings, 5, 6, 50
interpretation of, 21, 23, 24, 42, 47, 71, 81, 97, 99
in law, 2
and lie detection, 3, 29, 183
limits of, 23
media coverage of, 23, 24, 82, 99, 101, 216
and mind control, 22
and mind-reading, 21, 25, 175
and neuroessentialism, 101, 105
and neuropolicy, 107
and neurorealism, 106
and personal identity, 105, 108–109
and phrenology, 113–114
validity of (*see* validity of neurotechnology)
Neurological criteria of death, 18, 139, 142, 144. *See also* Brain death
Neurological determinism. *See* Determinism
Neuromarketing, 24, 103, 107, 182
Neuropharmaceuticals, 10, 14, 83–84, 87. *See also* Neuropharmacology
Neuropharmacology, x, xi, 4, 10–14, 34, 216, 218. *See also* Neuropharmaceuticals
Neurophilosophy, 24, 109, 191
Neuropolicy, 82, 101, 113, 118, 180, 215. *See also* fMRI; Neuroimaging
definition of, 107, 212
examples of, 107

Neurorealism, 24, 82, 101, 107, 113, 118, 212. *See also* fMRI; Neuroimaging
definition of, 24, 106
examples of, 106
Neuroscience of ethics. *See also* Theoretical neuroethics
dangers of, 189, 212–213
and the definition of neuroethics, 31–33, 36, 39, 51, 86, 93, 94
and emergentism, 194, 195, 200–201
and holism, 192, 194
and naturalism, 59
and the naturalistic fallacy, 204–205
and pragmatic neuroethics, ix, 73–74, 189–190, 201, 215
precursors of, 181
and reductionism, 194, 211
and semantic dualism, 205–206
and social neuroscience, 180–182
and theoretical neuroethics, 9, 93
Neuroscience revolution, 218–219
Neurostimulation. *See also* DBS
ethical aspects of, 4, 16, 25, 216
media coverage of, 99–101, 110
Neurosurgery, 4, 14, 15, 16, 33, 40
Neurotransmission, 10
Nonmaleficence, 124, 126. *See also* Moral acceptability
Normative ethics, 60, 62, 64–65, 67

Obsessive compulsive disorder (OCD), 15, 17
Owen, Adrian, 19–20, 140, 147, 151–153, 154

Parens, Erik
and the definition of neuroethics, 28, 72, 74, 75, 77, 78, 81, 84, 88, 89
and cognitive enhancement, 135, 136
Parkinson's disease (PD), 2, 6, 14–16, 100
Pediatric intensive care unit. *See* PICU
Penfield, Wilder, 219

Performance enhancement, xii, 29, 84,
121, 124, 127, 134, 218. *See also*
Cognitive enhancement
Permanent vegetative state, 147.
See also DOC; PVS; VS
Persistent vegetative state. *See* PVS
Personal identity (self-identity)
discussion of in media coverage of
neuroscience, 99, 105, 107, 108,
109, 110
and neuroscience, 31, 32, 81
and communication of neuroscience,
114, 117, 118
discussion of in neuroethics litera-
ture, 33, 37, 41, 42, 43, 45, 83,
88, 92
Persons, respect for, 37, 50, 211
PET
and ethics, 21, 82
in MCS,156
media coverage of in neuroscience
research, 104, 107, 110
in PVS, 140, 152, 155, 156
Phenomenology, 198, 206
Phrenology, 112, 113, 181, 219.
See also Neuroimaging
PICU, 171
Plum, Fred, 18, 141, 145–146, 170
Pontius, Anneliese A., 28–30, 34, 76,
80, 86
Positron emission tomography. *See*
PET
Posner, Jerome, 141, 145
Post-traumatic stress disorder, 122
Potter, Van Rensselaer
and the definition of bioethics, 31,
59, 201
and naturalism, 31–32, 54–57,
65–67, 182
Pragmatic naturalism (moderate prag-
matic naturalism), 54, 65, 66–68,
69, 71, 73, 94, 96, 134, 138, 182,
204, 206. *See also* Antinaturalism;
Naturalism; Pragmatic neuroethics
Pragmatic neuroethics, ix–xiii, xvi, 27,
34, 51, 69, 71, 73, 96, 189, 201,

215. *See also* Neuroscience of
ethics; Pragmatic naturalism
Pragmatism. *See also* Moral praiseworthiness; Pragmatic naturalism;
Pragmatic neuroethics
and bioethics, 53, 54, 56, 57, 58, 64
and cognitive enhancement, 131, 134
and the culture wars, 121
and naturalism, 53, 57
and neuroethics, 76, 86, 98
and philosophy of mind, 198, 200
Prefrontal cortex. *See* DLPFC; Dorsomedial frontal cortex; MPFC;
VMPFC
Prescription abuse (prescription drug
abuse), 10, 12, 14, 83–84, 87. *See
also* Cognitive enhancement; Neuropharmaceuticals; Neuropharmacology; Prescription misuse
Prescription misuse, 11–14, 122.
See also Cognitive enhancement;
Neuropharmaceuticals; Neuropharmacology; Prescription abuse
President's Council on Bioethics, 2–3,
122, 123
Privacy. *See also* Brain privacy;
Thought privacy
in cognitive enhancement, 121, 127
discussion of in media coverage of
neuroscience, 103, 104
discussion of in neuroethics literature, 6, 25, 31, 37, 40, 41–43, 45,
48, 50, 51
Properties
biological, 183, 189, 195, 199
biophysical, 183
brain, 195, 206
emergent, 176, 193, 195, 196, 198,
201, 202, 203, 205, 210
and emergentism, 193, 194
global, 145, 196
higher-order, 183, 193, 195, 199, 200,
209, 210, 212
and holism, 192, 194
mind (mind-level), 183, 189, 193,
195, 206, 208

natural, 60, 61, 63, 64, 65
neuronal, 183
physical, 89
qualitative, 192, 193
and reductionism, 190, 194
relational, 196, 199, 200, 202
Propositional attitude psychology. *See*
Folk psychology
Provigil, 84
Proxy (decision making), 6, 7, 162, 175
Psychosurgery, 16, 83, 114. *See also*
Lobotomy
Psychotherapy, 24
Public and cultural neuroethics, 4, 5,
7–8
Public debate, 31, 44, 104, 119, 121,
218. *See also* Public dialogue
Public dialogue, 80, 107, 118. *See also*
Public debate
Public health, x, 2, 11, 12, 14, 87, 91,
216
Public involvement, 41, 42, 44–45,
104, 115, 119
Public understanding of neuroscience,
7, 24, 42, 98, 215, 216
PVS. *See also* DOC; fMRI; Multi-
Society Task Force on PVS; Neuro-
imaging; Terri Schiavo; VS
behaviors in, 18, 146–147, 175
diagnosis of, 18, 20, 139, 145–147
history of, 145–146
media coverage of, 154, 168–170
perception of pain in, 19, 174
prognosis of, 139, 174

Qualia, 207–208
Qualitative research, 53, 93, 208, 209
Quality of life, 123, 161, 162, 163,
165, 166, 169, 170, 172

RC explanation. *See* Epistemology
RD explanation. *See* Epistemology
Readiness of neurotechnology
in cognitive enhancement, 127
discussion of in media coverage of
neuroscience, 102

discussion of in neuroethics literature, 2, 3, 37 40, 44
Reductionism
biological, 25, 74, 101, 210, 209
disciplinary, 74, 75, 87, 93
eliminativist, 190, 191, 193, 194
and emergentism, 193, 194
methodological, 92
mind-body, 72, 93, 103, 189, 190,
191
noneliminative, 108
ontological, 92, 93
philosophical, 24
Reid, Lynette, 71, 81, 88, 89
Relational-causal explanation. *See*
Epistemology
Relational-descriptive explanation.
See Epistemology
Research ethics, 83, 143,
Research neuroethics, 5–6
Resource allocation
in cognitive enhancement, 127
in DBS, 14–15
discussion of in media coverage of
neuroscience, 104
discussion of in neuroethics literature, 7, 40, 41, 42, 49
Responsibility
discussion of in media coverage of
neuroscience, 45, 104
discussion of in neuroethics literature, 41, 42, 44, 45, 47, 217
and neuroscience research, 2–3, 37,
59, 83, 109, 201, 207, 219
Ricoeur, Paul, 192, 206–207
Ritalin, 11, 12, 43, 44, 84, 112. *See
also* Methylphenidate; Stimulants
Roskies, Adina, 9, 30, 31, 32, 33, 34,
39, 54, 59, 79, 83, 86, 92, 93, 181
Rousseau, Jean-Jacques, 132–133

Safety, 41, 42, 46, 102, 124, 127
Safire, William, 38, 39, 40, 44, 45,
46, 49
Sandel, Michael J., 124–125, 126
Sartre, Jean-Paul, 54, 57, 212

Schiavo, Terri (Theresa)
  behavioral repertoire of, 168–169,
    174
  controversies surrounding, 7, 121,
    167, 175
  and end-of-life (EOL) decision
    making, 121, 175, 177
  media coverage of, 161, 163,
    167–170, 216
  and the persistent vegetative state
    (PVS), 7, 161, 163, 173
  and prognosis, 168, 174
Schiff, Nicholas, 20–21, 148, 149,
    150, 152, 153, 156, 157, 158
Schindler, Mary and Robert, 168,
    169
Science communication. *See* Com-
  munication; Multidirectional
  communication; Unidirectional
  communication
Scientific image, 108, 109, 159, 191.
  See also Manifest image
Self-identity. *See* Personal identity
Self-understanding, 77, 98, 108, 109.
  See also Personal identity
Sellars, Wilfred, 108
Semantic dualism. *See* Dualism
Shared decision making, 163
Sherrington, Charles, 219
Shevell, Michael, 42, 161, 171
Single-photon emission computerized
  tomography. *See* SPECT
Social neuroscience, xiii, 109, 179–183,
    201, 213, 216
SPECT, 98–99, 101, 114
Stem cell, 81, 83, 84, 90, 121
Stigma, ix, 1–2, 7–8, 90, 91, 99.
  See also Stigmatization
Stigmatization, 41–42, 47. *See also*
  Stigma
Stimulants, 10, 11, 12, 13, 84, 122,
    218. *See also* Methylphenidate;
  Ritalin
Stroke, 18, 32, 100, 147, 149, 152
Stupor, 139, 141, 149
Substance dualism. *See* Dualism

System. *See also* CNS; Cognitive
  system; Nervous system
  biological, 1, 74, 195, 196, 199, 200,
    202, 203, 211
  inorganic, 201, 203
  social, 1, 195, 196, 200, 210

Taylor, Charles, 117, 130
Temporal cortex, 187, 189
Temporal gyrus, 156, 188
Temporal lobe, 151, 187
Temporo-parietal junction, 184, 185
Thalamus, 142, 155, 185, 188
Theoretical neuroethics, 4, 5. *See also*
  Neuroscience of ethics
Theory of mind, 185, 186, 187
Thought privacy, 37, 51. *See also* Brain
  privacy
TMS, 46, 99, 102,
Tourette syndrome. *See* TS
Tovino, Stacey A., 21
Transcranial magnetic stimulation.
  See TMS
Traumatic brain injury, 147, 149, 150,
    168
Trolley problem, 8, 181–182
TS, 15, 17

UDDA, 144, 155
Unidirectional communication, 115,
    116, 118, 216. *See also* Commu-
  nication; Multidirectional commu-
  nication
Uniform Determination of Death Act.
  See UDDA

Validity of ethical norms 68, 133, 134
Validity of neurotechnologies
  discussion of in media coverage of
    neuroscience, 99, 102, 212
  discussion of in neuroethics litera-
    ture, 41, 42, 46
  in functional neuroimaging, 2, 23
Values
  and facts, 57, 60, 62
  family, 47, 121

human, 218, 219
moral, 107, 136
religious, 103
shared, 131
social, 90
Vegetative state. *See* VS
Ventromedial prefrontal cortex. *See*
    VMPFC
Virtues, 138. *See also* Moral
    excellence
Visual cortex, 187
VMPFC, 184, 185, 186
VS, 18, 20, 140, 145, 146, 147, 148,
    149, 150, 151, 153, 155, 156, 158,
    172

Wallis, Terry, 150
Wijdicks, Eelco F., 18, 139, 144,
    174–175
Williams, James, 57
Wolf, Susan, 54, 56, 57
Wolpe, Paul
  and the definition of neuroethics, 4,
    32, 33, 34, 36, 37, 75, 79, 94
  and lie detection, 3, 23–24
World Health Organization (WHO),
    ix, 7–8

Basic Bioethics

Arthur Caplan, editor

Peter A. Ubel, *Pricing Life: Why It's Time for Health Care Rationing*

Mark G. Kuczewski and Ronald Polansky, eds., *Bioethics: Ancient Themes in Contemporary Issues*

Suzanne Holland, Karen Lebacqz, and Laurie Zoloth, eds., *The Human Embryonic Stem Cell Debate: Science, Ethics, and Public Policy*

Gita Sen, Asha George, and Piroska Östlin, eds., *Engendering International Health: The Challenge of Equity*

Carolyn McLeod, *Self-Trust and Reproductive Autonomy*

Lenny Moss, *What Genes Can't Do*

Jonathan D. Moreno, ed., *In the Wake of Terror: Medicine and Morality in a Time of Crisis*

Glenn McGee, ed., *Pragmatic Bioethics*, 2d edition

Timothy F. Murphy, *Case Studies in Biomedical Research Ethics*

Mark A. Rothstein, ed., *Genetics and Life Insurance: Medical Underwriting and Social Policy*

Kenneth A. Richman, *Ethics and the Metaphysics of Medicine: Reflections on Health and Beneficence*

David Lazer, ed., *DNA and the Criminal Justice System: The Technology of Justice*

Harold W. Baillie and Timothy K. Casey, eds., *Is Human Nature Obsolete? Genetics, Bioengineering, and the Future of the Human Condition*

Robert H. Blank and Janna C. Merrick, eds., *End-of-Life Decision Making: A Cross-National Study*

Norman L. Cantor, *Making Medical Decisions for the Profoundly Mentally Disabled*

Margrit Shildrick and Roxanne Mykitiuk, eds., *Ethics of the Body: Post-Conventional Challenges*

Alfred I. Tauber, *Patient Autonomy and the Ethics of Responsibility*

David H. Brendel, *Healing Psychiatry: Bridging the Science/Humanism Divide*

Jonathan Baron, *Against Bioethics*

Michael L. Gross, *Bioethics and Armed Conflict: Moral Dilemmas of Medicine and War*

Karen F. Greif and Jon F. Merz, *Current Controversies in the Biological Sciences: Case Studies of Policy Challenges from New Technologies*

Deborah Blizzard, *Looking Within: A Sociocultural Examination of Fetoscopy*

Ronald Cole-Turner, ed., *Design and Destiny: Jewish and Christian Perspectives on Human Germline Modification*

Holly Fernandez Lynch, *Conflicts of Conscience in Health Care: An Institutional Compromise*

Mark A. Bedau and Emily C. Parke, eds., *The Ethics of Protocells: Moral and Social Implications of Creating Life in the Laboratory*

Jonathan D. Moreno and Sam Berger, eds., *Progress in Bioethics: Science, Policy, and Politics*

Eric Racine, *Pragmatic Neuroethics: Improving Treatment and Understanding of the Mind-Brain*